西安文庙航拍总平面
Aerial photograph of Confucian Temple in Xi'an

西安东岳庙大殿次间梁栿彩画大样图
Caihua of side-bay beams of main hall, Dongyue Temple of Xi'an

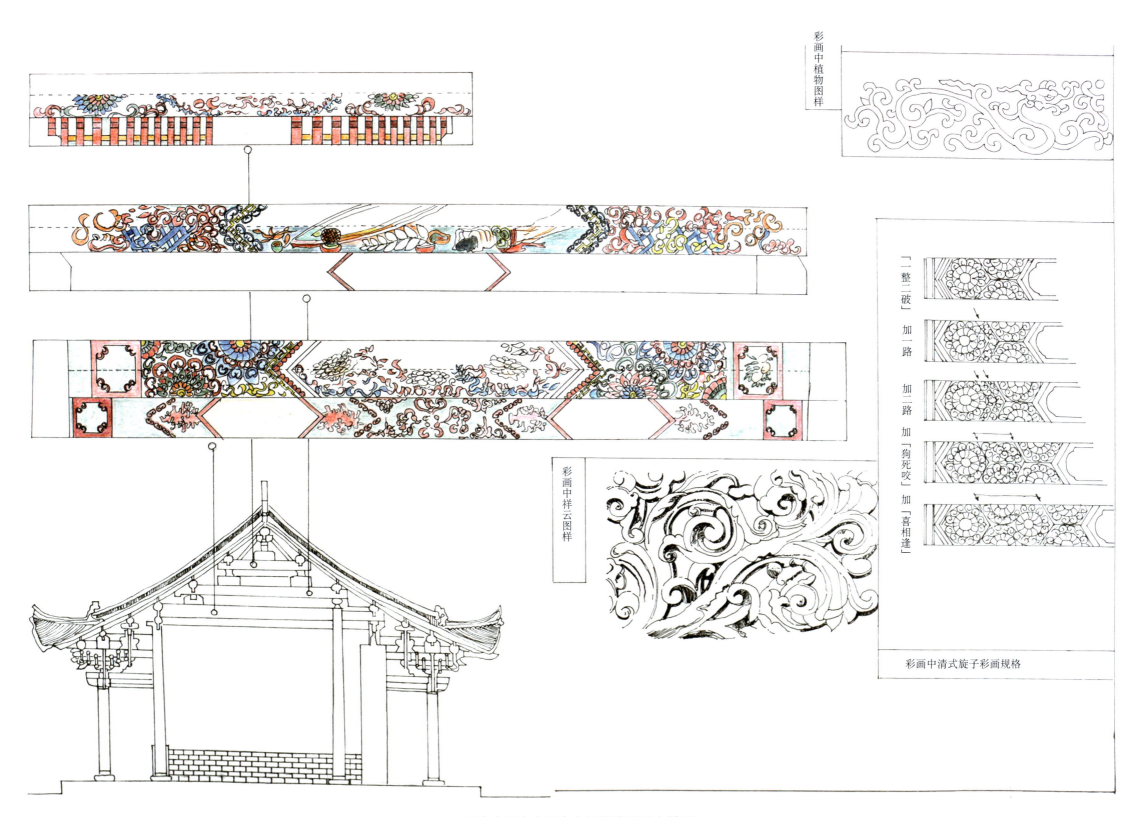

西安东岳庙大殿当心间梁枋彩画大样图
Caihua of central-bay beams of main hall, Dongyue Temple of Xi'an

中国古建筑测绘大系·祠庙建筑

陕西祠庙

西安建筑科技大学建筑学院 编写
林源 喻梦哲 岳岩敏 主编

国家出版基金项目

"十二五"国家重点图书出版规划项目

中国建筑工业出版社

Traditional Chinese Architecture Surveying and
Mapping Series:
Shrines and Temples Architecture

SHAANXI SHRINES AND TEMPLES

Compiled by School of Architecture, Xi'an University of Architecture and Technology
Edited by LIN Yuan, YU Mengzhe, YUE Yanmin

China Architecture & Building Press

Editorial Board of the Traditional Chinese Architecture Surveying and Mapping Series

Editorial Advisory Board: FU Xinian, HOU Youbin
Editorial Director: SHEN Yuanqin
Deputy Editorial Director: WANG Lihui
Editors in Chief: WANG Qiheng, WANG Guixiang, CHEN Wei, CHANG Qing

Editorial Team Members (Characters arranged according to stroke counts):
DING Yao, WANG Nan, WANG Wei, WANG Mo, BAI Ying, BAI Chengjun,
FENG Di, ZHU Lei, ZHU Yuhui, LIU Chang, LIU Yang, LIU Daping,
LIU Tongtong, LI Luke, YANG Jing, XIAO Dong, WU Cong, WU Xiaomin,
HE Jie, HE Beijie, WANG Zhiyang, ZHANG Long, ZHANG Shiqing,
ZHANG Fengwu, ZHANG Xingguo, ZHANG Chunyan, LIN Yuan, YUE Yanmin,
SHI Fei, YAO Hongfeng, HE Congrong, JIA Jun, GUO Xuan, GUO Huazhan,
ZHUGE Jing, CAO Peng, YU Mengzhe, CHENG Fei, LIAO Huinong

Contents

Introduction	001
Confucian Temple in Xi'an (Stele Forest Museum)	005
'Capital' City God Temple in Xi'an	037
Dongyue Temple of Xi'an	081
The Offering Hall of Dongyue Temple (Huayang Temple) in Hu County	097
City God Temple of Sanyuan	111
Confucian Temple in Jingyang	145
Confucian Temple in Hancheng	165
Xiyue Temple of Huayin	203
Survey Record	244
Attachment: Existing Temple in Shaanxi region	245

目　录

概述——〇〇一

西安文庙（碑林博物院）——〇〇五

西安都城隍庙——〇三七

西安东岳庙——〇八一

户县东岳庙（化羊庙）——〇九七

三原城隍庙——一一一

泾阳文庙——一四五

韩城文庙——一六五

华阴西岳庙——二〇三

测绘工作记录——二四四

附表　陕西地区现存祠庙建筑一览表——二四五

Introduction

Shaanxi has preserved many shrines and temples dedicated to different Chinese popular deities, deified historical figures, and personified forces of nature including Confucius, Chenghuang (City God), Dongyue (East Peak, referring to Mount Tai, the East Mountain of the Five Great Mountain of China), and Xiyue (West Peak i.e. Mount Hua). Confucian temples make up the majority. They are dispersed throughout the province, but primarily concentrated in two main areas: in Xi'an, Xianyang, Jingyang, Xingping, Hu county, Yao county, Heyang, and Hancheng in the Central Shaanxi Plain; and Hanzhong, Yang county, Hanyin, and Chengu in southern Shaanxi. The second largest group are the temples dedicated to local city gods, located in Xi'an, Sanyuan, Wugong, Chengcheng, Fufeng, and Hancheng in the Central Shaanxi Plain, and in Yang county and Chenggu in southern Shaanxi. Next in number are the temples to nature deities, but only one Temple to the West Peak (in Huayin at the foot of Mount Hua) and two temples to the East Peak (in Xi'an and in Hu county [known as Huayang Temple]) have survived. Finally, there are a handful of other Chinese popular shrines and temples found throughout the province such as the temples dedicated to the Cangjie in Baishui, Duke of Zhou in Qishan, Sima Qian in Hancheng, Zhuge Liang in Mian county, Zhang Liang in Liuba as well as the temples in Hancheng dedicated to the Jade Emperor (Yuhuang), Queen of the Earth (Houtu), Yu the Great (Dayu), Sima Qian, Fawang, and the nine maidens (*jiulang*). (See also the table at the end of this volume P221.)

These sites are preserved in varying degrees. Some have maintained an almost intact layout with only a few buildings demolished or reconstructed at a later date. For example, Xiyue Temple in Huayin, the City God temples in Sanyuan and Hancheng, the Confucian Temple in Hancheng, Zhuge Liang Temple in Mian county, and Zhang Liang Temple in Liuba are all possessed

概述

陕西地区保存至今的祠庙建筑类型颇为丰富，如文庙、城隍庙、岳庙，以及先贤祠等。就现存数量而言，文庙建筑最多，有西安文庙（碑林博物院）、咸阳文庙、泾阳文庙、兴平文庙、户县文庙、耀县文庙、合阳文庙、韩城文庙（以上主要分布在关中地区）、汉中文庙、汉阴文庙、城固文庙、洋县文庙（以上分布在陕南地区）等；其次是城隍庙，有西安城隍庙、三原城隍庙、武功城隍庙、澄城城隍庙、扶风城隍庙、韩城城隍庙（以上主要分布在关中地区）以及洋县城隍庙、城固城隍庙等（以上分布在陕南地区）；西岳庙，一处，在华山脚下的华阴市；东岳庙现存的只有西安东岳庙和户县东岳庙（化羊庙）两处；先贤祠及其他祠庙现存尚为数不少，有白水仓颉庙、岐山周公庙、韩城司马迁祠、勉县武侯祠、留坝张良庙、韩城法王庙、韩城大禹庙、韩城九郎庙等等，广泛分布在关中和陕南地区（详见245页附表）。

这些祠庙建筑保存状况差异甚大，有些建筑组群的整体格局保留基本完整，仅有少量单体建筑损毁或为晚近时期新建，如华阴西岳庙、三原城隍庙、韩城城隍庙、韩城文庙、勉县武侯祠、留坝张良庙等；有些是建筑组群的主要部分或大殿所在的中心院落被较为完好地保存下来，如泾阳文

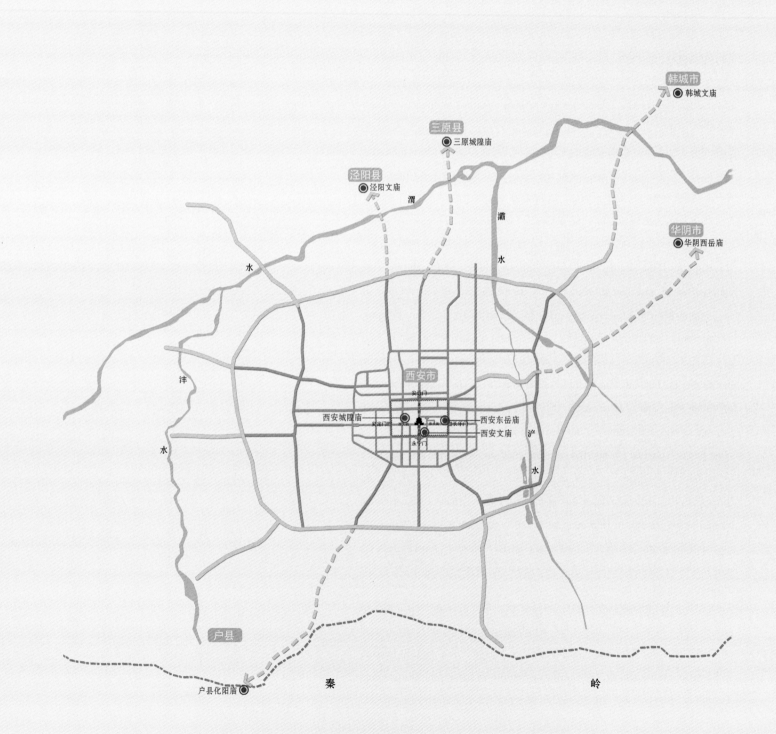

of near intact layouts. Others such as the Confucian Temple in Jingyang and Dongyue Temple in Xi'an have managed only to keep the central structures or the principal hall of the complex from falling into decay. While even others have lost their architectural structures forever, except perhaps for one or two scattered buildings. Examples include the Lingxing (Star) Gate and Pond at the Confucian Temple in Hanzhong, Dacheng Hall(Great Achievement) at the Confucian Temple in Xingping, the offering hall at the Dongyue Temple in Hu county, or the main hall at Jiulang Temple in Hancheng, etc.

This volume of the *Traditional Chinese Architecture Surveying and Mapping Series* introduces eight cultural heritage sites in Shaanxi province: three sites situated in Xi'an, namely the Confucian Temple (Stele Forest Museum), City God Temple, and Dongyue Temple; Dongyue Temple (Huayang Temple) in Hu county; City God Temple in Sanyuan; the Confucian Temple in Jingyang , the Confucian Temple in Hancheng, and Xiyue Temple in Huayin. Over the past two decades, we have accumulated several hundred measured drawings from many places throughout Shaanxi province, but for this volume, we have selected these eight sites according to the following criteria: first, the site must have been important and representative, either in terms of size, current state and condition, or as an embodiment of outstanding architectural achievement; second, the site must have been measured comprehensively, resulting in a complete set of high-quality architectural drawings produced not later than in the last ten years.

The drawings were carefully compiled and meticulously edited by us together with our colleagues, as well as by postgraduate students who have spared no effort in completing the work. We would like to thank all of them for their commitment. We also owe special gratitude to the students who took part in the surveying and measuring fieldwork over the past few decades. Their hard work is what has made this publication possible in the first place.

本卷共收录了陕西的八处祠庙建筑——西安文庙（碑林博物院）、西安城隍庙、西安东岳庙、户县东岳庙（化羊庙）、三原城隍庙、泾阳文庙、韩城文庙和华阴西岳庙。从累积了二十年的几十处祠庙建筑的测绘图纸中，选择出这八处建筑的几百张图纸，殊为不易。我们主要是依据下述标准进行图纸的遴选工作的：一是建筑物本身的重要性和代表性，如组群规模大且完整，或是保存状况较为完好，或是建筑品质突出；二是全套图纸内容与质量的齐整，且是近十年来测绘完成的。

本卷图纸整理的工作量巨大，能够如期完成全赖教研室各位老师及研究生们的全力投入与辛苦付出。更更要感谢当年跟着我们去测绘的同学们，没有他们的认真工作就没有如今这些测绘图纸。

西安文庙（碑林博物院）

Confucian Temple in Xi'an (Stele Forest Museum)

Location: Sanxue Street, Xi'an, Shaanxi province

Construction Date: Ming and Qing dynasties

Protection Level: National Priority Protected Site (first batch)

地　　址：西安三学街

建造年代：明—清

保护级别：全国重点文物保护单位（第一批）

Introduction

Located at Sanxue Street in Xi'an, the Confucian Temple or Wenmiao, also known as the Stele Forest Museum, was declared a National Priority Protected Site in 1961. The site was first established in 1087 during the Northern Song dynasty (960-1279) to house two Tang-period (618-907) steles—*Kaicheng shijing* and *Shitai xiaojing*. In 1103, the steles were relocated along with the Confucian Temple and the prefecture school to its present location. The new architecture was described as consisting of "five hundred columns" and having assumed "a dimension and size unrivaled at the time".

Zhongxiu Xi'an fuxue wenmiao ji, a Ming-dynasty (1368-1644) document from 1475, gives an account of the temple renovation:

"…the site was expanded. First was built the seven-bay Dacheng (Great Achievement) Hall, 4.5 *zhang* high, 5 *zhang* long, and 9.2 *zhang* wide. Its wings, both comprised of thirty-bay structures, are only half as high and long as the main hall but several times as wide. Other buildings include Ji (Halberd) Gate, Lingxing Gate (named after a star), Wenchang (Culture and Literature) Shrine, Qixian (Seven Saints) Shrine, a holy kitchen (*shenchu*), a fasting dormitory (*zhaisufang*), and Pan (School) Pond…"

These structures, along with *Taihe yuanqi* (Supreme Harmony and Primordial Energy) Archway (built in 1592; Ming) and seven Qing-period (1616-1912) stele pavilions, have formed and still form the basic layout of the Confucian Temple in Xi'an as we know it today. Dacheng (Great Achievement) Hall was unfortunately destroyed by a fire caused by a lightening strike in 1959, while other buildings including the Ji (Halberd) and Lingxing (Star) gates and the water pond have survived until today.

Zhu Wei'ao, a member of the Ming imperial family, funded the erection of the monumental archway in 1592. The name of the structure alludes to *Zhouyi* (*Book of Changes*; in English sometimes known as *I Ching*) and suggests that the primordial energy (or breath; *qi*) ultimately harmonizes and justifies everything in the world. The archway was not used as an entrance gate, because it stood too close to the city wall. Instead, two smaller "real" gates, positioned at a short distance from and 90-degree angle to the archway, took up this function—to the west, Li (Courtesy) Gate and to the east, Yi (Righteousness) Path. Additionally, the city wall section located south of the archway was

概述

西安碑林为全国重点文物保护单位，位于西安市三学街，宋哲宗元祐二年（1087年）为保存唐《开成石经》与《石台孝经》而建，徽宗崇宁二年（1103年）将文庙、府学最终迁建于今址，"总五百楹，宏模廓度，伟冠一时。"

按明成化十一年（1475年）《重修西安府学文庙记》称：当时"扩其旧址，首建大成殿七间，崇四丈有五、深五丈，袤九丈有二。两庑各三十间，崇深视殿半之，袤且数倍。次作戟门，又次棂星门，又次文昌祠、七贤祠、神厨、斋宿房、泮池……"加上明万历二十年（1592年）增建的"太和元气"牌坊和清代的七座碑亭，构成了西安孔庙的基本格局。其中大成殿1959年毁于雷火，戟门、棂星门、泮池等皆保存完好。

太和元气坊建于明万历二十年（1592年），由皇族朱惟𣏌捐资修建，取"合会大利，利贞万物"之意。因牌坊之南紧邻城墙，不便出入，故在其东西两面开辟"礼门"、"义路"二门以供出入，而以牌坊南侧之墙为"塞门"，影壁之上刻有清末著名书画家刘晖手书"孔庙"二字。

图1 西安文庙（碑林博物院）航拍总平面

Fig.1 Site plan of Confucian Temple in Xi'an (Stele Forest Museum)

used as a protective screen or gate with a shielding function (*saimen*). It was inscribed with two Chinese characters—*Kong* (Confucius) and *miao* (temple)—by the famous late-Qing calligrapher Liu Hui.

The pond behind the archway was originally dug in the Yuan period (1271-1368) but underwent repair on several later occasions.

Lingxing Gate consisted of two bays in the Yuan period but was enlarged into a three-bay structure in the Qing period. The horizontal plaque installed above the central doorway bears an inscriptions that reads "*depei tiandi*" (his morality matches heaven and earth), the plaque above the eastern doorway reads "*Wenmiao*" (Confucian Temple), and the plaque above the western doorway reads "*daoguan gujin*" (his teachings are unrivalled for all eternity).

The ornamental pillar (*huabiao*) was produced no earlier than the Ming period.

Ji Gate, also named Yi (Courtesy) Gate or Zhisheng (Sacrosanct) Gate, dates to the Ming dynasty. The path leading from the gate inside the temple is flanked by six octagonal Qing stele pavilions housing precious relics such as Jingyun (Auspicious Cloud) Bell from the Tang dynasty and a stone horse from the Central-Asian region of Bactria (Daxia).

泮池最早开凿于元代，后几经修葺。

棂星门在元代为两间，到了清代改为三间，中门额书『文庙』、东门额刻『德配天地』、西门额刻『道冠古今』。

华表刻制于明清时期。

戟门又称仪门、至圣门，建于明代。戟门之内，道路两侧分布清代所建八角碑亭六座，陈列包括唐景云钟、大夏石马等重要文物。

图2 西安文庙棂星门

图3 西安文庙戟门

图4 西安文庙八角亭

图5 西安文庙唐《石台孝经》亭

Fig.2 Lingxing Gate of Confucian Temple in Xi'an
Fig.3 Ji Gate of Confucian Temple in Xi'an
Fig.4 Octagonal pavilion of Confucian Temple in Xi'an
Fig.5 Tang-period (*Shitai xiaojing*) stele pavilion, Confucian Temple in Xi'an

Survey and Mapping Information

Responsible Department: Department of Architecture (Class of 2011), School of Architecture, Xi'an University of Architecture and Technology

Team Members: SHI Yongpeng, CHEN Baoxin, JIN Xuan, LI Hanchun, ZHU Kecheng, CENG Jianqing, QU Sijia, ZHANG Yuhan, GENG Lantian, BAI Siyu, YANG Ziyi, NAN Mingyue, XU Xin, XU Lu, GUO Jingyu, JING Fenglin, YANG Ying, ZHANG Guanglong, ZHANG Yike, WANG Xin, WANG Jingyi, HAO Ning, XIE Yuejiao, BAI Shuaishuai, WANG Yingjie, TANG Mengying, HUANG Tingyu, LI Yifan, JING Siyuan, PAN Wendian, HAO Xinyang, WANG Pengbo, SHI Chao, ZHANG Henghui, LEI Hao, BAI Jiang, WU Tao, LI Fangbo, XU Duo, HONG Zhen, ZHANG Pengju, LI Ang, QU Bike, WANG Xu, GU Qianqian, WANG Ruoya, WANG Yunfeng, SONG Chen, ZENG Zehua, ZHENG Siyu, XING Jingyue, LI Jiaxi, PENG Fan

Supervisors: SONG Hui, LI Shuangshuang

Editors of Drawings: LI Shuangshuang, LEI Honglu

Survey Time: October 2015

西安文庙（碑林博物院）测绘的人员名单

测　绘：西安建筑科技大学建筑学院建筑学2011级

史永鹏　陈宝鑫　李菡纯　朱可成　曾健清　瞿思嘉　张雨晗
耿蓝天　金璇　杨子依　南明玥　徐欣　郭境钰　景枫林
杨英　柏思宇　张一可　王信　王婧仪　郝宁　谢月皎　白帅帅
王英杰　张光龙　唐梦莹　黄庭玉　李艺帆　景思远　潘文典　郝歆旸　王鹏波
史超　张恒晖　雷浩　白江　吴涛　李方博　许铎　洪祯
张鹏举　李昂　屈碧珂　王旭　顾倩倩　王若雅　王云峰　宋晨
甄泽华　郑思雨　邢竞月　李佳熹　彭帆
指导教师：宋辉　李双双
图纸整理：李双双　雷鸿鹭
测绘时间：2015年10月

参考文献 References

[一] 国家文物局主编. 中国文物地图集·陕西分册. 西安：西安地图出版社, 1998.

[二] 路远. 明代西安碑林、文庙及府县三学整修述要. 文博. 1996 (1). 11-15.

[三] 路远. 西安碑林初创时期若干问题的再探讨. 文博. 1995 (6). 27-32.

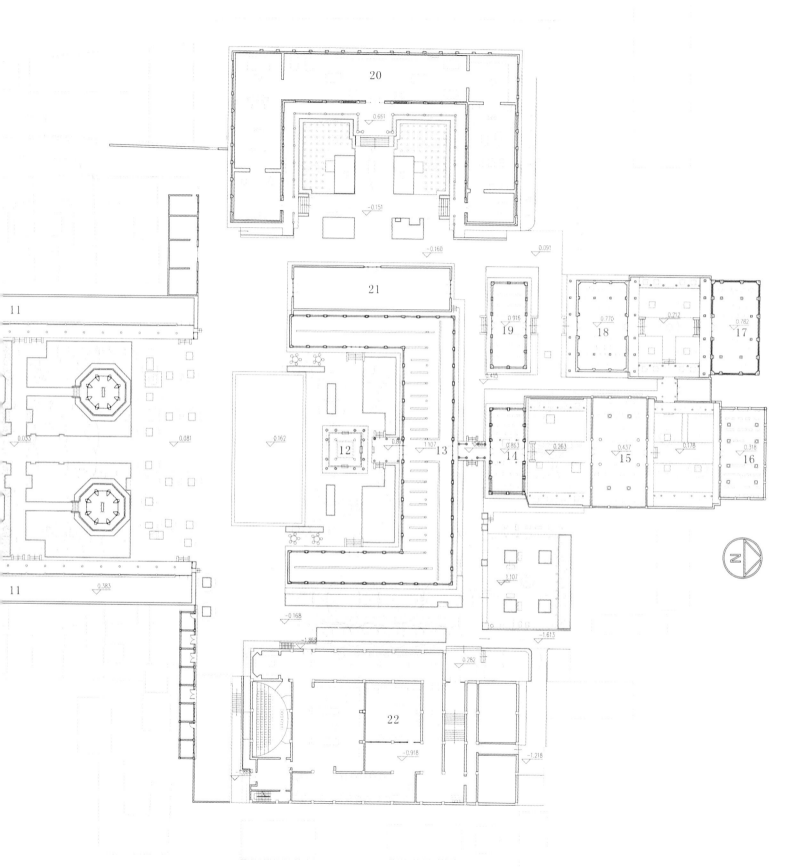

1	照壁	Screen wall
2	太和元气坊	"Taihe yuanqi" archway
3	义路门	Yilu Gate
4	礼门	Li Gate
5	泮池	Pond
6	棂星门	Lingxing Gate
7	望云堂	Wangyun Hall
8	（增建）碑林艺术品商店	Stele Forest Art Shop (later addition)
9	戟门	Ji Gate
10	八角御碑亭	Octagonal stele pavilion
11	临时展室	Temporary showroom
12	孝经亭	Xiaojing Pavilion
13	碑林一室	Stele room 1
14	碑林二室	Stele room 2
15	碑林三室	Stele room 3
16	碑林四室	Stele room 4
17	碑林五室	Stele room 5
18	碑林六室	Stele room 6
19	碑林七室	Stele room 7
20	（增建）石刻艺术馆	Stone Carving Gallery (later addition)
21	（增建）碑林旅游商店	Stele Forest Tourist Shop (later addition)
22	（增建）石刻艺术博术馆	Ten-thousand Carvings Museum (later addition)

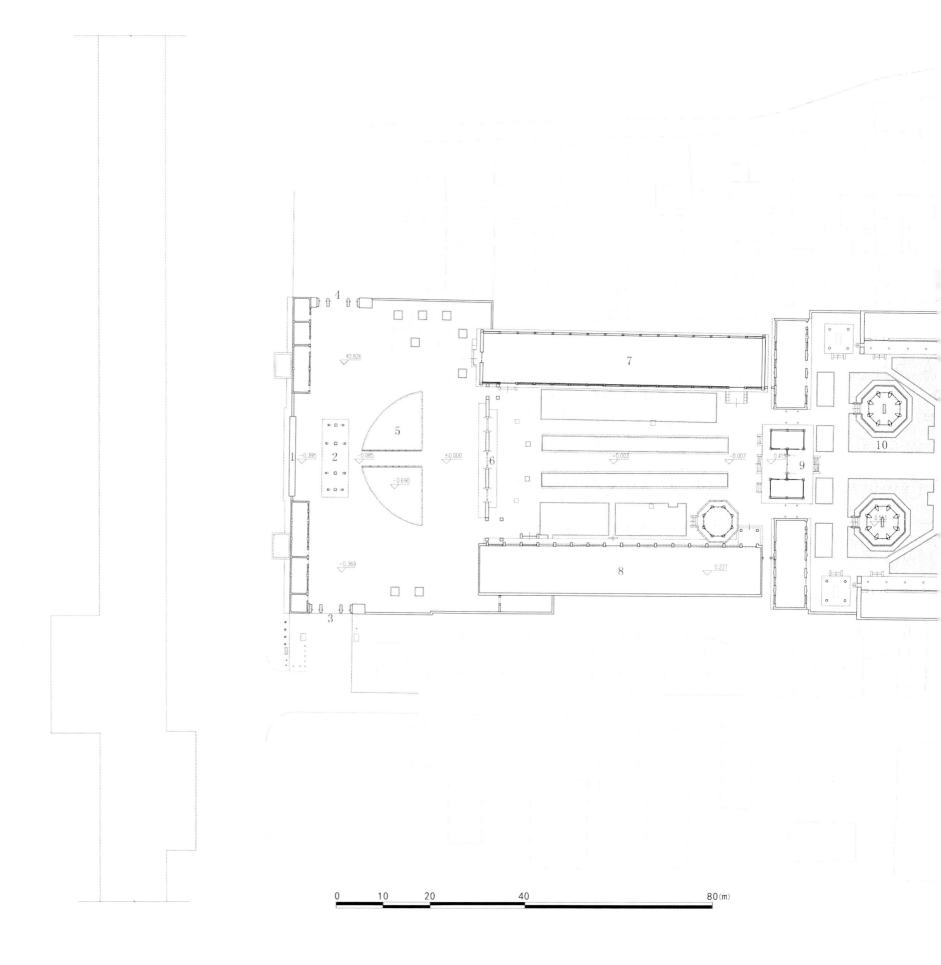

总平面图
Site plan

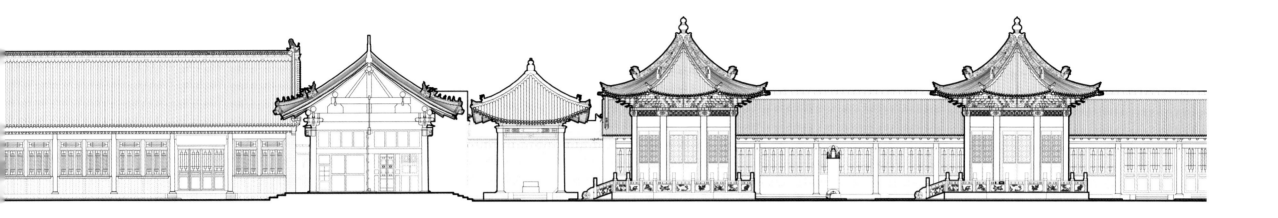
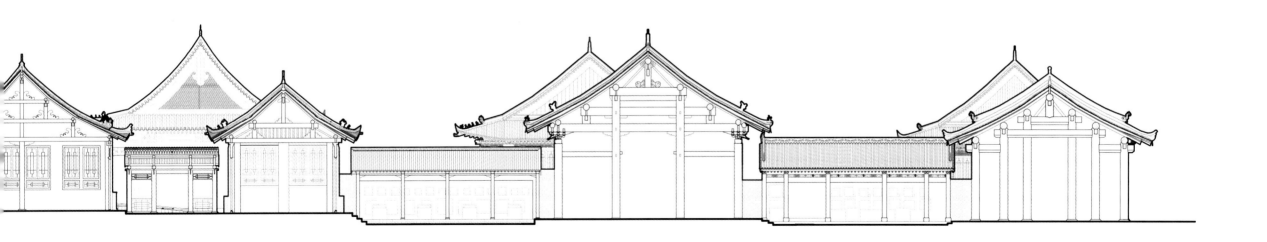

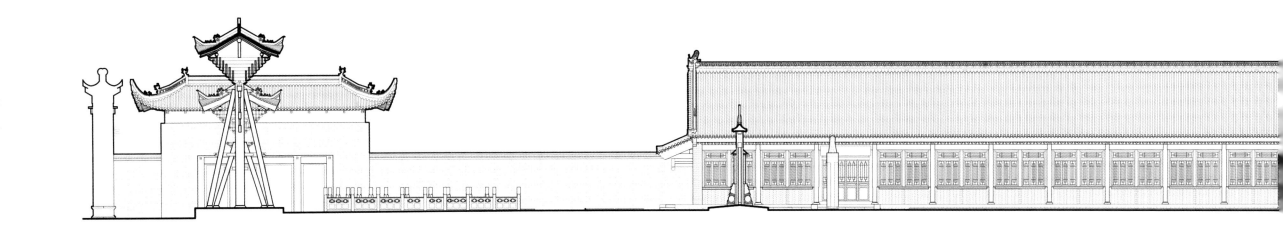

院落纵剖面图
Longitudinal section of courtyards
0 4 8 16(m)

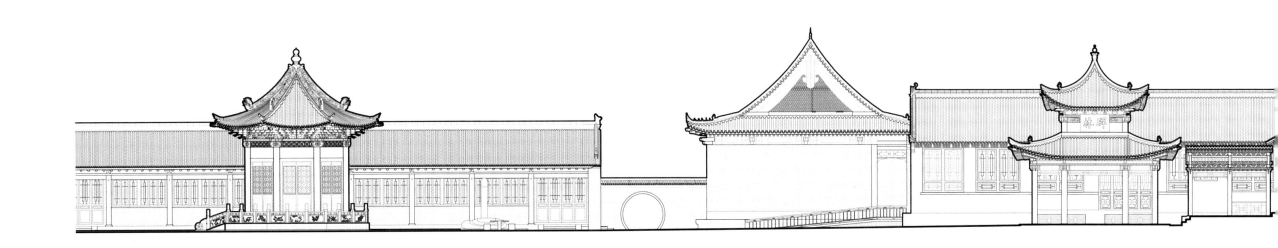

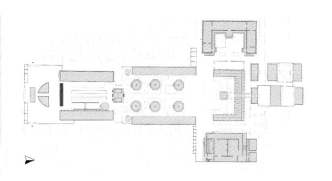

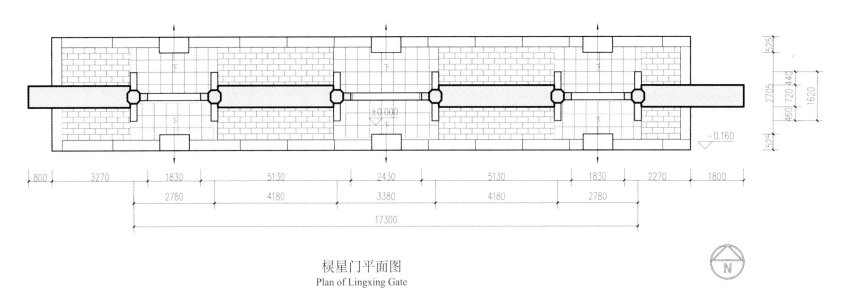

棂星门平面图
Plan of Lingxing Gate

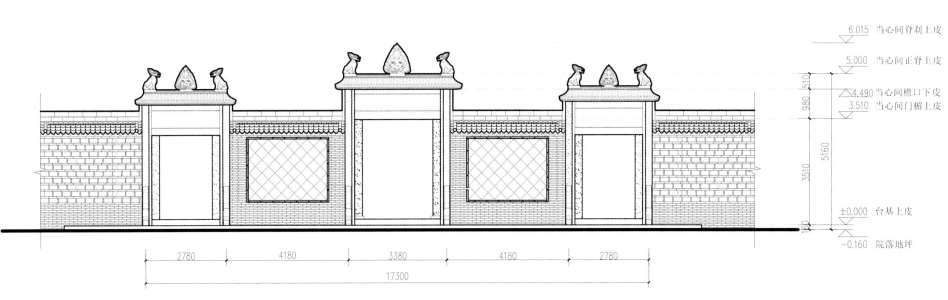

棂星门南立面图
South elevation of Lingxing Gate

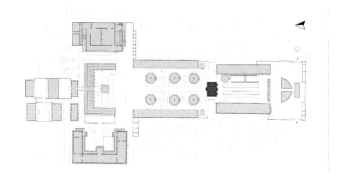

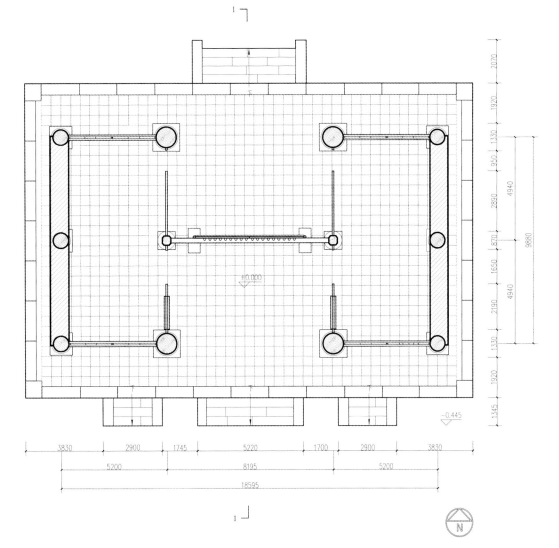

戟门平面图
Plan of Ji Gate

戟门梁架仰视图
Plan of framework of Ji Gate as seen from below

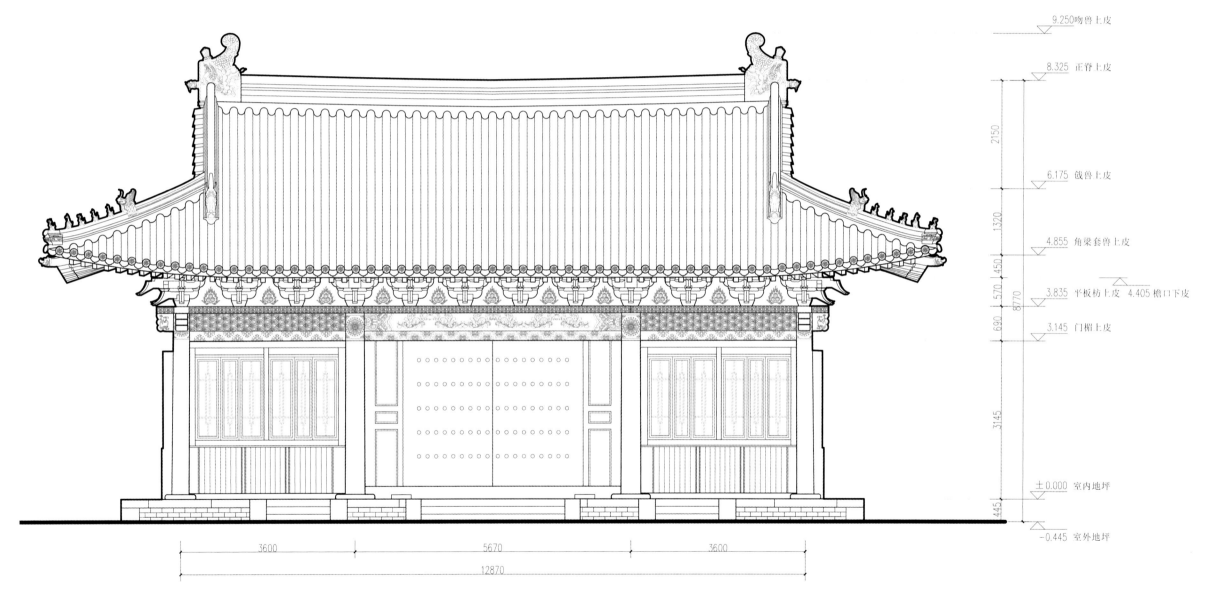

戟门南立面图
South elevation of Ji Gate

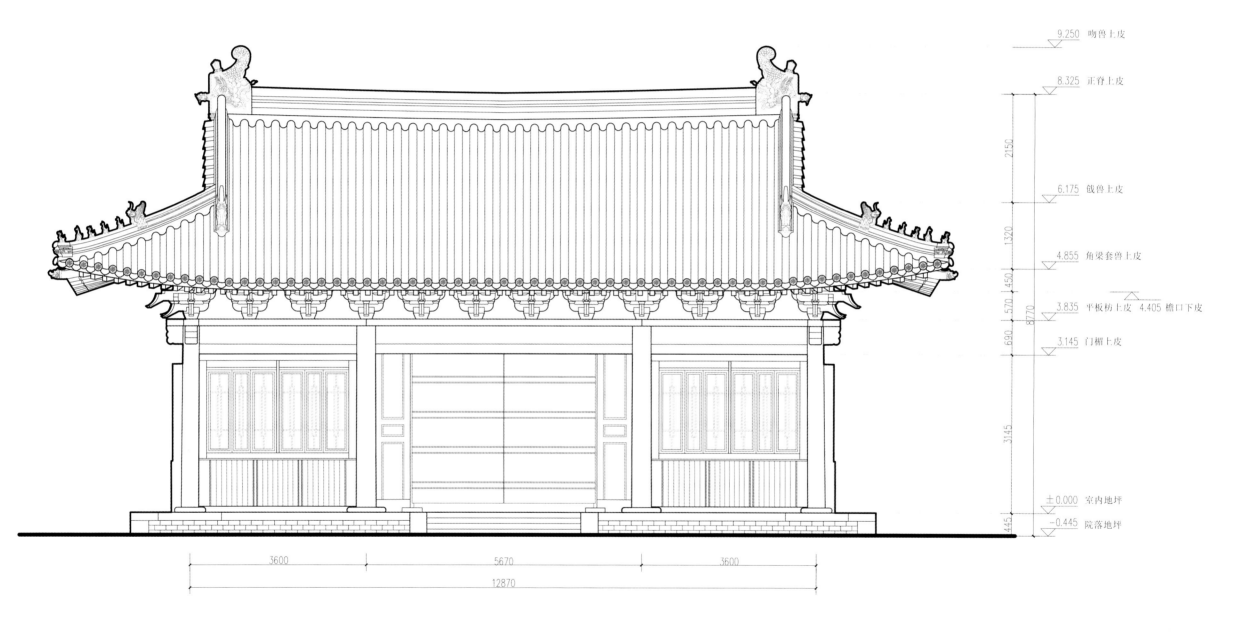

戟门北立面图
North elevation of Ji Gate

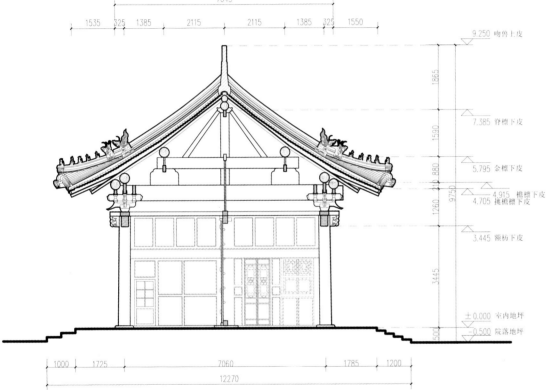

戟门 1-1 剖面图
Section 1-1 of Ji Gate

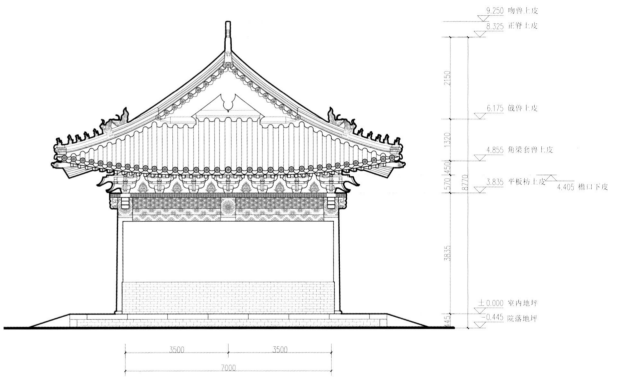

戟门西立面图
West elevation of Ji Gate

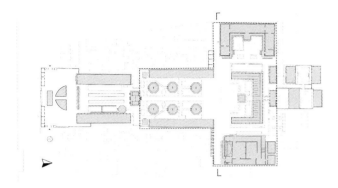
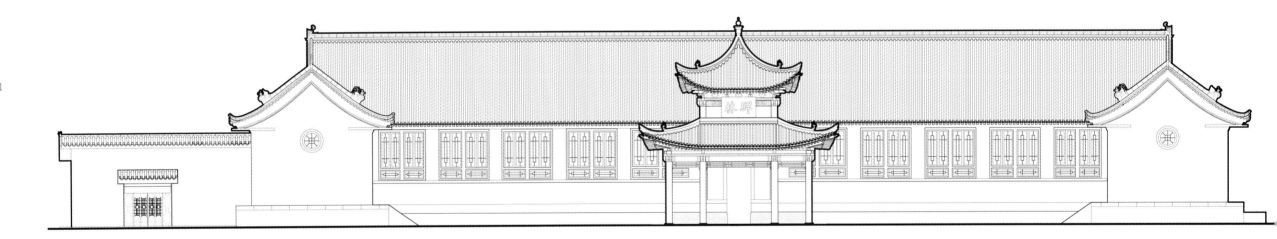

"石台孝经"亭院落横剖北视图
Cross-section of courtyard with *"shitai xiaojing"* stele pavilion as seen from the north

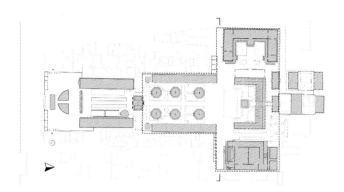

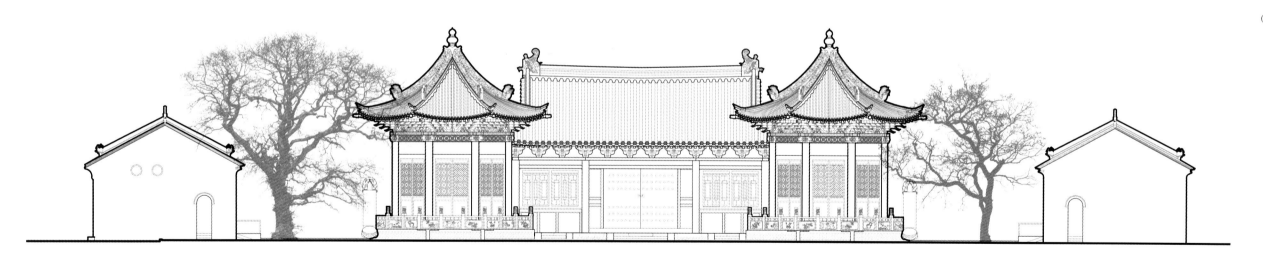

"石台孝经"亭院落横剖南视图
Cross-section of courtyard with "shitai xiaojing" stele pavilion as seen from the north

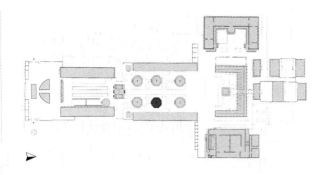

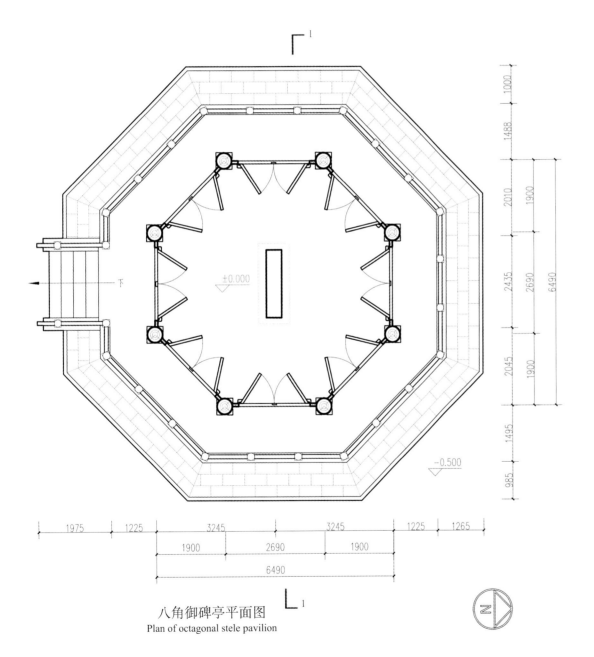

八角御碑亭平面图
Plan of octagonal stele pavilion

八角御碑亭梁架仰视图
Roof-framework as seen from below, octagonal stele pavilion

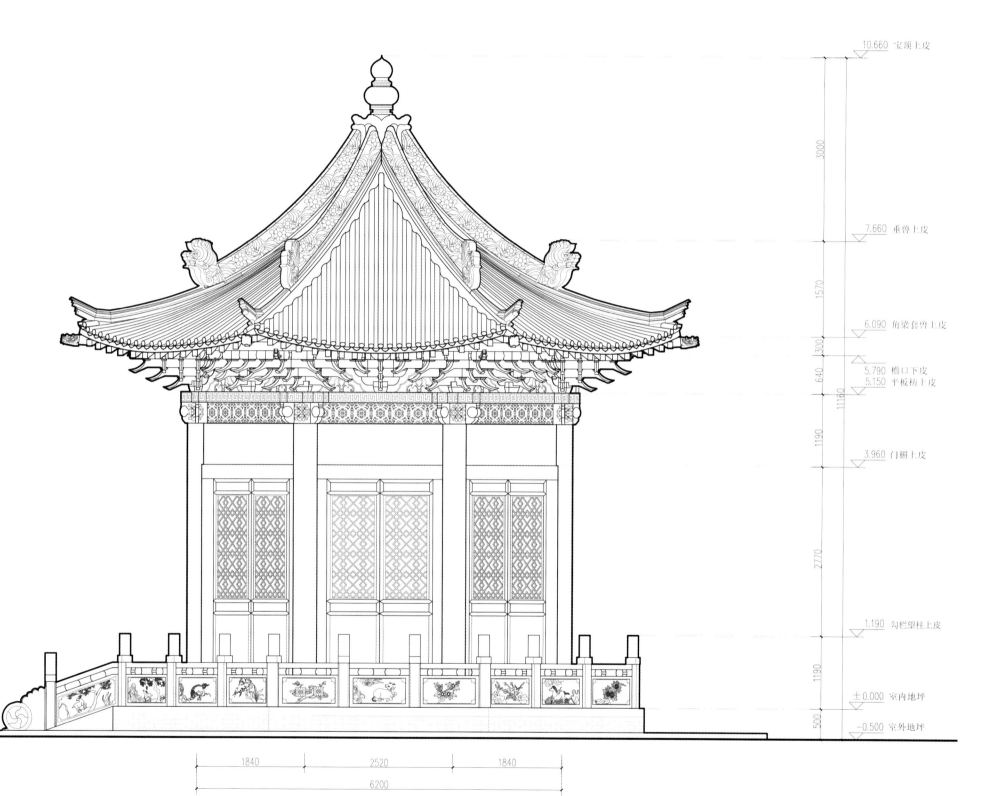

八角御碑亭东立面图
East elevation, octagonal stele pavilion

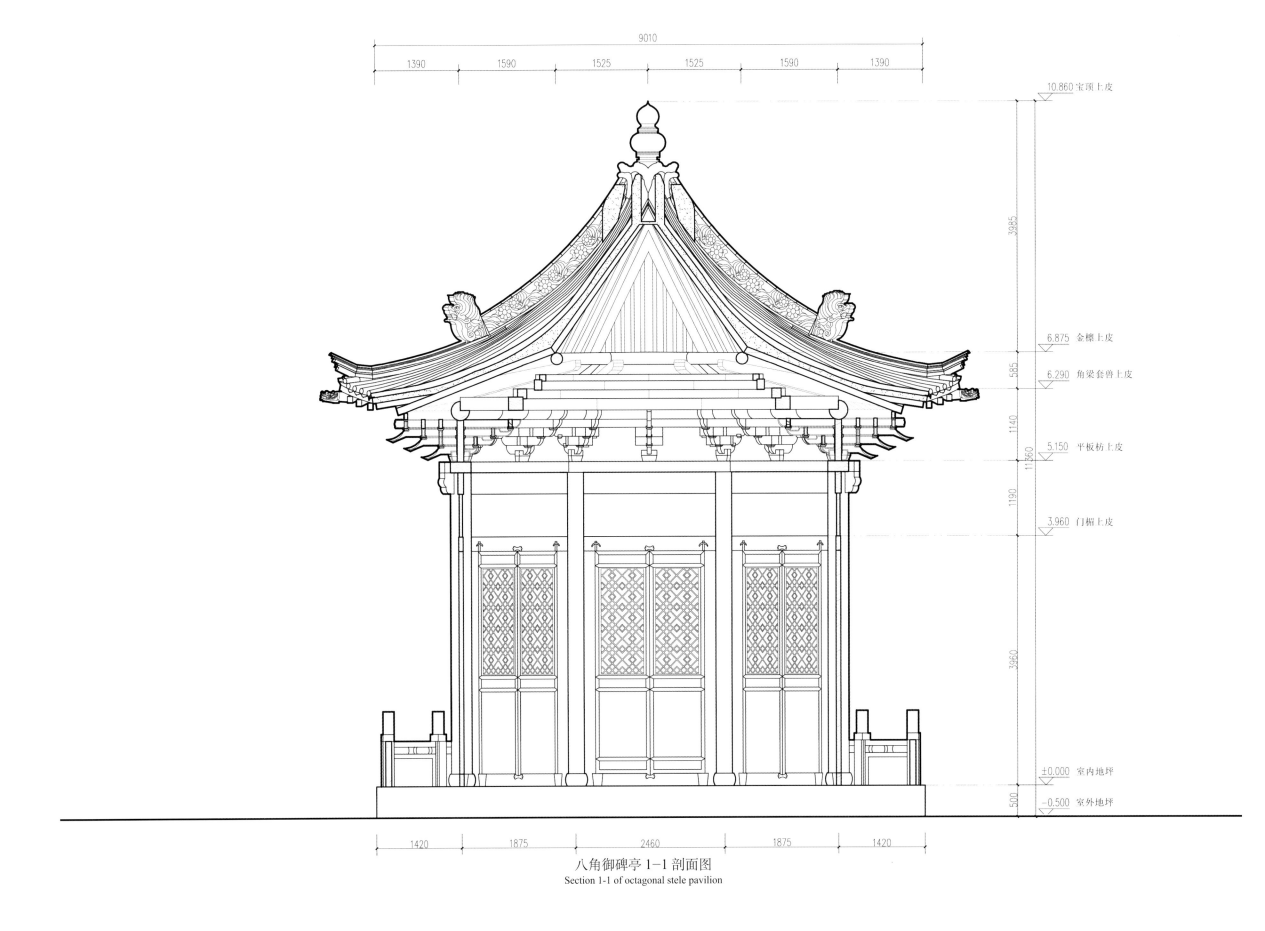

八角御碑亭 1-1 剖面图
Section 1-1 of octagonal stele pavilion

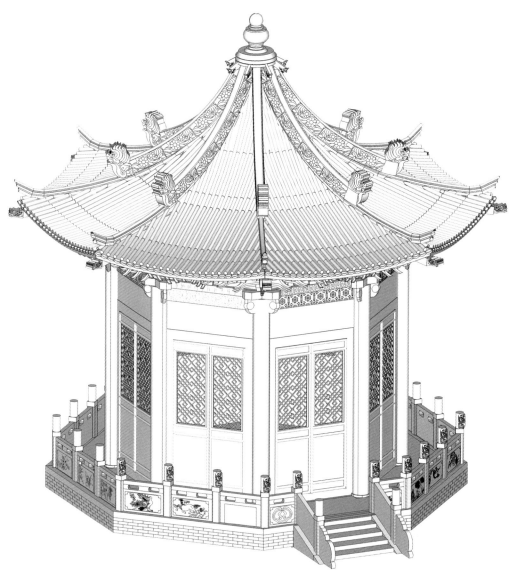

八角御碑亭模型
Reconstruction drawing of octagonal imperial stele pavilion

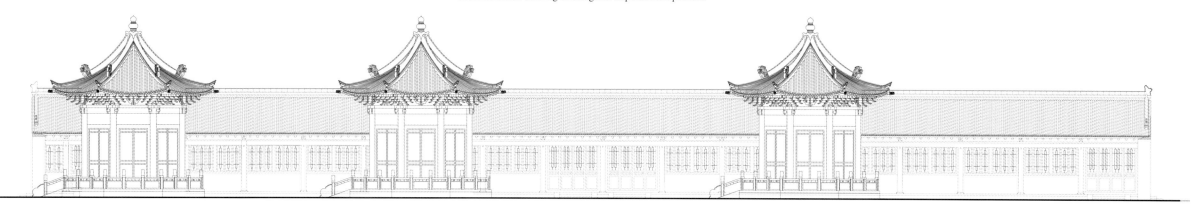

八角御碑亭院落西立面图
West elevation of courtyard with octagonal stele pavilions

八角御碑亭院落模型
Reconstruction drawing of courtyard with octagonal stele pavilions

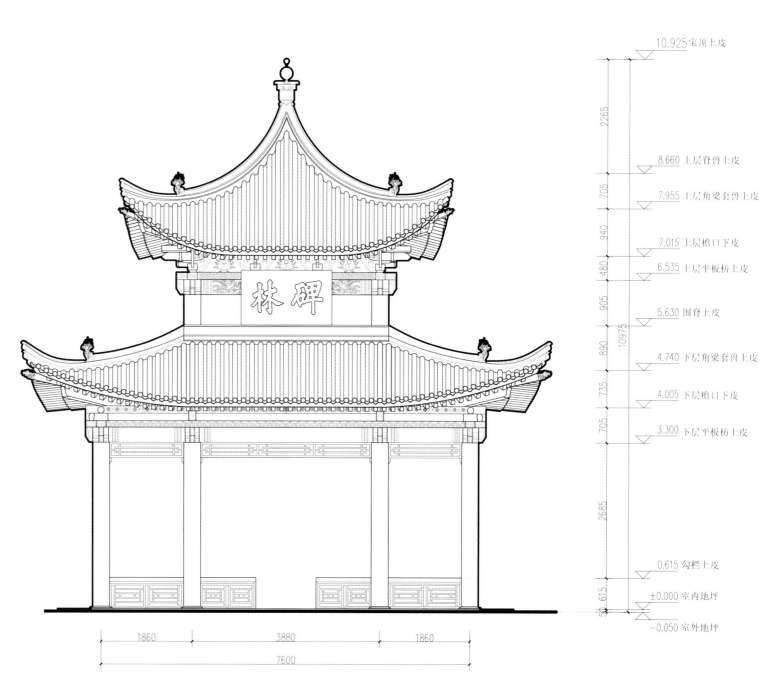
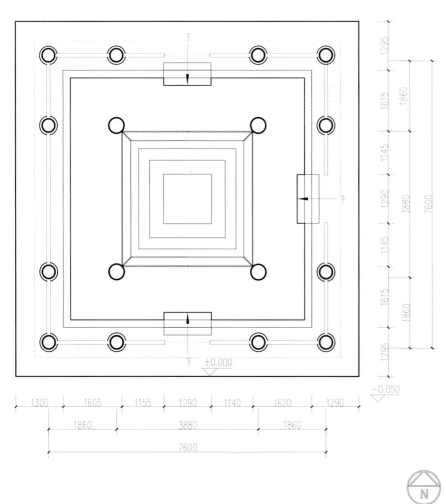

唐《石台孝经》亭平面图
Plan of Tang-dynasty *"shitai xiaojing"* stele pavilion

唐《石台孝经》亭南立面图
South elevation of Tang-dynasty *"shitai xiaojing"* stele pavilion

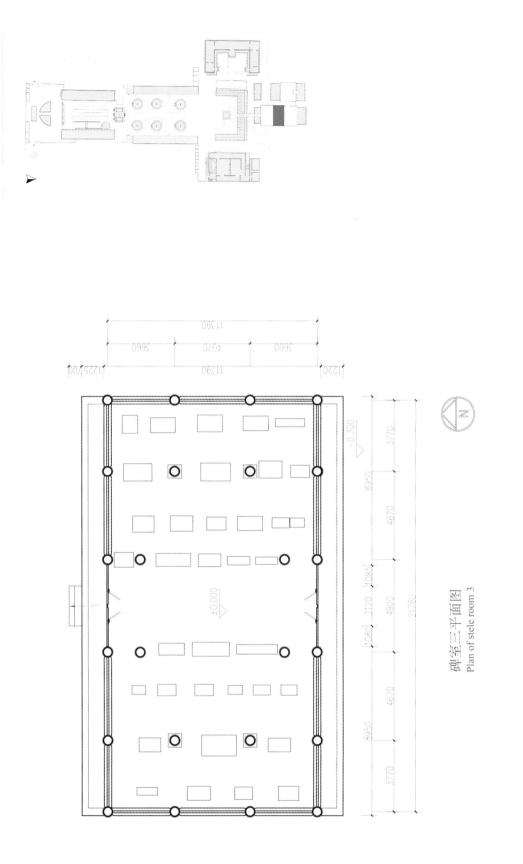

碑室三平面图
Plan of stele room 3

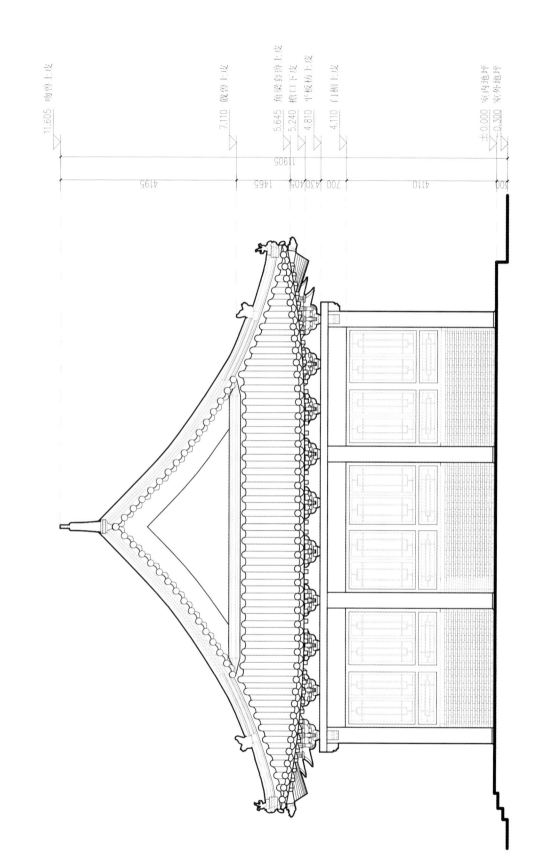

碑室三西立面图
West elevation of stele room 3

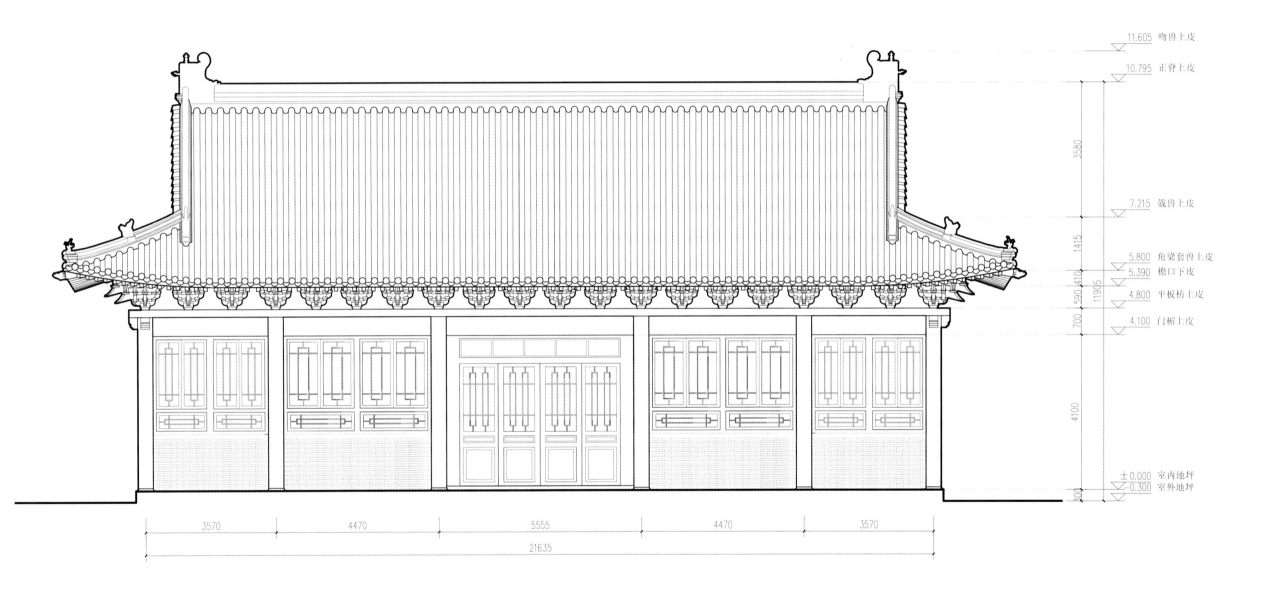

碑室三南立面图
South elevation of stele room 3

碑室三模型
Reconstruction of stele room 3

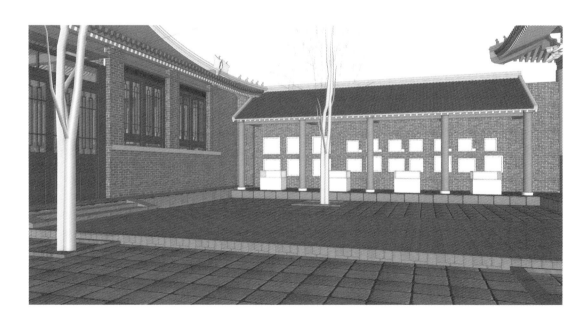

碑室三庭院模型
Reconstruction of courtyard of stele room 3

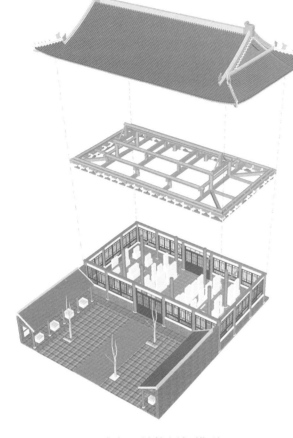

碑室三结构拆解模型
Exploded view of structure of stele room 3

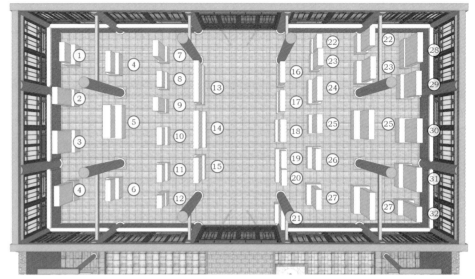

1. 德应侯碑	9. 广武将军产碑	17. 武都太守残碑	25. 邓太尉祠碑
2. 大观圣作之碑	10. 熹平石经残石	18. 曹全碑	26. 熹平石经残石
3. 孟显达碑	11. 邓太尉祠碑	19. 篆书千字文序碑	27. 广武将军弓产碑
4. 郭家庙碑	12. 昌公晖福寺碑	20. 篆书目录偏旁字源	28. 李憨碑
5. 智永真草千字文	13. 述圣颂碑	21. 唐公房碑	29. 道德寺碑
6. 惠坚禅师碑	14. 颜勤礼碑	22. 严勤礼碑	30. 惠坚禅师碑
7. 道德寺碑	15. 唐公房碑	23. 述圣颂碑	31. 智永真草千字文
8. 李憨碑	16. 仓颉庙碑	24. 宕昌公晖福寺碑	32. 郭家庙碑

碑室三藏碑索引图
Annotated plan of stele room 3 as seen from above

碑室三室内模型
Reconstruction of interior of stele room 3

碑室三檐下模型
Reconstruction of eaves of stele room 3

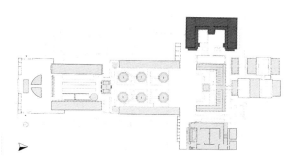

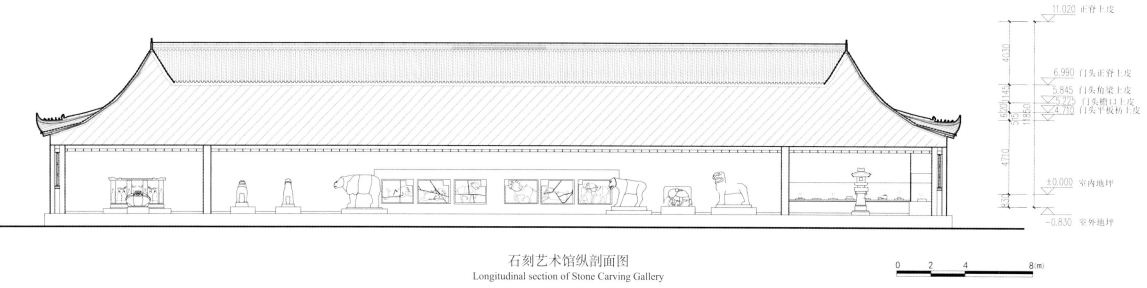

石刻艺术馆纵剖面图
Longitudinal section of Stone Carving Gallery

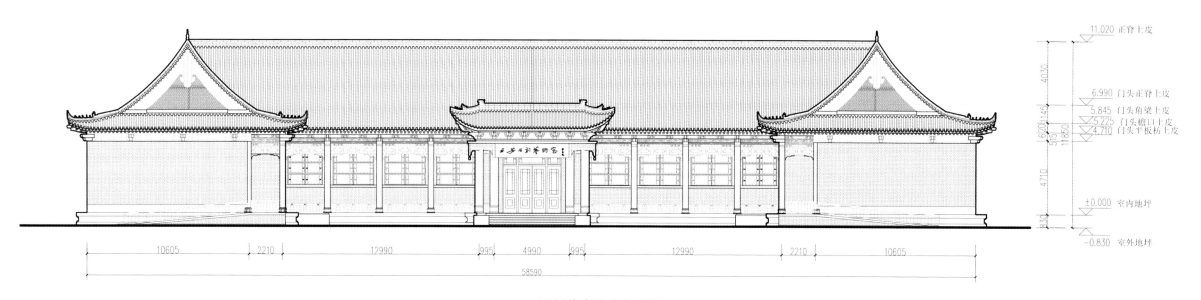

石刻艺术馆东立面图
East elevation of Stone Carving Gallery

石刻艺术馆南侧拴马桩大样图
Carved posts of southern side of Stone Carving Gallery

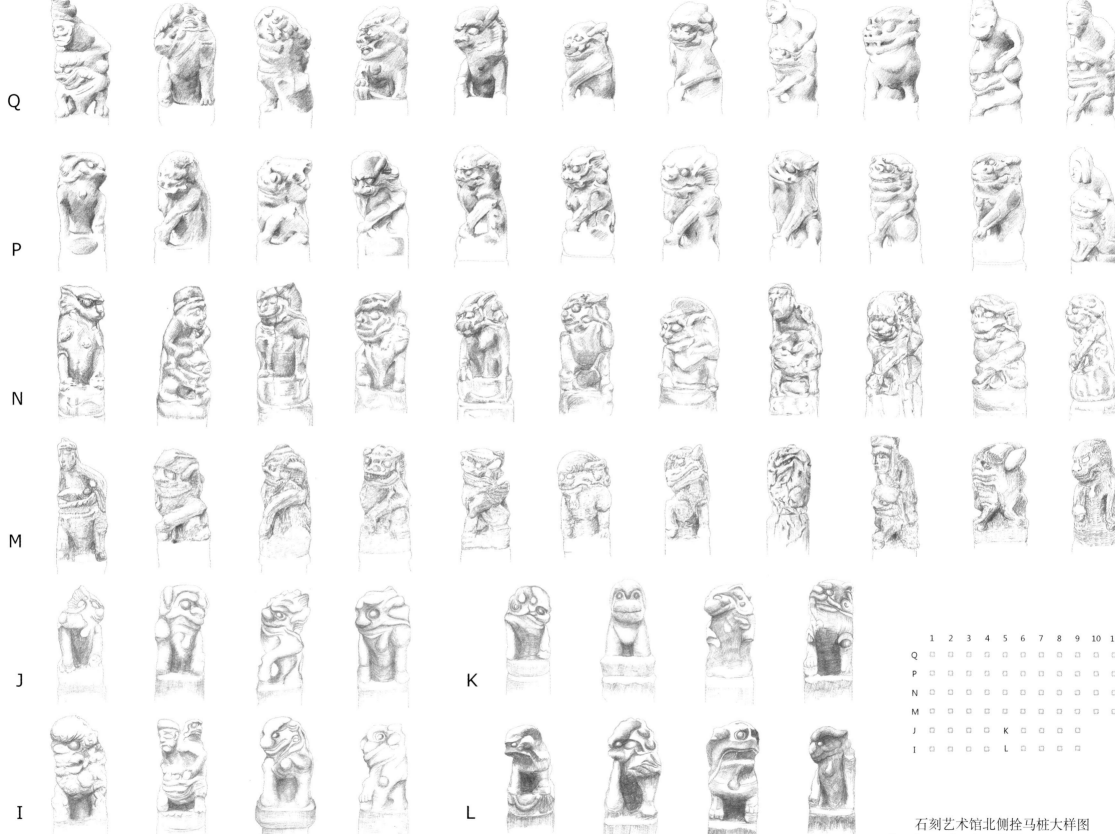

石刻艺术馆北侧拴马桩大样图
Carved posts of southern side of Stone Carving Gallery

西安都城隍庙

'Capital' City God Temple in Xi'an

Location: Western Street, Xi'an, Shaanxi province

Construction Date: Ming and Qing dynasties

Protection Level: National Priority Protected Site (fifth batch)

地　　址：陕西省西安西大街

年　　代：明—清

保护级别：全国重点文物保护单位（第五批）

Introduction

When it was built in 1387, the City (Chenghuang; "Walls and Moats") God Temple in Xi'an was one of the three most important temples of this kind in the Ming dynasty. Thanks to its unrivaled position among architectural monuments in China's northern western provinces, the character *du* (capital) was added to its name. The temple was initially situated at Jiuyao Street inside the east city gate but was relocated in 1433 to its present-day location at West Street. In 1723, the temple was destroyed by fire but in the same year, it was reconstructed by order of Nian Gengyao, governor of Shaanxi and Gansu. The artisans used material (stone and wood) from the former residence of Prince Qin of Ming and built a new complex with a gigantic layout and magnificent structures unmatched by any other on the central Shaanxi Plain (Guanzhong).

The Temple was dedicated to Ji Xin who served as a military general under Liu Bang, founder of the Han dynasty and later known as emperor Gaozu (r. 206-195 BCE) of Han. In 204 BCE, Xiang Yu, Liu Bang's archenemy and rival in an internal struggle for power, led an army of 40,000 men to Henan and successfully laid siege to Xingyang. Taking advantage of a resemblance in appearance, Ji Xin disguised himself as Liu Bang and feigned surrender. Liu Bang was able to escape, but after finding out the truth, Xiang Yu burnt Ji Xin to death. Owing to his martyrdom, Ji Xin, as an embodiment of loyalty for generations as an embodiment of loyalty. Various posthumous titles were conferred on him including the Song-dynasty title of "Zhongyou an Han gong" (Duke of Loyalty Blessing the Han), the Yuan-dynasty (1271-1368) title of "Fude xianzhong kangji wang" (Prince of Benevolence Serving Morality and Showing Loyalty), and the Ming-dynasty titles of "Zhongliehou" (Marquis of Loyalty and Martyrdom) and "City God of Xi'an". Additionally, Ji Xin's deeds became the subject of poetry. Li Tang, a county magistrate of Xichong in the Qing period, once visited the temple and composed the following lines:

"Hundreds of battles paved the way to the founding of Han dynasty.
A noble title was not on his mind when he dedicated himself to fire.
To fool the enemy, he dared to put on his master's guise.
Heavier than Mount Tai, that was his sacrifice.
On a lone mount, he (Gaozu) escaped from demise.
Xiang sneered at the martyr, amusement in his eyes.
Concealed in weeds, the temple now lies in desolation.
Yet the loyal soul will enjoy eternal memory."

Yu Youren, a famous politician of the Republican era, wrote:
"The grass at the foot of Guangwu Hill embodies the promise of spring.
For the fate of the state, the general was burnt to death.

概述

西安都城隍庙始建于明洪武二十年（1387年），是当时全国三大城隍庙之一，统辖西北数省，故称『都城隍庙』。初建时在东门内九曜街，明宣德八年（1433年）移建西大街现址。清雍正元年（1723年）庙毁于火，同年由川陕总督年羹尧移用明代秦王府砖石木料重修，建成后『规模宏大，栋宇崇宏，雄伟壮观，甲于关中』。

都城隍庙所供奉城隍为刘邦麾下大将纪信。公元前204年，项羽率四十万大军围刘邦于荥阳，纪信因外貌与刘邦相似，献计假扮刘邦出降，刘邦则趁乱逃脱。项羽发现中计后将纪信烧死，纪信也因此被视为忠臣，世受祭享。宋时封为『忠佑安汉公』、元朝封为『辅德显忠康济王』，明朝改为『忠烈侯』，署理西安府城隍。清时西充县令李棠访城隍庙，吟咏其事曰：『汉业艰难百战秋，隆准单骑从此脱，重瞳双眼笑谁酬？于今荒草空祠宇，一片忠魂万古留。』民国时于右任先生也曾题诗：『广武山前望草春，将军为国焚此身。敢于诳楚乘黄幄，焚身原不为封侯。刘兴项扑成陈迹，独有忠臣庙貌新』。

清光绪十三年（1887年），庙前商户不慎失火，烧失山门及民居商铺众多，时任陕西巡抚叶伯英募资重修。民国时陕西省政府主席邵力子也曾拨专款修葺。1942年，侵华日军空袭西安，向都城隍庙投掷炸弹两枚，炸毁了二殿及藏经阁，庙内珍藏数百年的文物毁于一旦。中华人民共和国

Fig.1 Old photograph of 'Capital' City God Temple in Xi'an from the Republican era
Fig.2 "*Yougan youying*" timber archway of 'Capital' City God Temple in Xi'an
Fig.3 Stage building of 'Capital' City God Temple in Xi'an

图一 西安都城隍庙民国时期旧影

图3 西安都城隍庙戏楼

图2 西安都城隍庙『有感有应』木牌坊

Liu (Bang) rose and Xiang (Yu) became a thing of the past.
With a brand new appearance, the temple of the loyal martyr will last."

In 1887, during late Qing period, a fire accidentally caused by vendors outside the City God Temple destroyed the main gate of the complex along with many houses and stores. Shortly afterwards, the provincial governor Ye Boying commissioned repair. In the Republican era, the governor of Shaanxi Shao Lizi allocated a special fund for temple renovation. In 1942, two bombs were dropped on the site during a Japanese air raid, destroying two halls and the Buddhist library along with the cultural relics that had been housed there for centuries. Religious activities came to a sudden halt during the early years of the Peoples' Republic of China. The resting hall (*qindian*) was repurposed as Miaohou Street Office. The open square in front of the temple was transferred into a wholesale market for small commodities after 1979. In 2001, the temple was declared a National Priority Protected Site, and the Xi'an municipal government provided the necessary funds to remove traces of Communist activity from within the temple perimeter and return the property to the Taoist Association. In 2005, the transformation was finally completed.

The City God Temple of Xian is famous for its vast size as well as its delicately built, magnificent buildings. A monumental archway (*pailou*), five bays wide, marks the temple entrance. A plaque is attached to it saying "*ni lai le me*" (have you come?). The archway columns are embellished with a couplet saying "*shanlai cidi xinbukui, eguo wumen danzihan*" (at my door good-doers are free of shame, whereas evil-doers will be responsible for their own disaster). Behind the *pailou*, the front gate (*shanmen*) of the temple opens into a 100-meter corridor paved with limestone leading to Fangsheng (Life Freeing) Pond. The corridor is flanked by (grain?) stores and the two-story Wenchang Pavilion dedicated to the God of Culture and Literature (Wenchangwang). The pavilion roof connects to the roof of the building in front of it (i.e. an undulating roof; *goulianda*) through a built-in "valley" that carries off rainwater at the intersection of the two roof slopes. Behind the pond stands Yi Gate. After passing through Yi Gate, there is a two-story stage building (*xilou*) that is located opposite to the main hall to its north. In-between them stands another timber-framed archway, this time three bays wide (with four columns). This *pailou* has plaques attached on both sides, with the southern one saying "*yougan youying*" (he listens and answers) and the northern one saying "*congming zhengzhi*" (bright and upright). A large timber board is suspended above the plaques, bearing an inscription that reads "*rensuan buru tiansuan*" (god outwits man). A pair of bronze lions, forged in 1559, used to stand flanking the central bay of the *pailou* but has now been moved to the Provincial Museum of Shaanxi. The main hall is a seven-bay, ten-rafter structure with hip roof and surrounding corridor. Inside are installed statues of the City God, the legendary civil and military officials in charge of afterlife judgment (Wenwu panguan), and the Four Meritorious Officers who guard time by day, month, year, and season (Sizhi gongcao). The sidewalls depict stories of the City God, the Ten Courts of Hell (Shidian yanjun), and the Six Realms of Samsara (Sisheng liudao lunhui).

国建立后，宗教活动一度中断，后将寝殿用作庙后街办事处，改革开放以后将庙前广场改为小商品批发市场，2001年列为全国重点文物保护单位，2003年由西安市政府出资，迁出庙内商贩，将庙产归还道教协会，2005年庙前广场改造工程完工。

都城隍庙范围广大，建筑精宏。山门处立有五间牌楼一座，高悬『你来了么』牌匾，楹联为『善来此地心不愧，恶过吾门胆自寒』，牌楼后为山门，入内为百米长之青石甬道，道旁为店铺及二层高勾连搭文昌阁一座，其后为放生池，池后即是仪门。进入仪门，有二层戏楼一座，与大殿南北对峙，两者之间立有四柱三间木牌楼一座，正背面分别匾书『有感有应』『聪明正直』，匾下悬巨大的木算盘一个，上书『人算不如天算』，其下置立明嘉靖三十八年（1559年）铸造铜狮一对（现迁置陕西省博物馆）。大殿庑殿顶，七间十椽，周围回廊开敞，内奉城隍，配祀文武判官与四值功曹，两壁绘城隍巡城图、十殿阎君图、四生六道轮回图等。

图5 西安都城隍庙大殿内部梁架（维修前）

图4 西安都城隍庙大殿（维修前）

Fig.4 Main hall (before restoration) of 'Capital' City God Temple in Xi'an
Fig.5 Interior framework (before restoration) of 'Capital' City God Temple in Xi'an

Survey and Mapping Information

Responsible Department: Department of Architecture (Class of 2011), School of Architecture, Xi'an University of Architecture and Technology

Team Members: ZHAO Nansen, FU Rong, WANG Jialiang, WANG Jiangning, GE Yingchao, QIU Lei, ZHANG Chi, WANG Xinyi, XIAO Xiong, LI Chuan, LIU Yuan, QU Pengjing, HAO Lihui, FU Jiaming, LAN Xi, LI Xiao, WANG Jing, WEI Xiaoyu, FAN Liye, HOU Tian, HAO Shan, ZHANG Yuxin, SU Bowen, HOU Qing, XUE Jiajia, XU Pengfei, QIN Yujie, GOU Rui, HU Kun, MA Tong, XUE Peng, HU Jiahao, HU Yuan, LI Zeyu, JI Qian, HONG Jianli, WANG Haotian, NAN Yuesong, YIN Tong

Supervisors: YU Mengzhe, HUANG Sida

Editors of Drawings: LI Shuangshuang, TONG Mengfei

Survey Time: October 2015

西安都城隍庙测绘的人员名单

测 绘：西安建筑科技大学建筑学院建筑学2011级

赵南森 付蓉 王家梁 葛应超 仇磊 张箎 王心怡
肖雄 李川 刘源 屈鹏菁 郝力慧 符佳鸣 兰西 李潇
王品 魏晓雨 樊李烨 侯天 郝姗 张雨馨 苏博文 侯青
薛佳佳 徐鹏飞 秦宇洁 勾瑞 胡坤 马通 薛鹏 胡家灏
呼源 李泽宇 计倩 洪建力 王浩天 南岳松 尹彤

指导教师：喻梦哲 黄思达

图纸整理：李双双 仝梦菲

测绘时间：2015年10月

参考文献 References

［一］赵立瀛主编. 陕西古建筑. 西安：陕西人民出版社. 1992.

［二］国家文物局主编. 中国文物地图集·陕西分册. 西安：西安地图出版社. 1998.

［三］刘征. 西安城隍庙建筑研究. 西安建筑科技大学硕士学位论文. 2006.

［四］袁晓东. 西安城隍庙历史街区保护与更新研究. 西安建筑科技大学硕士学位论文. 2004.

［五］刘磊, 金璐. 寻找逝去的记忆——西安都城隍庙掠影. 城建档案. 2008（4）.32-36.

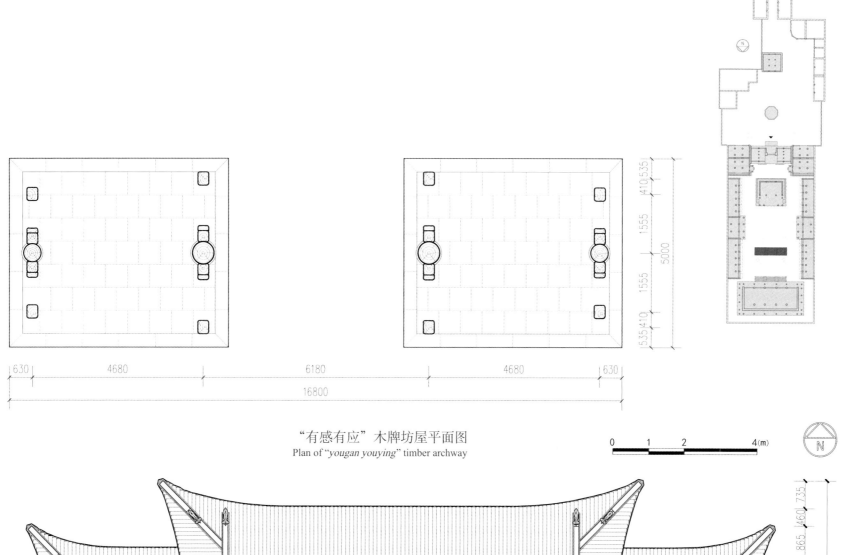

"有感有应"木牌坊屋平面图
Plan of *"yougan youying"* timber archway

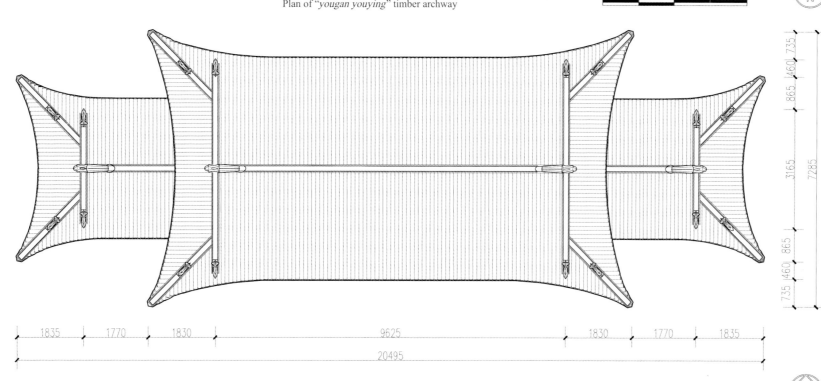

"有感有应"木牌坊屋顶平面图
Plan of roof of *"yougan youying"* timber archway

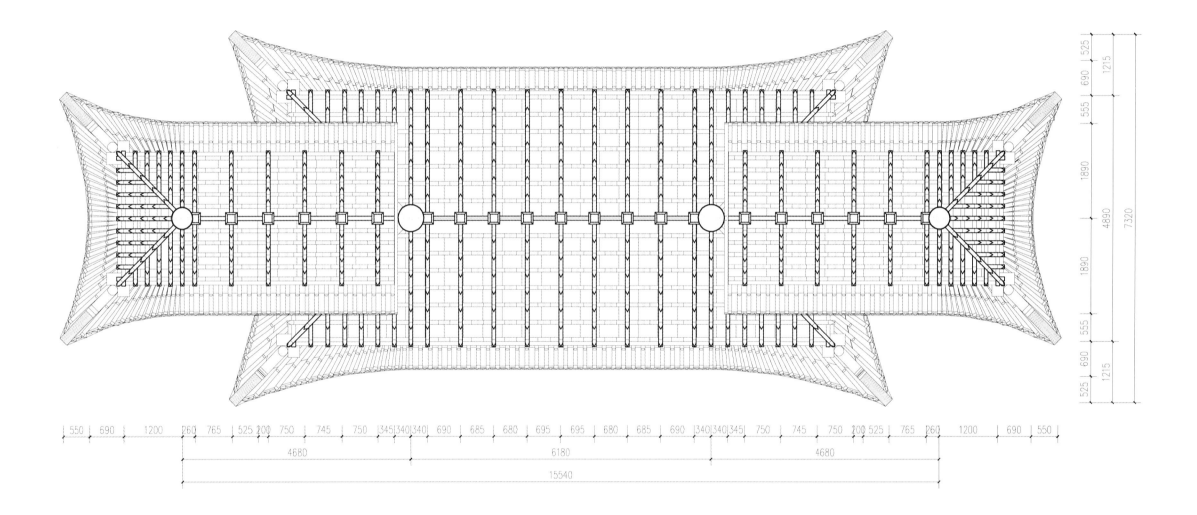

"有感有应"木牌坊梁架仰视图

Plan of framework of *"yougan youying"* timber archway as seen from below

中国古建筑测绘大系·祠庙建筑——陕西祠庙

"有感有应"木牌坊南立面图
South elevation of *"yougan youying"* timber archway

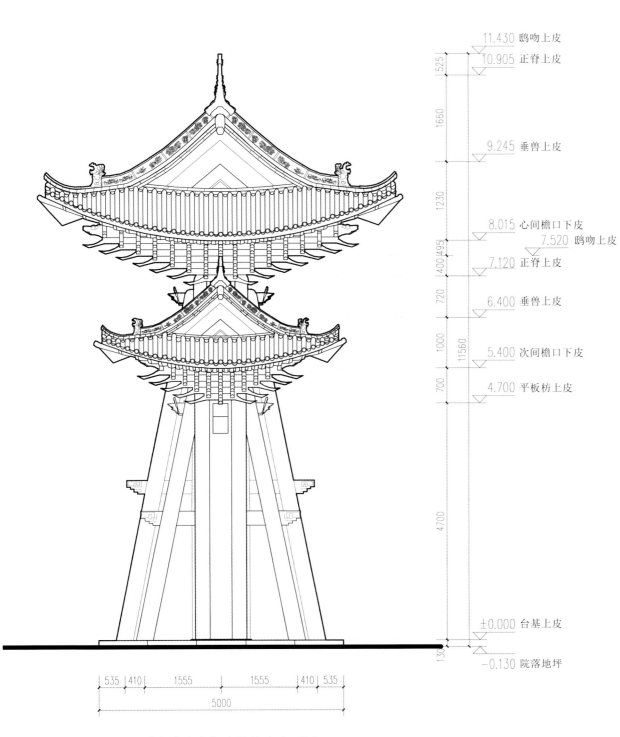

"有感有应"木牌坊东立面图

East elevation of *"yougan youying"* timber archway

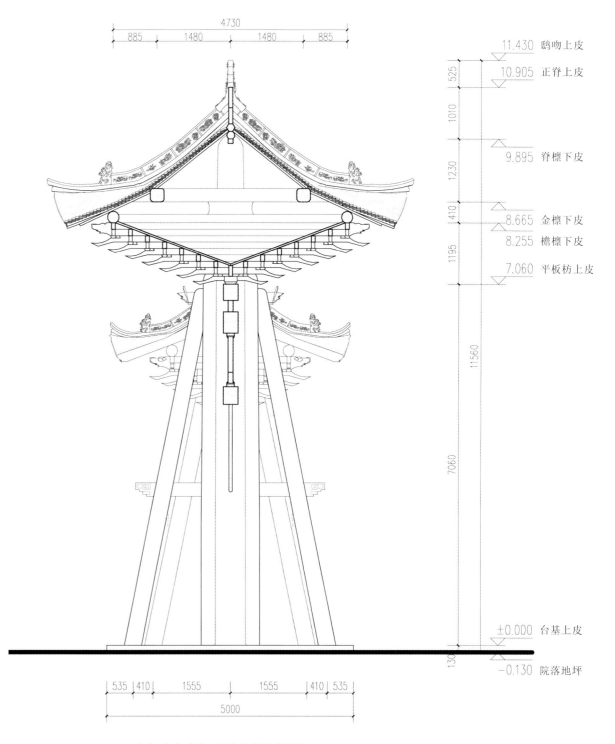

"有感有应"木牌坊横剖面图

Cross-section of *"yougan youying"* timber archway

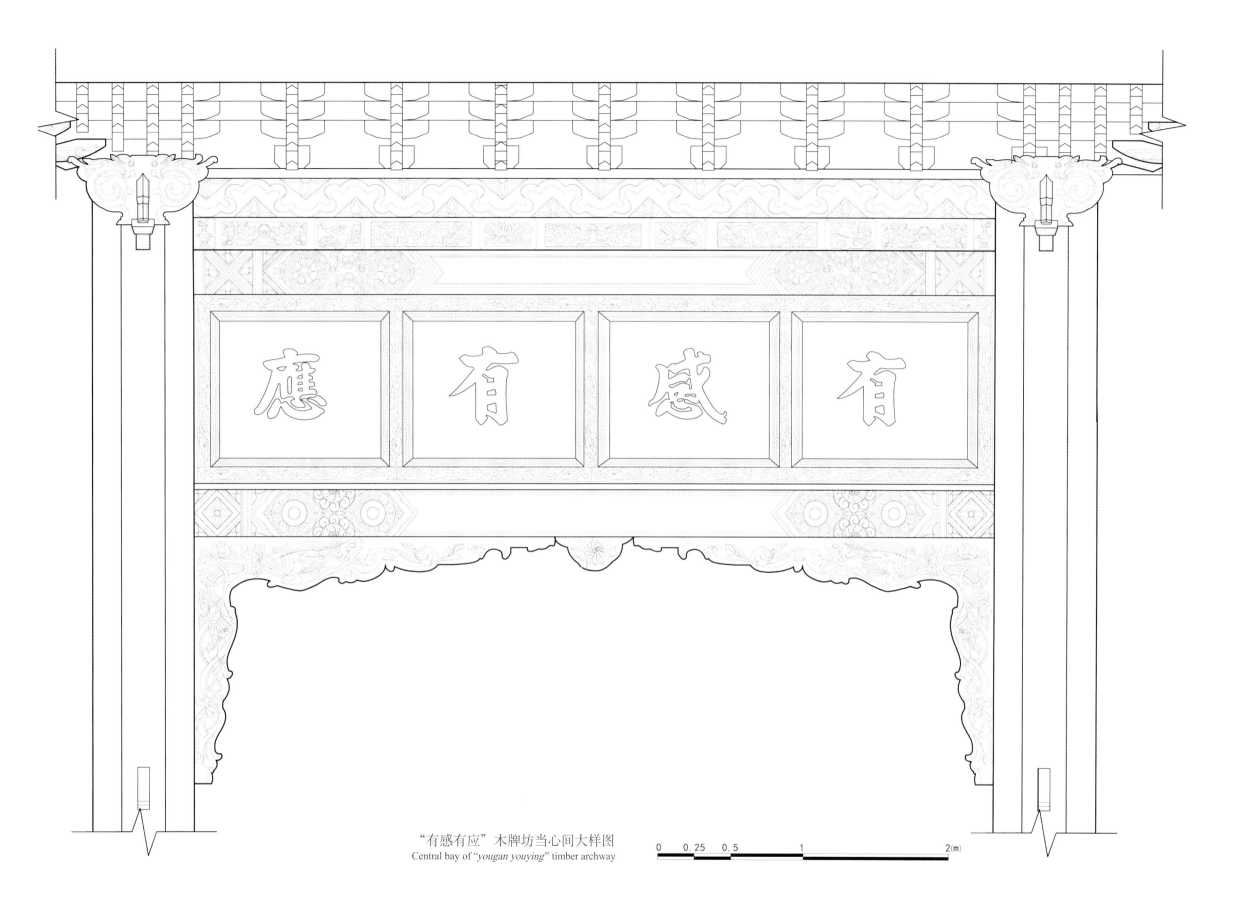

"有感有应"木牌坊当心间大样图
Central bay of *"yougan youying"* timber archway

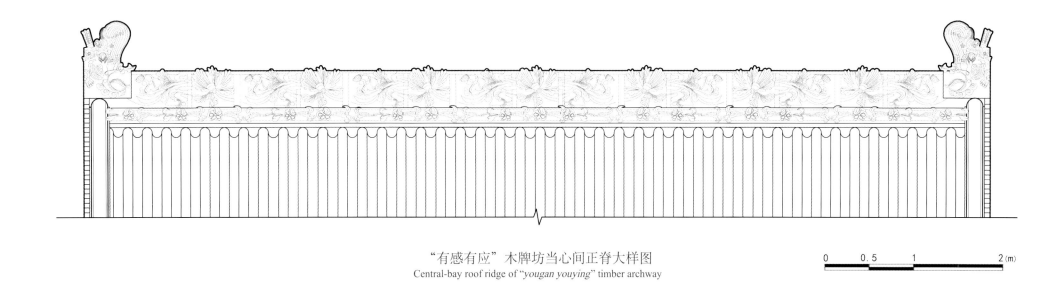

"有感有应"木牌坊当心间正脊大样图
Central-bay roof ridge of *"yougan youying"* timber archway

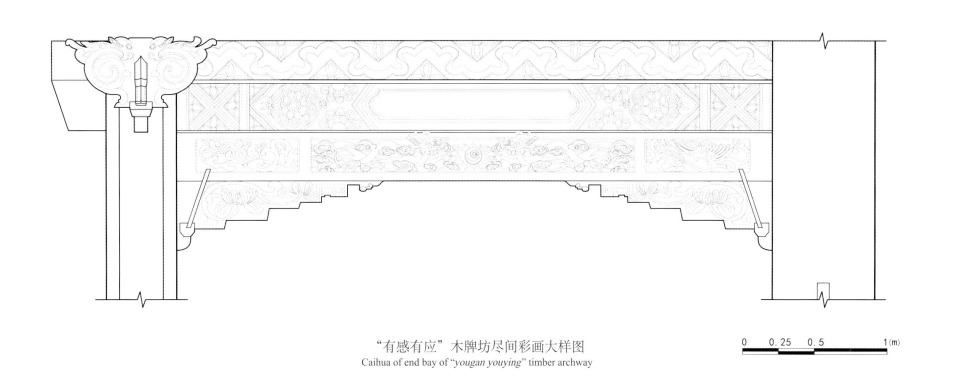

"有感有应"木牌坊尽间彩画大样图
Caihua of end bay of *"yougan youying"* timber archway

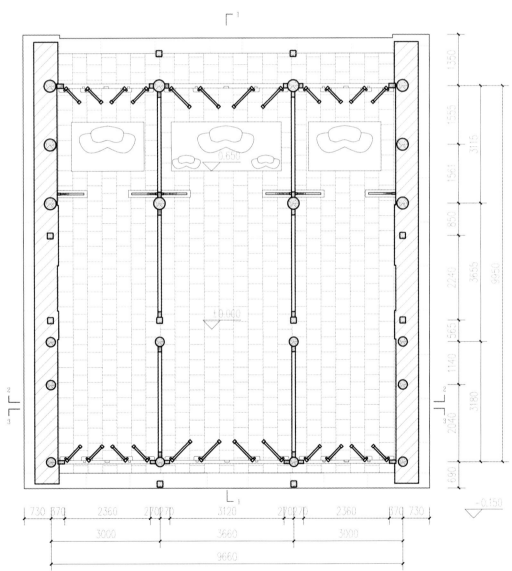

文昌阁一层平面图
Plan of first floor of Wenchang Pavilion

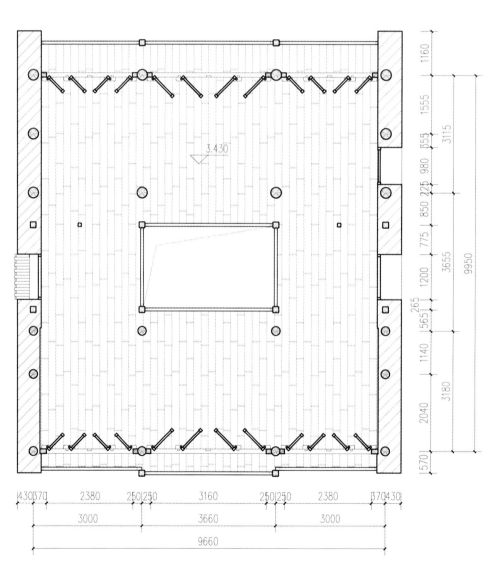

文昌阁二层平面图
Plan of second floor of Wenchang Pavilion

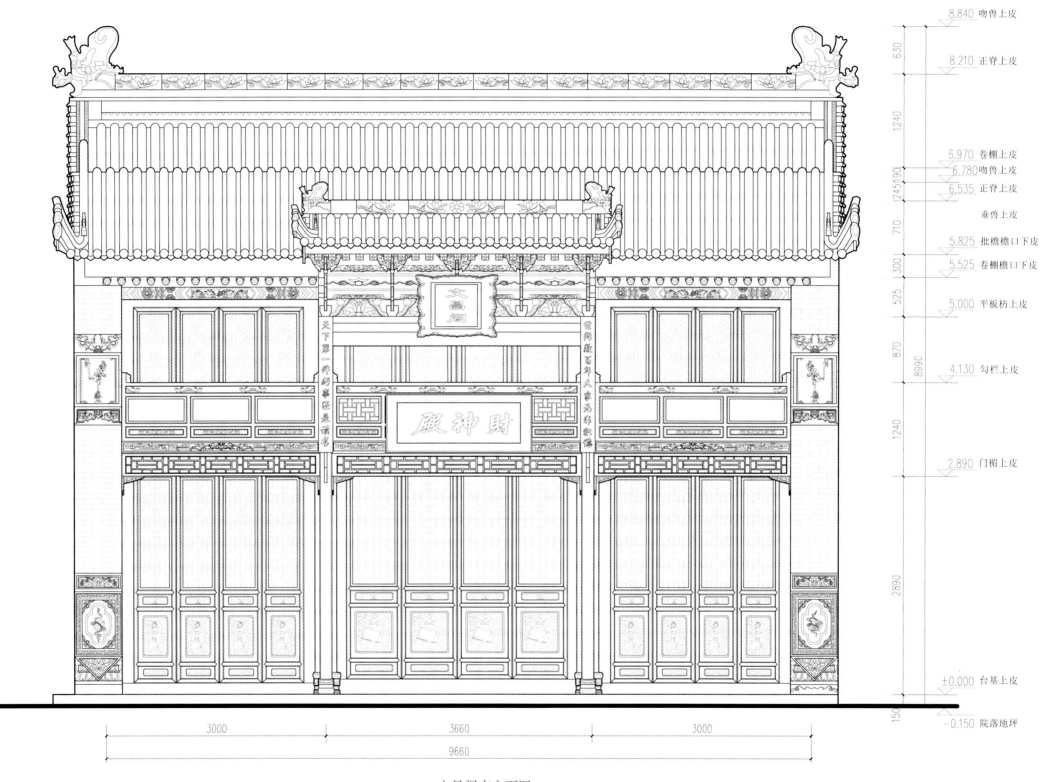

文昌阁南立面图
South elevation of Wenchang Pavilion

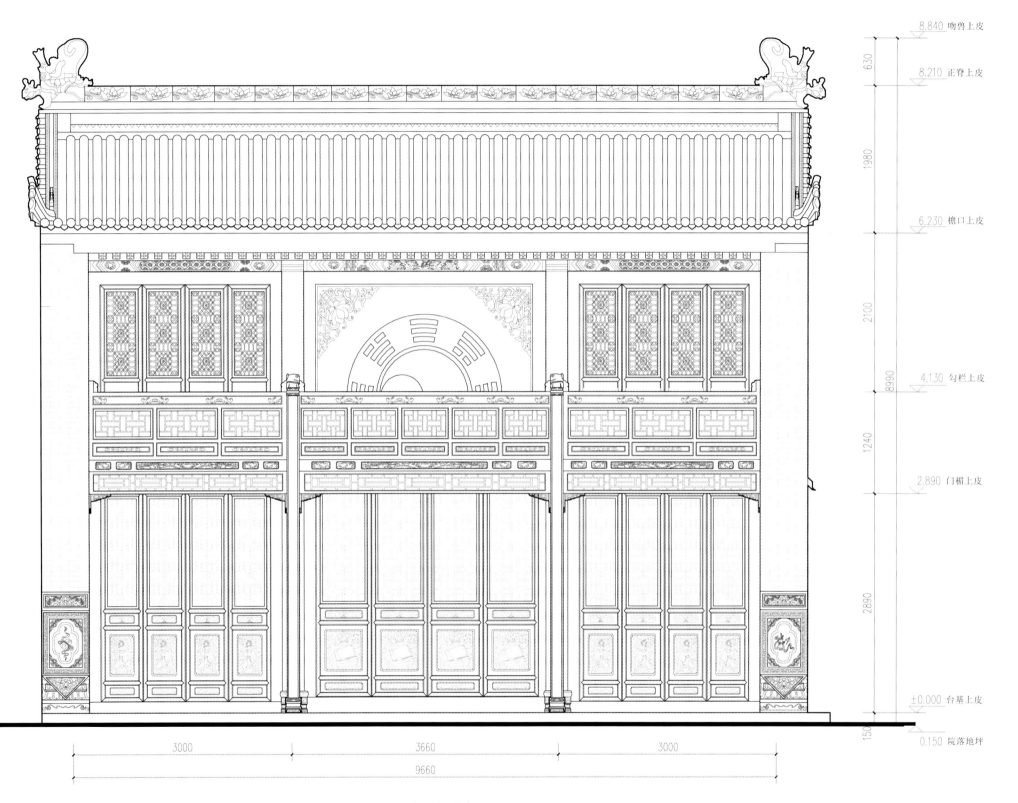

文昌阁北立面图
North elevation of Wenchang Pavilion

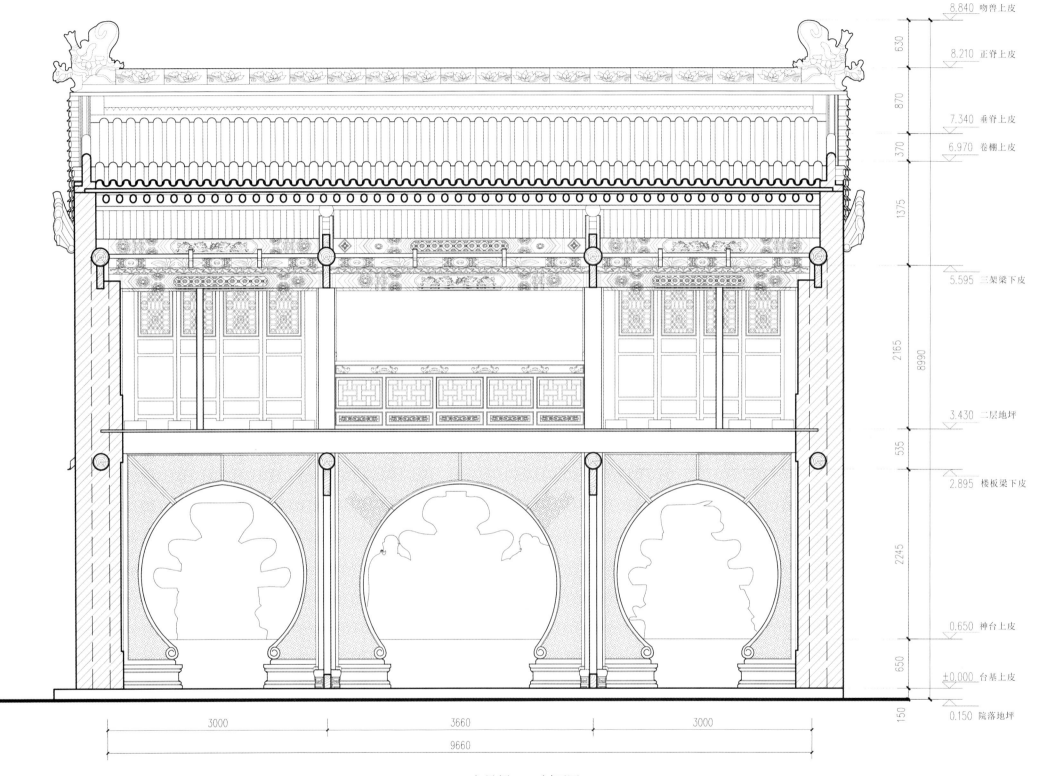

文昌阁 2—2 剖面图
Section 2-2 of Wenchang Pavilion

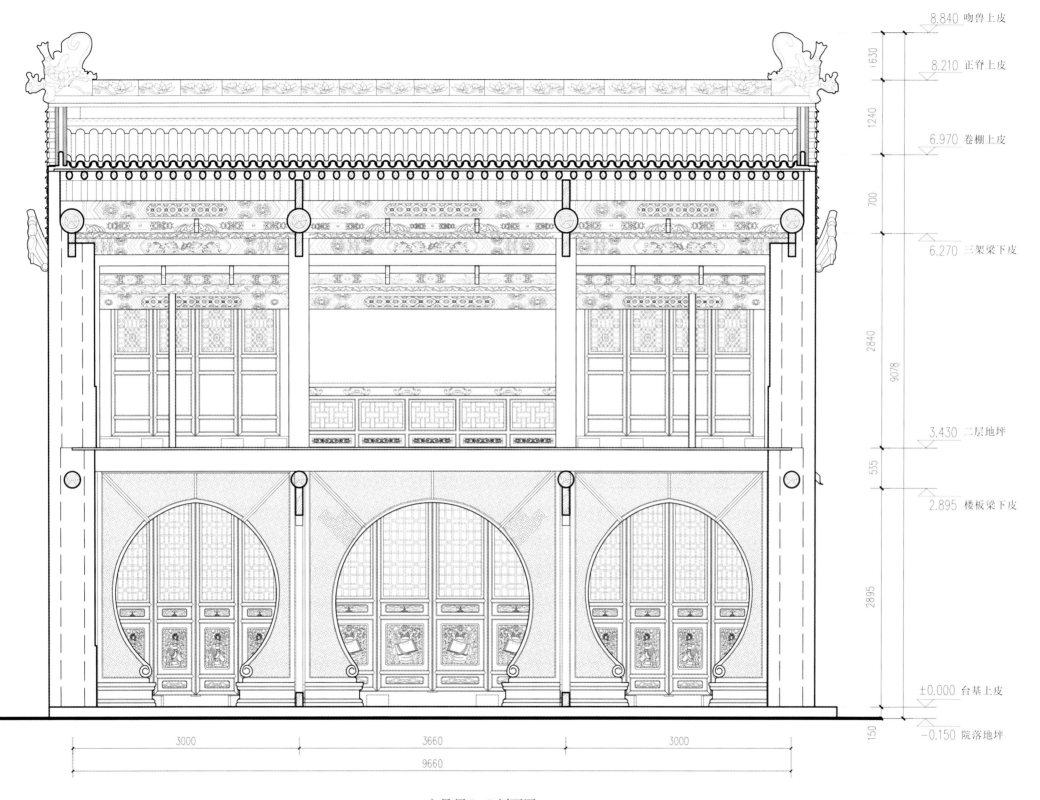

文昌阁 3-3 剖面图
Section 3-3 of Wenchang Pavilion

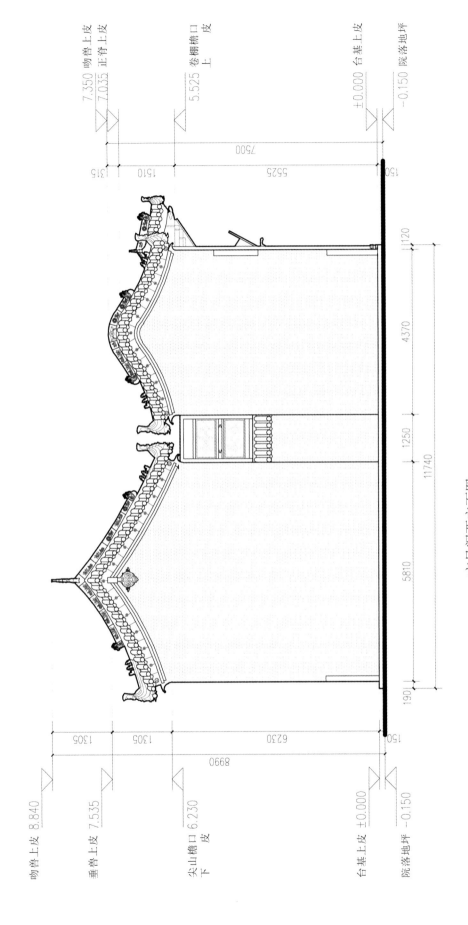

文昌阁西立面图
West elevation of Wenchang Pavilion

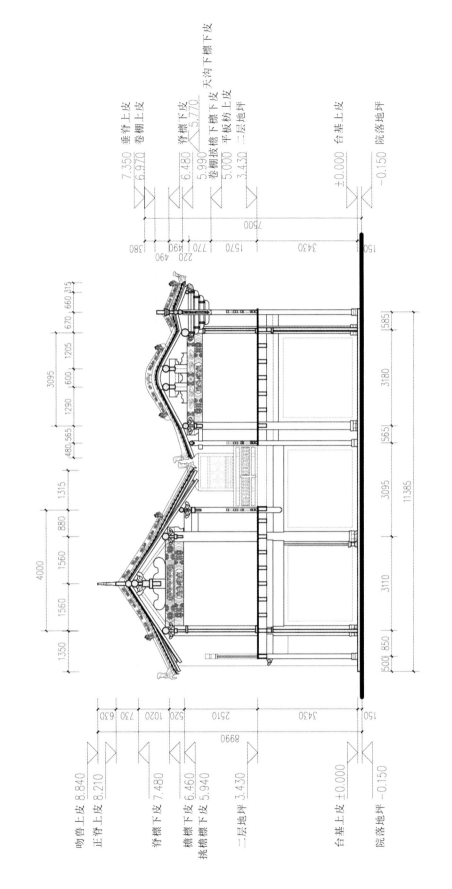

文昌阁1—1剖面图
Section 1-1 of Wenchang Pavilion

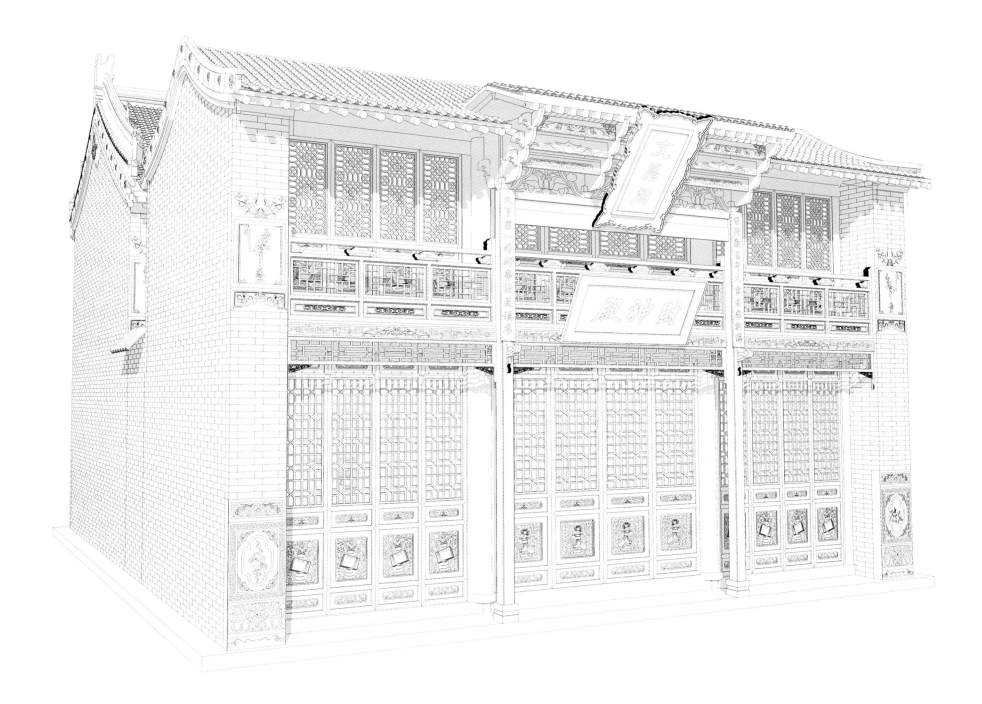

文昌阁——财神殿模型
Reconstruction of Caishen Hall of Wenchang Pavilion

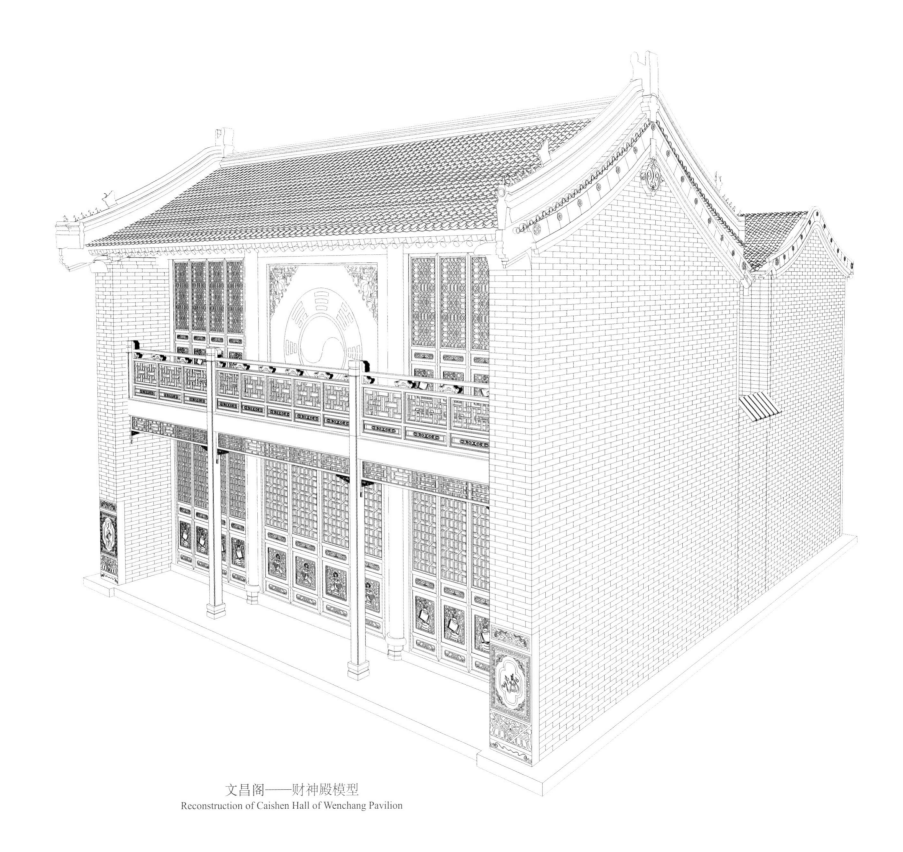

文昌阁——财神殿模型
Reconstruction of Caishen Hall of Wenchang Pavilion

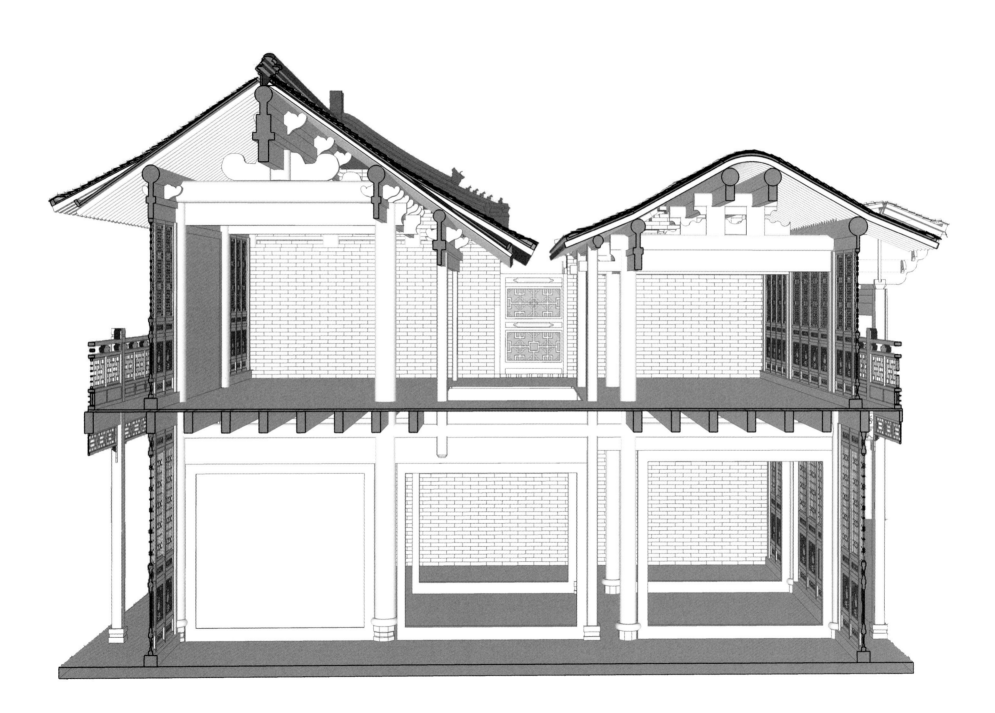

文昌阁——财神殿模型剖透视
Perspective section view of Wenchang Pavilion

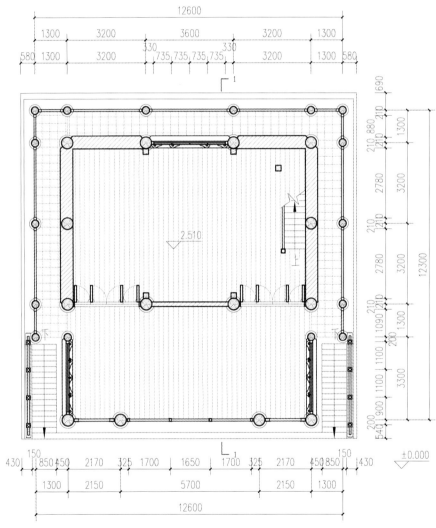

戏台一层平面图
Plan of first floor of stage building

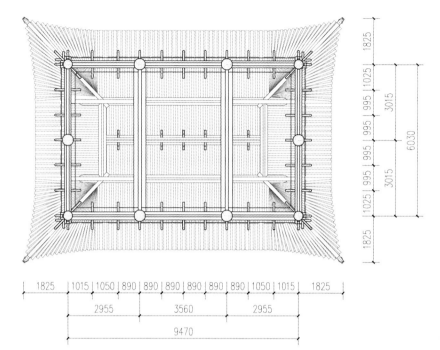

戏台二层梁架仰视图
Framework as seen from below, second floor of stage building

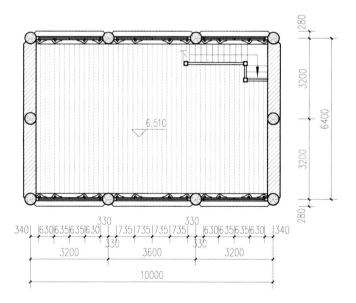

戏台二层平面图
Plan of second floor of stage building

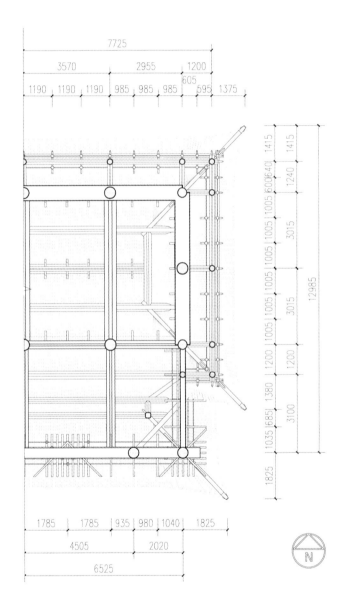

戏台一层梁架仰视图
Framework as seen from below, first floor of stage building

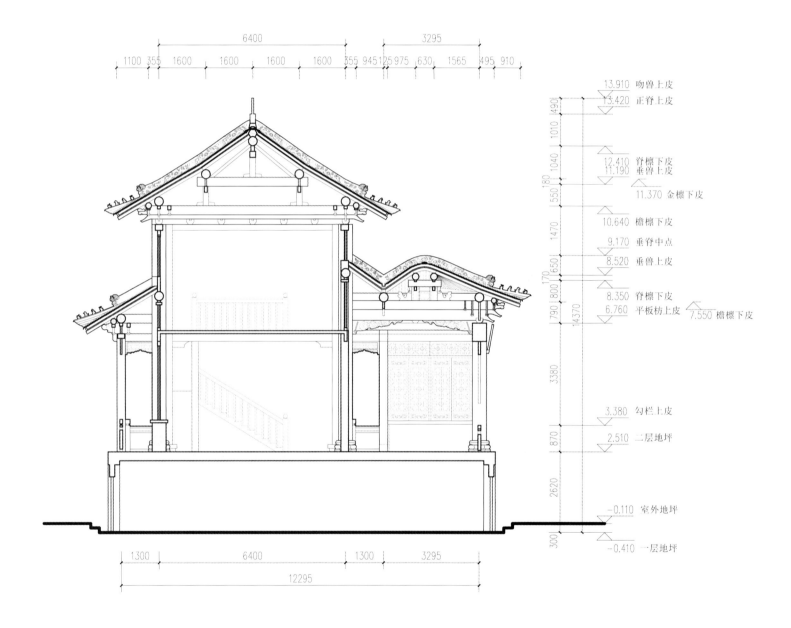

戏台 1-1 剖面图
Cross-section of central bay of stage building

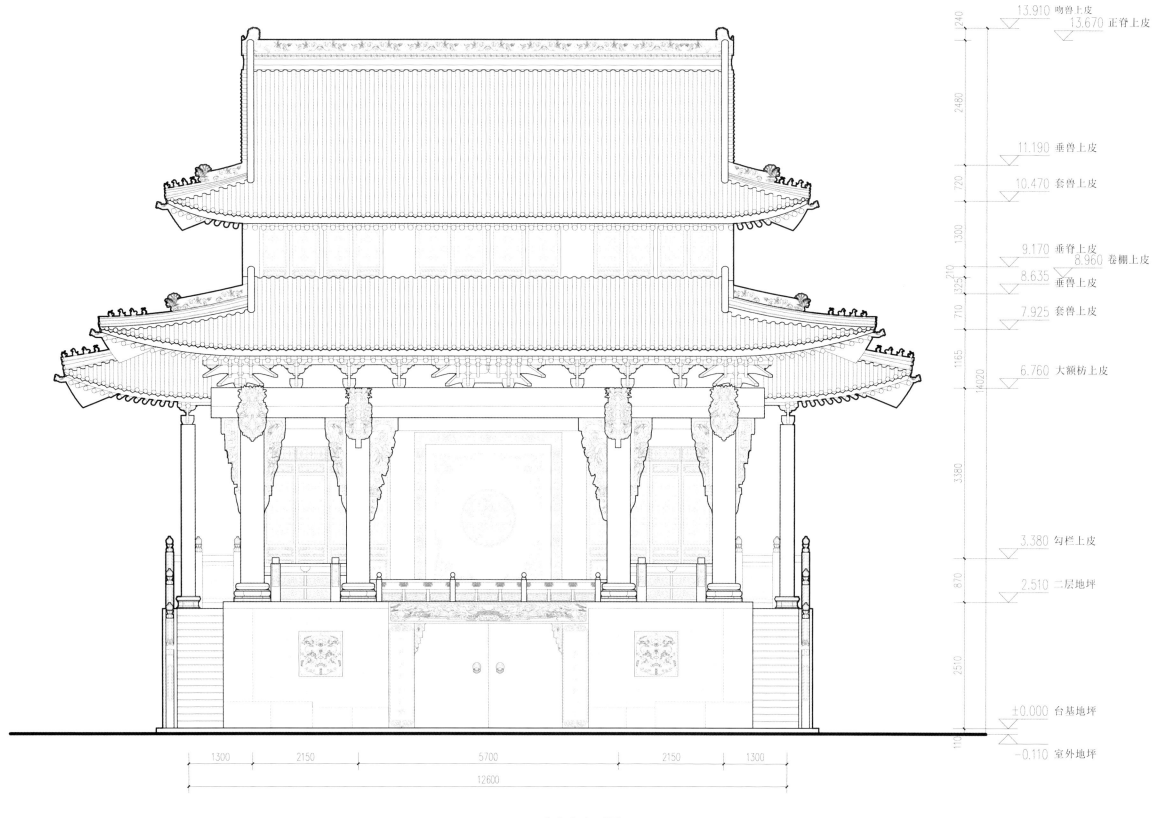

戏台北立面图
North elevation of stage building

戏台北侧二层后壁纹饰大样

Decoration of second-floor rear wall, northern side of stage building

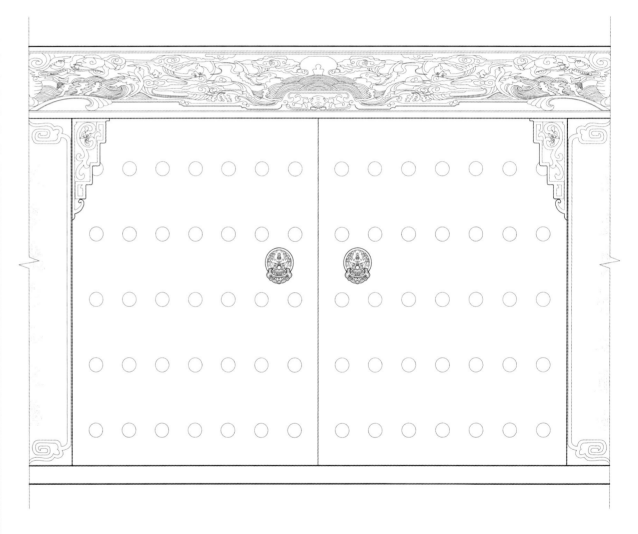

戏台北侧一层大门纹饰大样

Decoration of first-floor main gate, northern side of stage building

戏台北立面基座砖雕大样图

Carved brick base, northern side of stage building

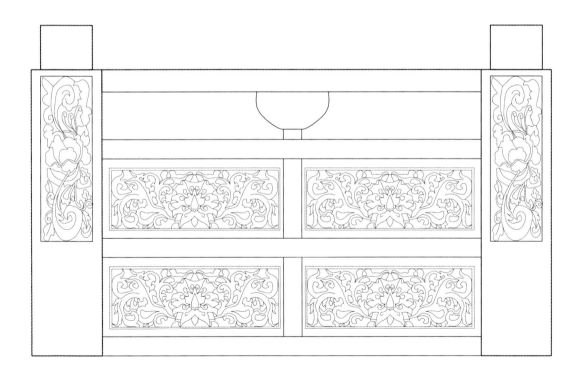

戏台北侧二层后壁纹饰大样

Decoration of second-floor rear wall, northern side of stage building

戏台北侧柱端大样图

Column end, northern side of stage building

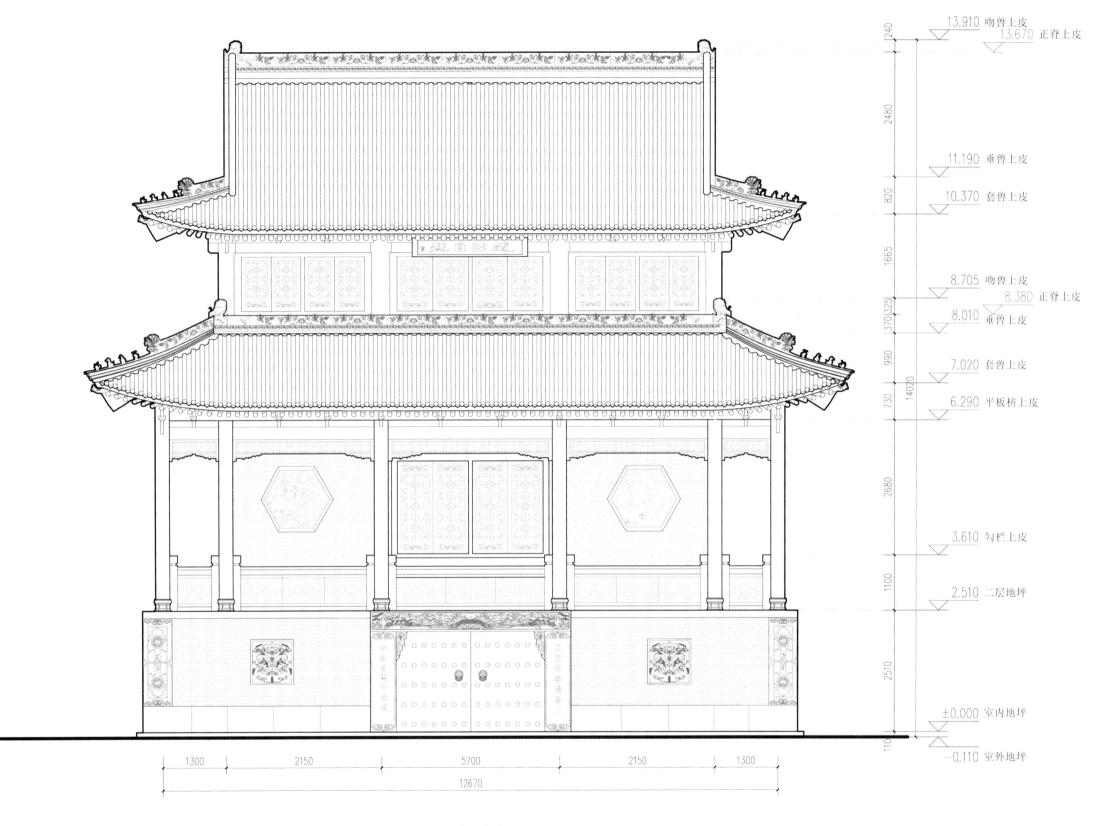

戏台南立面图
South elevation of stage building

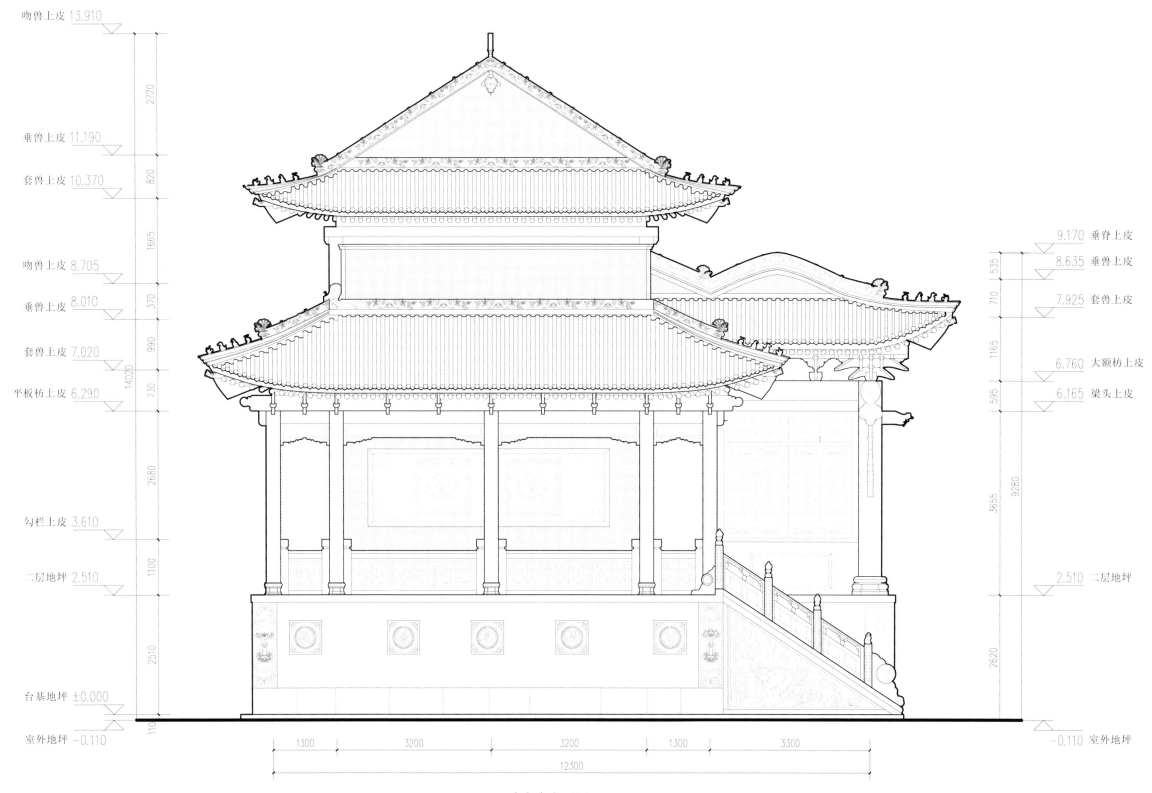

戏台东立面图
East elevation of stage building

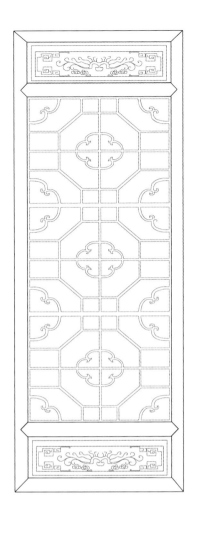
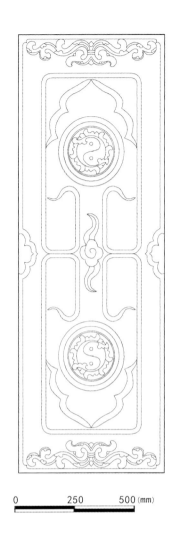

戏台南侧窗大样、东立面基座砖墙雕饰大样图
Carvings of southern window and eastern wall brick base of stage building

戏台东立面后壁雕饰大样图
Carving of rear wall, northern side of stage building

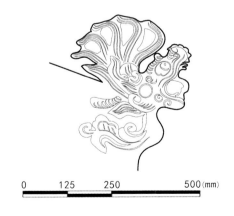

角兽大样图
Ridge-end decoration

戏台东立面基座砖墙纹饰大样图
Decoration of eastern wall brick base of stage building

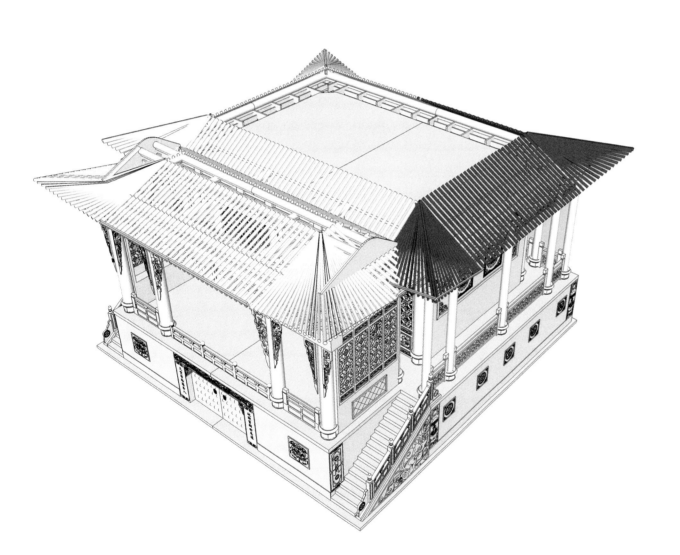

戏台模型

Reconstruction of stage building

仪门平面图
Plan of Yi Gate

仪门 1-1 剖面图
Section of central bay of Yi Gate

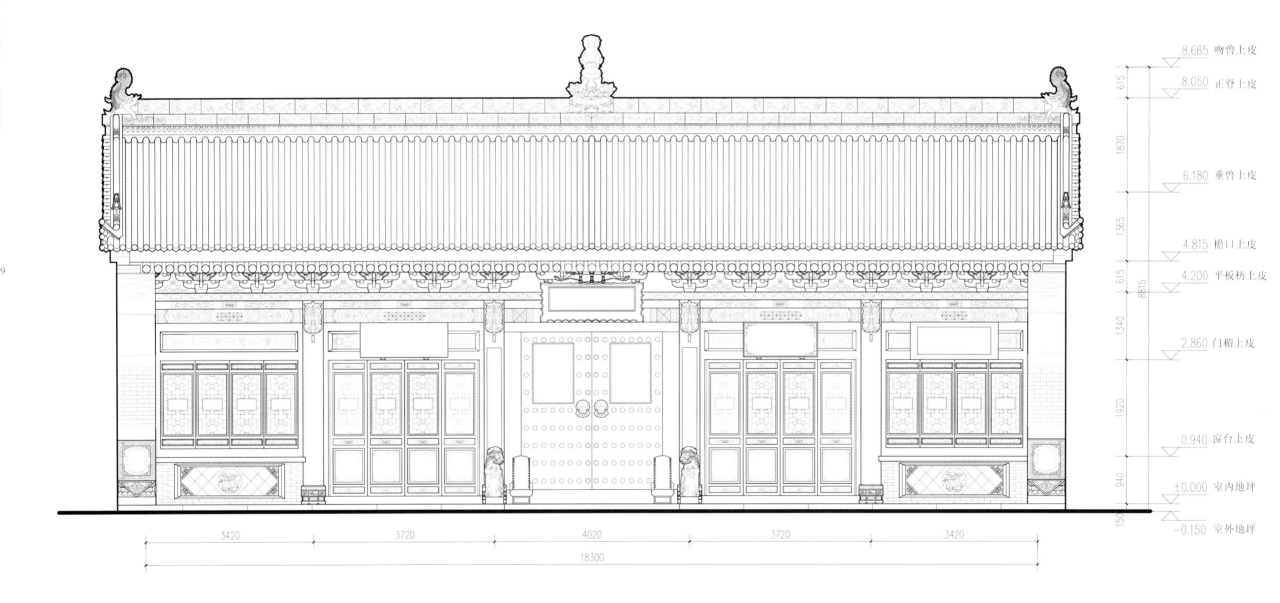

仪门南立面图
South elevation of Yi Gate

仪门南—剖立面图
South-Section elevation of Yi Gate

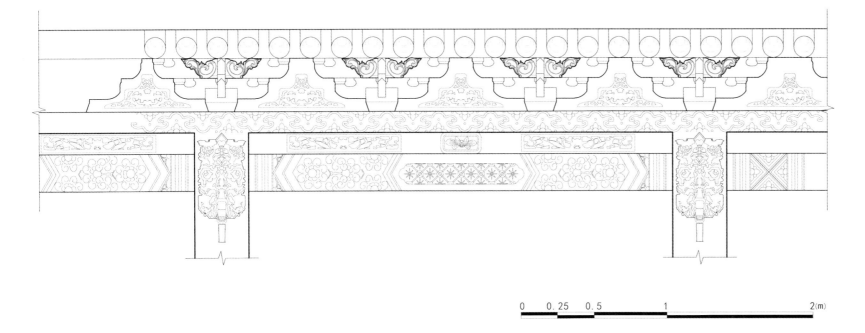

仪门檐下斗栱及彩画大样图
Lower eaves bracketing and *caihua* of Yi Gate

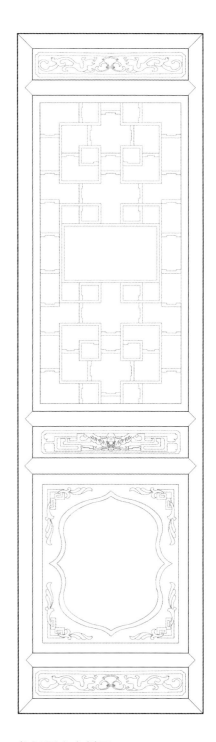

仪门隔扇大样图
Door shutters of Yi Gate

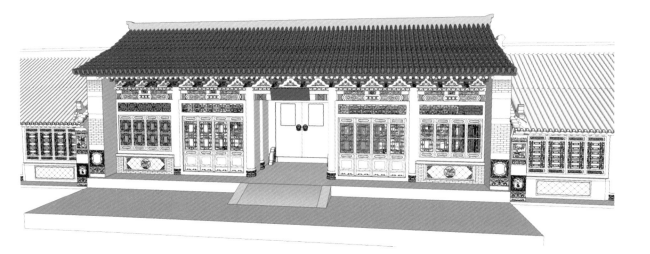

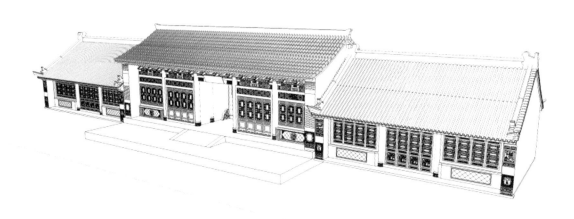

仪门模型
Reconstruction of Yi Gate

仪门室内模型
Reconstruction of interior of Yi Gate

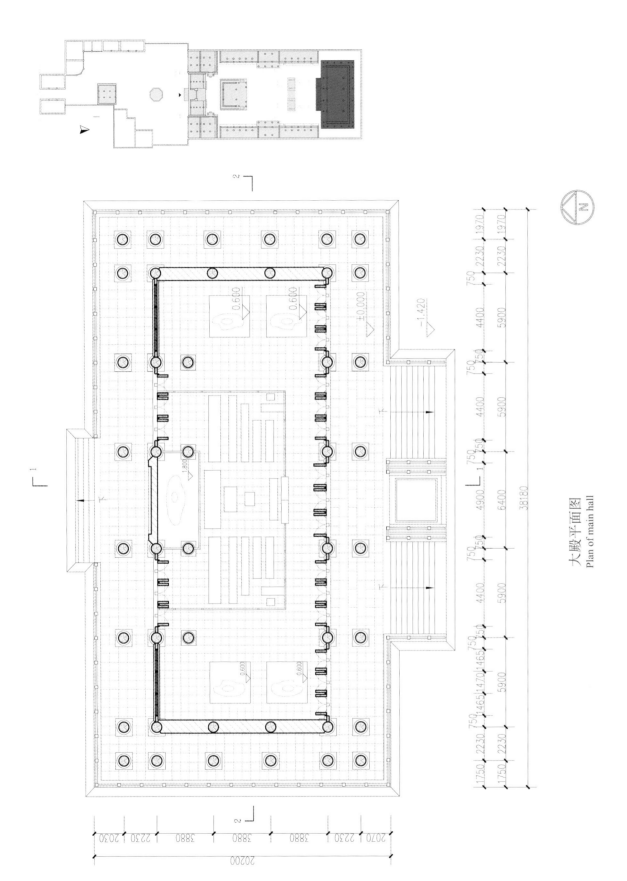

大殿平面图
Plan of main hall

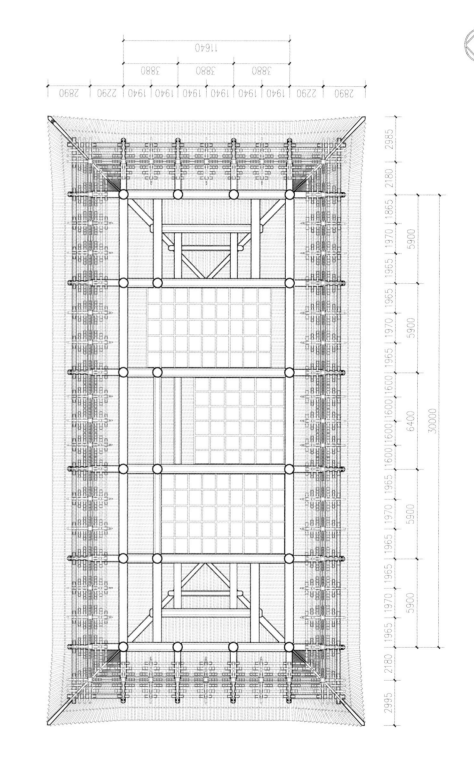

大殿梁架仰视图
Plan of framework of main hall as seen from below

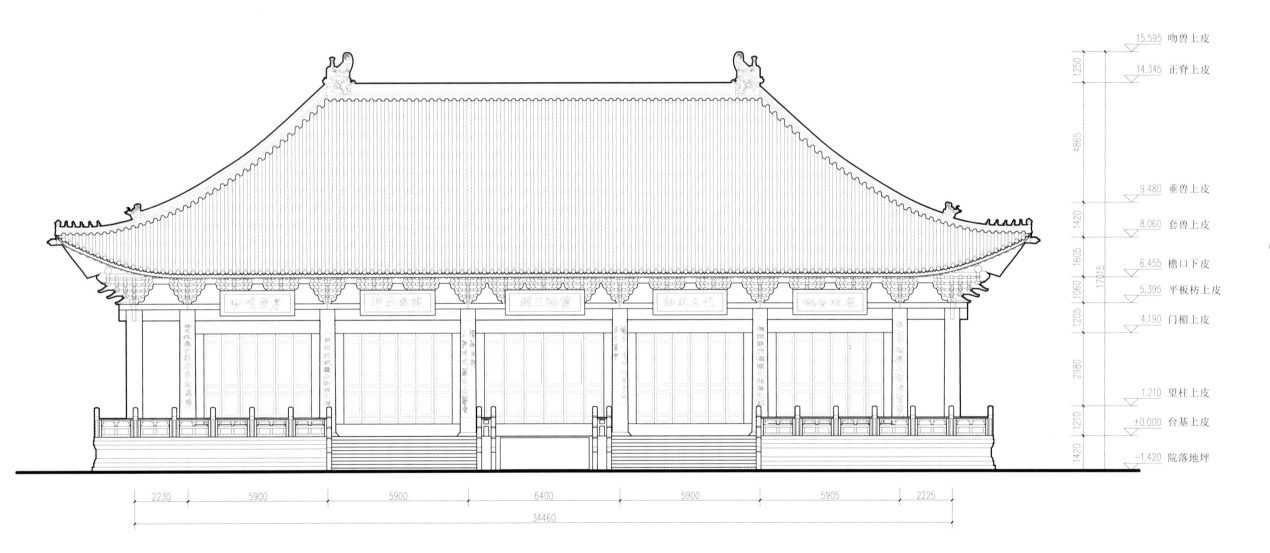

大殿南立面图
South elevation of main hall

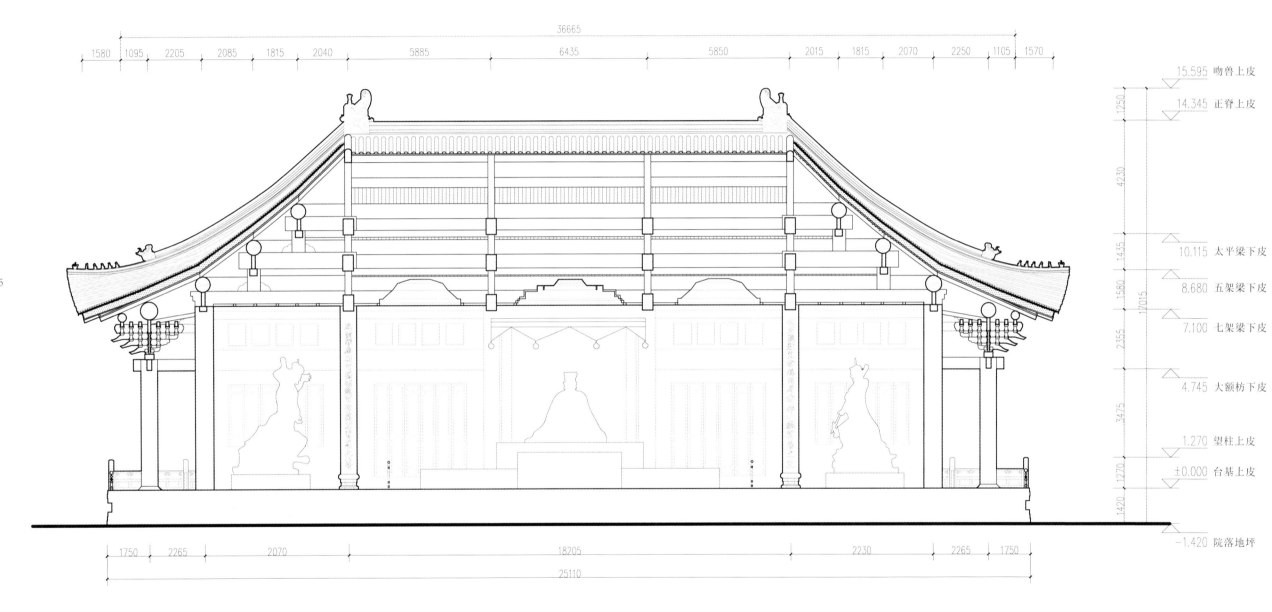

大殿 2-2 剖面图
Section 2-2 of main hall

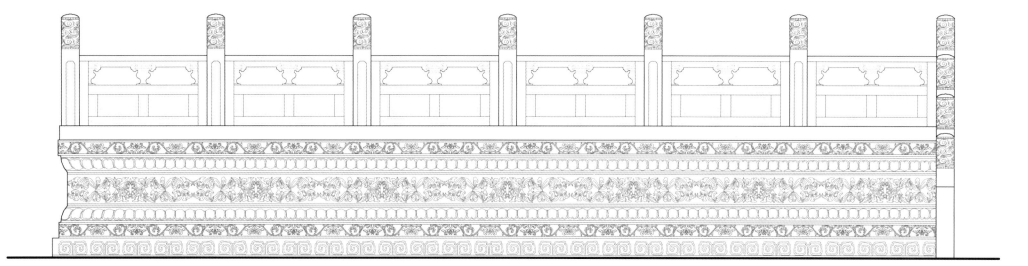

大殿须弥座大样图
Xumizuo of main hall

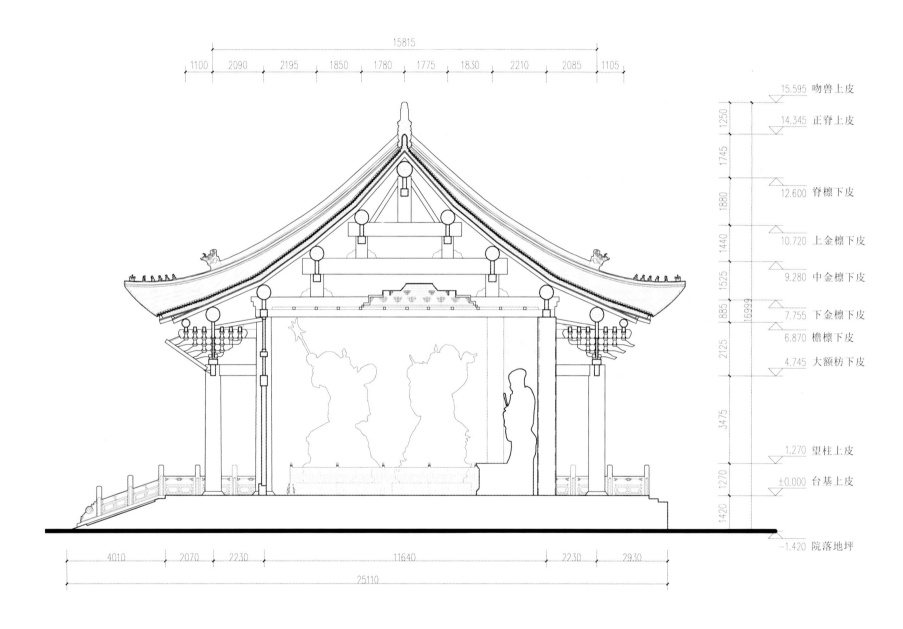

大殿 1-1 剖面图
Section 1-1 of main hall

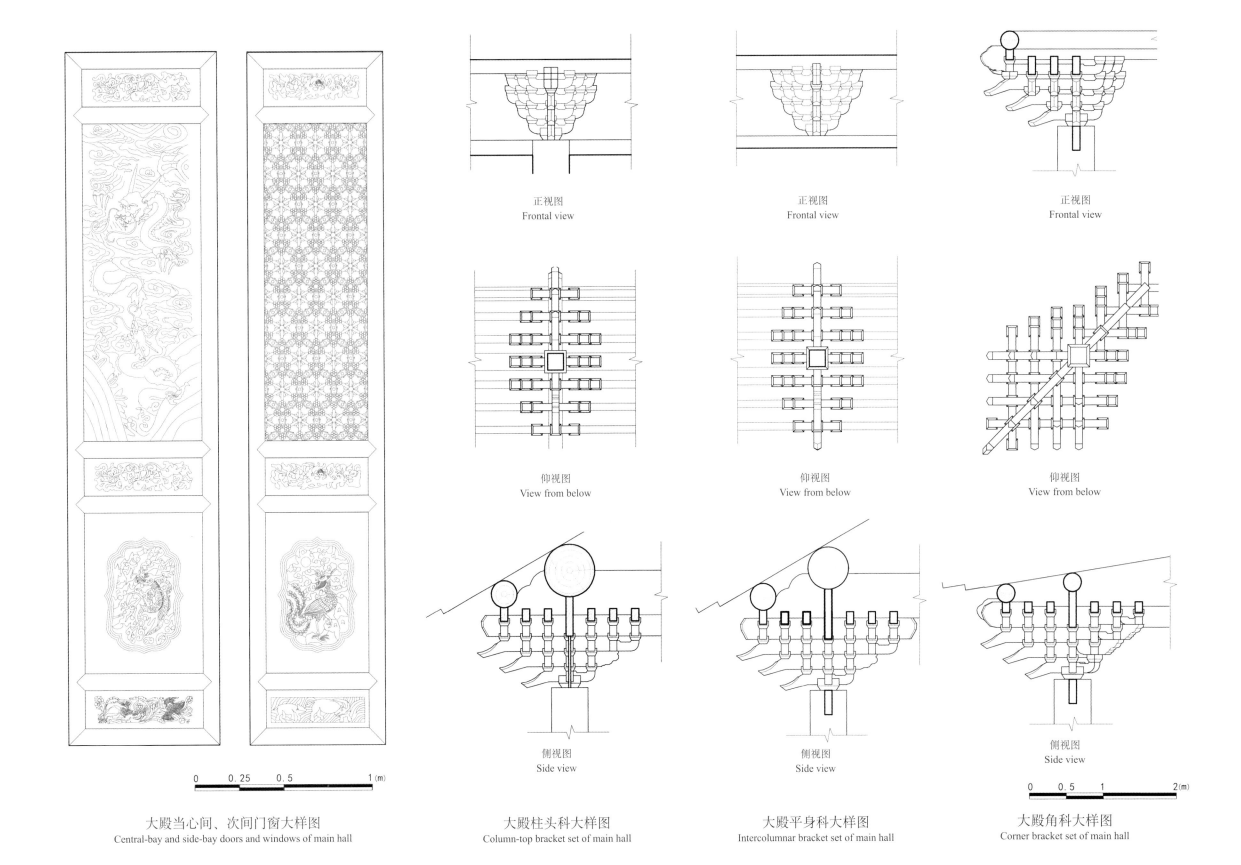

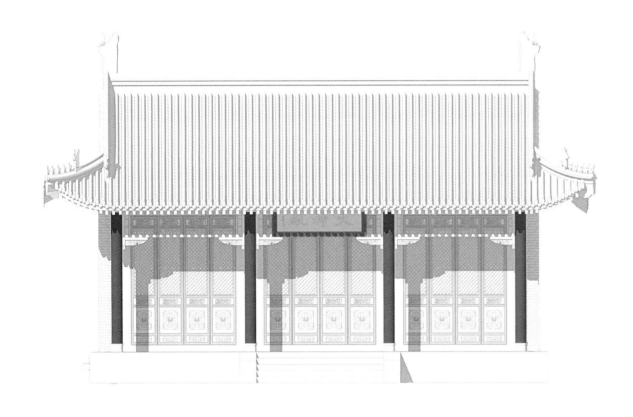
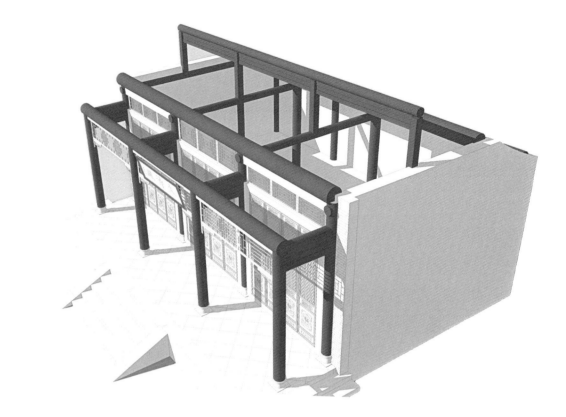
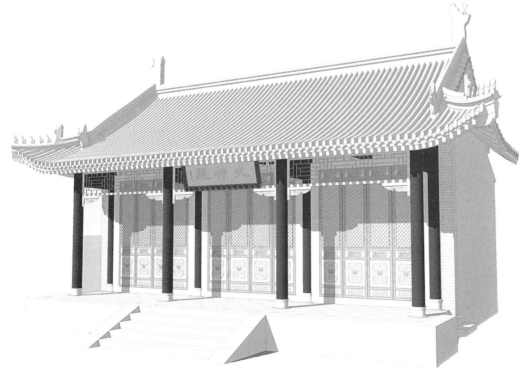
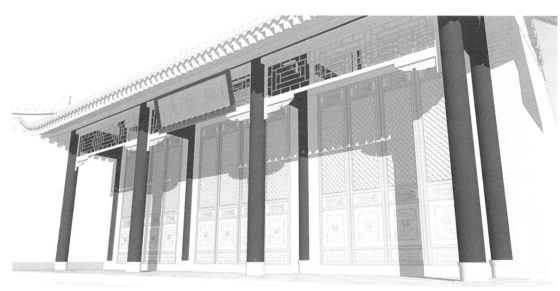

火神殿模型
Reconstruction of Huoshen Hall

西安东岳庙
Dongyue Temple of Xi'an

Location: Changrenli, near the eastern city gate in Xi'an, Shaanxi province

Construction Date: Ming and Qing dynasties

Protection Level: Shaanxi Province Protected Site

地　　址：陕西省西安东门内昌仁里

年　　代：明—清

保护级别：陕西省文物保护单位

Introduction

Dongyuemiao or Temple to the East Peak (referring to Mount Tai, the East Mountain of the Five Great Mountains or literally, the Five Peaks) of Xi'an is located inside the historical city walls near the eastern city gate (Changlemen). The entry in *Xianning Changan liangxian zhixu*[①] suggests that the temple was built in 1116 during the Song dynasty and repaired on several occasions afterwards—between 1488 and 1505 (emperor Hongzhi of Ming), in 1582 (emperor Wanli of Ming), and in 1895 (emperor Guangxu of Qing). The complex must have been designed on a large scale, but only four buildings have survived: the main hall, the middle hall, the rear hall, and Sanjiao (Three Religions) Hall situated east of the rear hall. All the other structures including the stone archway in front of the main hall were destroyed over the course of history. Many cultural relics were also lost forever, an example being the stone tablets and sculptures originally installed inside the halls. Today we can only speculate about the original layout and perimeter of the complex. The main hall dates to the Ming dynasty but was repaired in the succeeding Qing dynasty. Much of the northern, eastern, and western walls of the main and rear halls are still decorated with paintings that depict architecture, landscape, and figures. These paintings are rare and precious examples of large-scale Taoist temple murals in Shaanxi province.

① Song Juwu. *DONG Youcheng xuxiu*. 1936.

概述

东岳庙位于西安古城东门（长乐门）内。据《咸宁长安两县志续》[①]载东岳庙创建于北宋徽宗政和六年（1116年），明弘治年间（1488—1505年）、万历十年（1582年）、清光绪二十一年（1895年）曾大修。原组成规模宏大，现仅存大殿、中殿、后殿和后殿东侧的三教殿四座单体建筑，其他单体建筑及大殿前的石牌坊还有石碑、殿中塑像等文物今已不存，整个建筑群的格局、范围已不清晰。大殿建于明，清时重修。大殿和中殿内的东、西壁以及后壁保留有大面积的彩色壁画，绘山水、楼阁、人物等，是目前陕西地区保存不多的大幅道教宫观壁画之一。

（一）［清］宋菊坞撰，董祐诚续修，民国25年刊本。

图3 西安东岳庙大殿前檐柱头科斗栱

图2 西安东岳庙大殿前檐斗栱

图1 西安东岳庙大殿

图5 西安东岳庙中殿墀头

图4 西安东岳庙大殿角科斗栱

Fig.1　Main hall of Dongyue Temple in Xi'an
Fig.2　Front eaves bracketing of main hall of Dongyue Temple in Xi'an
Fig.3　Bracket set atop front eaves column, main hall of Dongyue Temple in Xi'an
Fig.4　Bracket set atop corner column, main hall of Dongyue Temple in Xi'an
Fig.5　Decorative carving at wall end, middle hall of Dongyue Temple in Xi'an

Survey and Mapping Information

Responsible Department: Department: Department of Architecture (Class of 2007), School of Architecture, Xi'an University of Architecture and Technology

Team Members: LUO Jing, ZHANG Qinan, LI Zefeng, SHI Xuanhao, LIAO Xi, SHI Kanghong, SONG Lu, JIA Yue, ZENG Chen, LI Bing, QIN Yanling, GAO Ling, TU Binghua, LIANG Qian, WANG Junna, WU Fengchen, ZHANG Chen, WANG Junhai, XING Junzhe, TANG Ge, GUAN Junqing, LI Nan, YUAN Chengmei, CHEN Lei, DONG Jing, WANG Tao, LIU Mingjia, YUAN Zhe, WANG Jie, LIU Shuting, WANG Yanshu, WANG Ning, LI Delu, XIE Jinfan, LEI Jing, PEI Chenchen, YAN Dichao, WU Chongshan, SHI Lin, CUI Yanzhao, LOU Yang, WANG Yusong

Supervisors: LIN Yuan

Editors of Drawings: TONG Mengfei

Survey Time: April 2010

西安东岳庙测绘的人员名单

测绘：西安建筑科技大学建筑学院建筑学2007级

罗　婧　张栖楠　李泽峰　史轩豪　廖　翕　石康宏　宋　露　贾　玥
曾　辰　李　兵　秦艳玲　高　岭　屠炳华　梁　倩　王军娜　吴风臣
张　琛　王俊海　邢俊哲　唐　歌　关俊卿　李　男　远成美　陈　蕾
董　婧　王　涛　刘明佳　苑　哲　王　捷　刘姝婷　王雁舒　王　宁
李德鲁　谢金机　雷　婧　裴辰辰　严迪超　吴崇山　施　琳　崔彦钊
楼　洋　王煜松

指导教师：林　源

图纸整理：仝梦菲

测绘时间：2010年4月

参考文献 References

[一] 西安市地方志编纂委员会编．西安市志．西安：西安出版社．1996．

[二] 赵立瀛主编．陕西古建筑．西安：陕西人民出版社．1992．

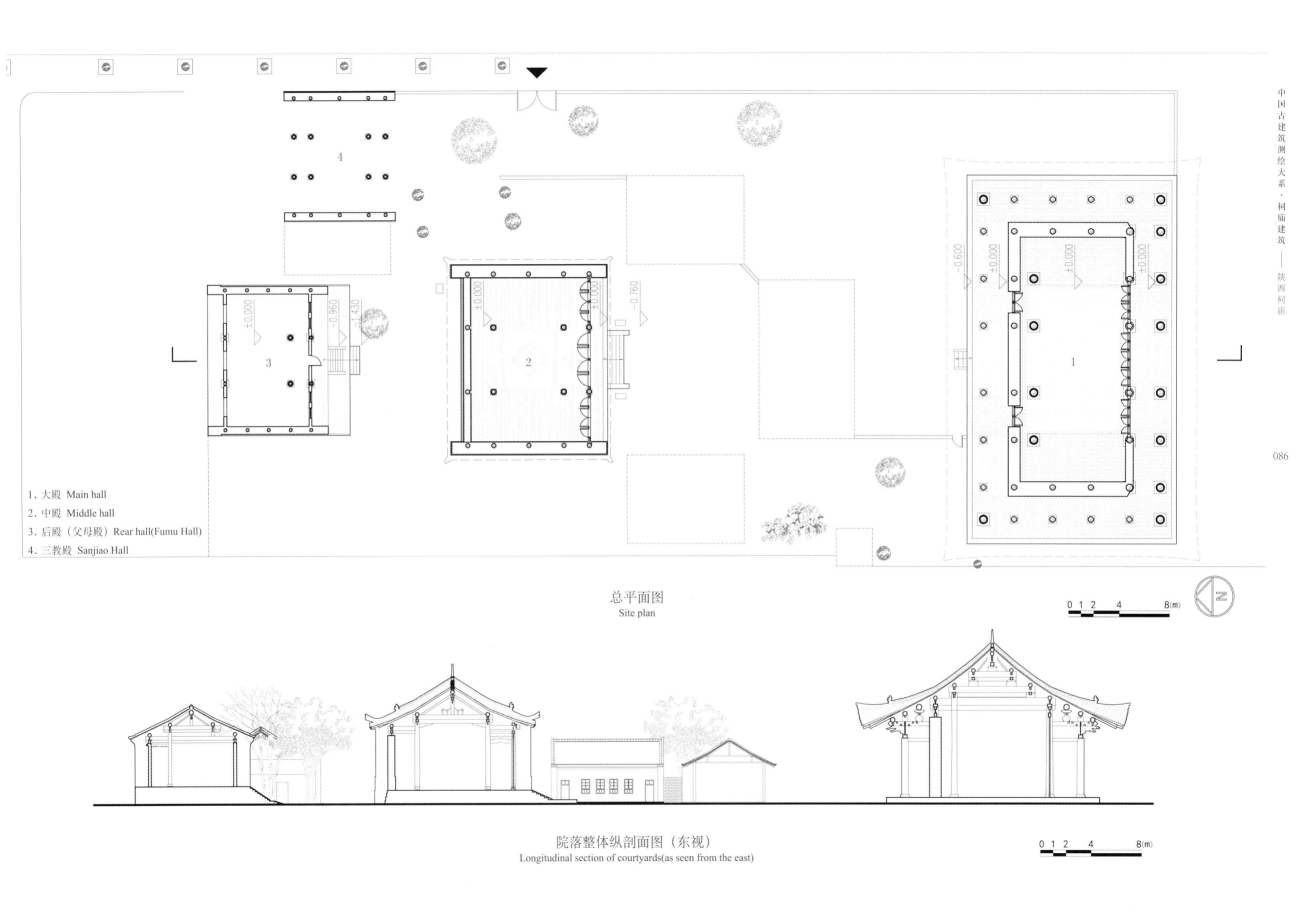

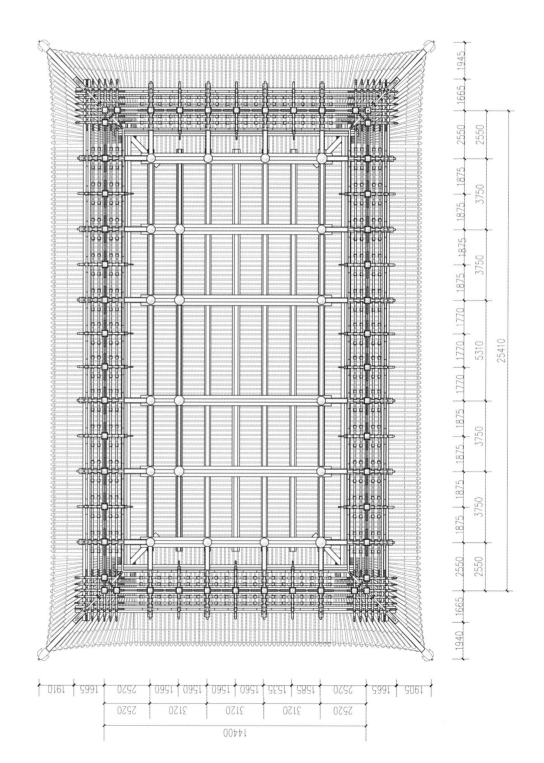

大殿平面图
Plan of main hall

大殿梁架仰视图
Plan of framework of main hall as seen from below

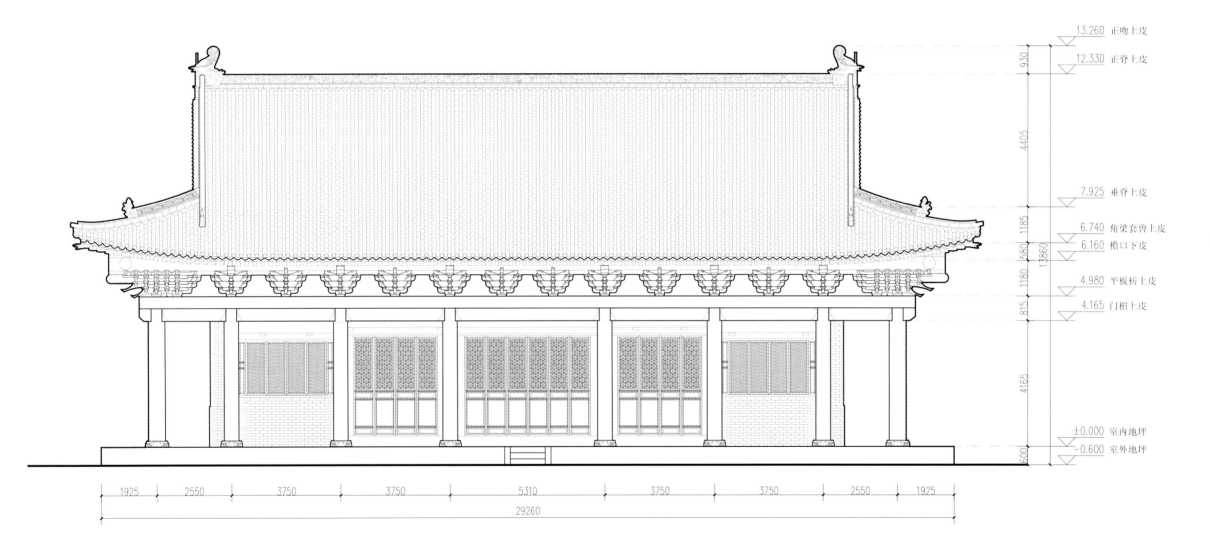

大殿南立面图
South elevation of main hall

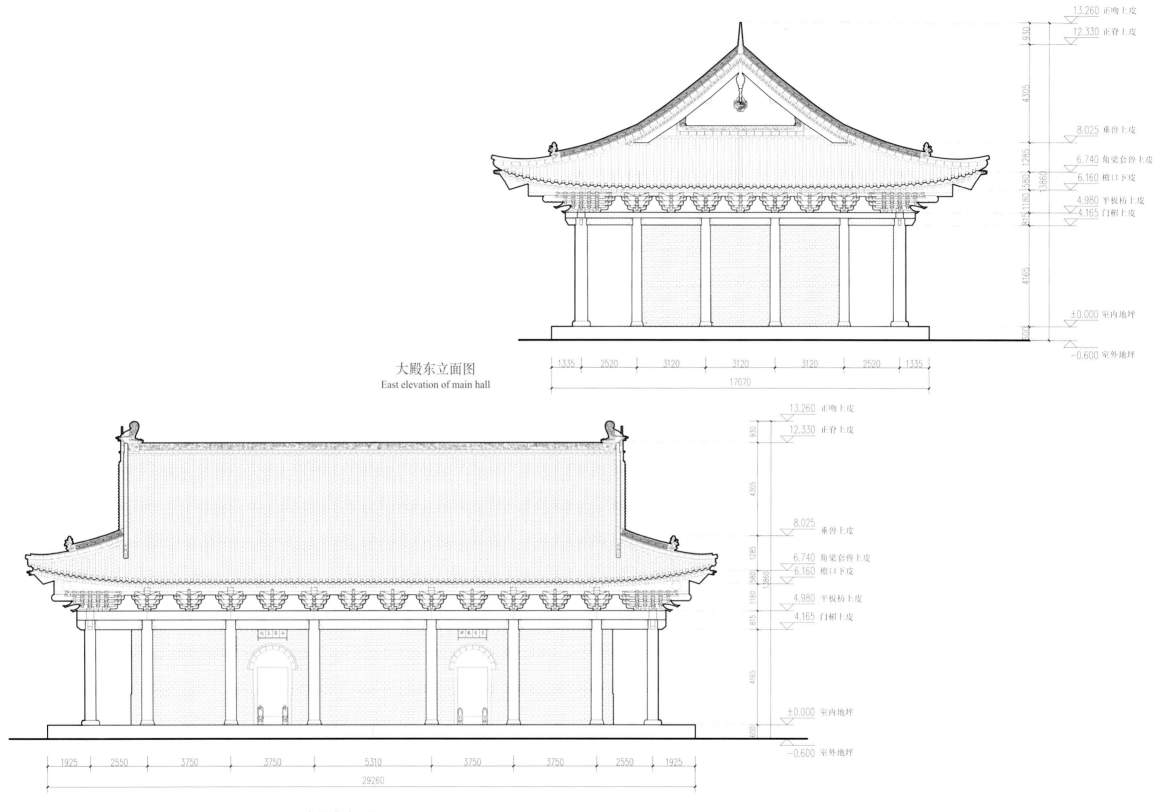

大殿东立面图
East elevation of main hall

大殿北立面图
North elevation of main hall

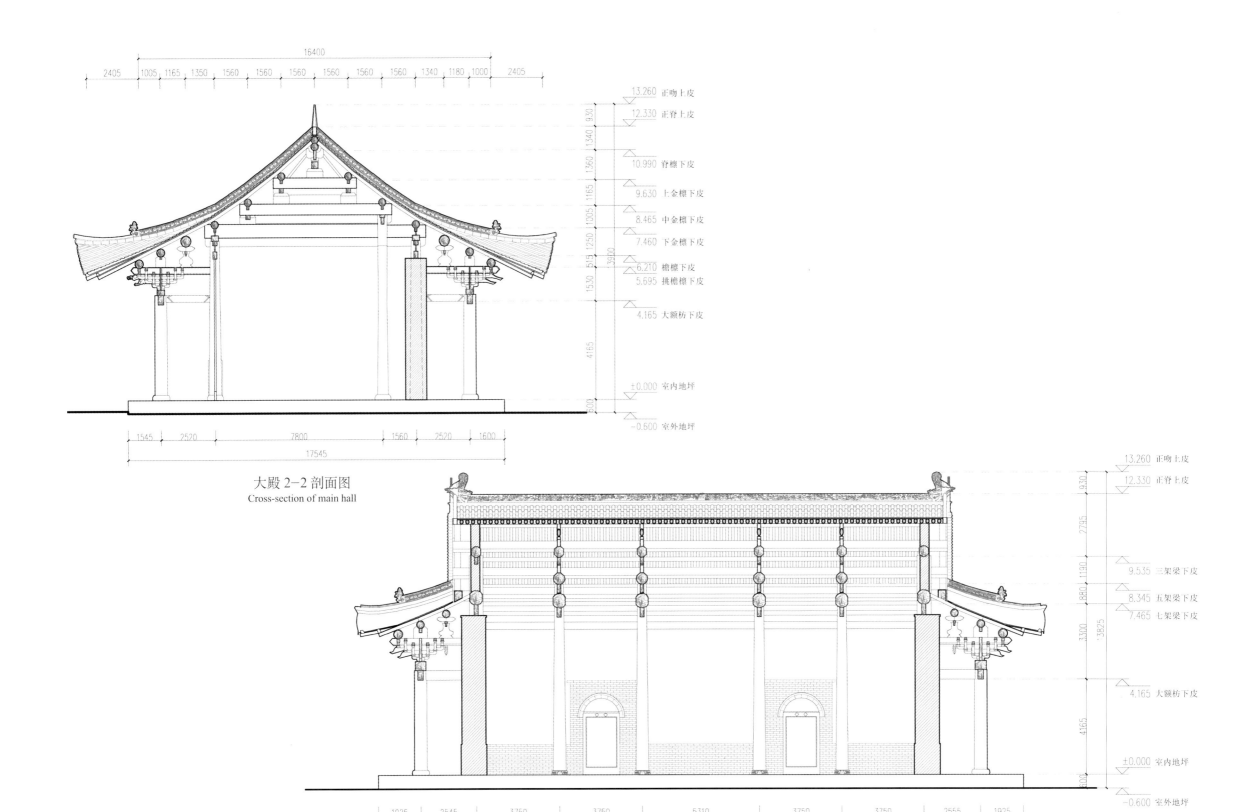

大殿 2-2 剖面图
Cross-section of main hall

大殿 1-1 纵剖面图
Longitudinal section of main hall

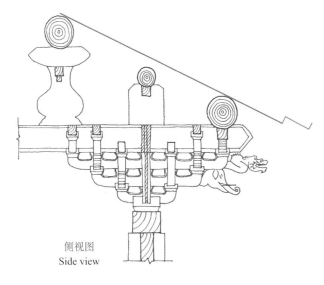
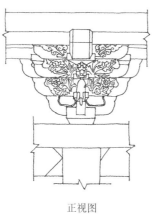

侧视图　　　　　　　　　正视图
Side view　　　　　　　　Frontal view

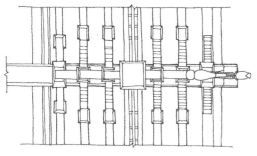

仰视图　　　　　　　　　后视图
View from below　　　　View from back

大殿正立面当心间柱头科大样图
Bracket set atop front central-bay columns of main hall

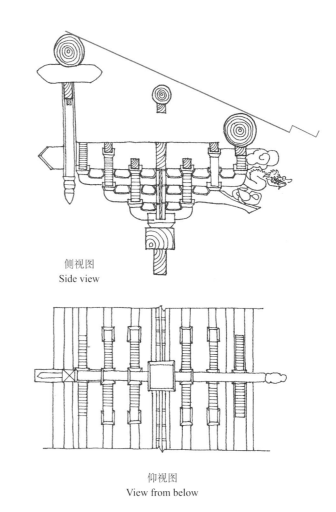

侧视图　　　　　　　　　正视图
Side view　　　　　　　　Frontal view

仰视图　　　　　　　　　后视图
View from below　　　　View from back

大殿正立面当心间平身科大样图
Bracket set between front central-bay columns of main hall

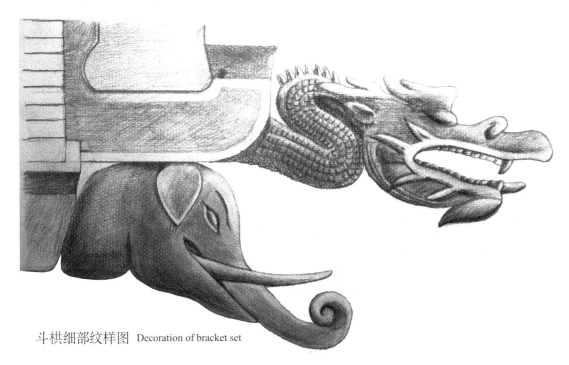

斗栱细部纹样图　Decoration of bracket set

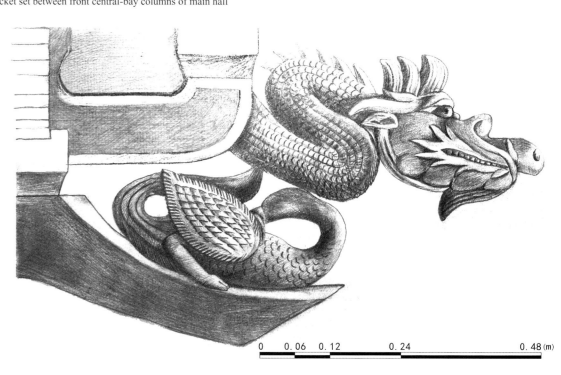

0　0.06　0.12　　0.24　　　　0.48(m)

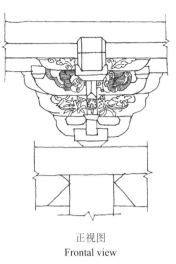

侧视图
Side view

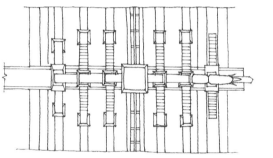

仰视图
View from below

大殿正立面当心间柱头科大样图
Bracket set atop front central-bay columns of main hall

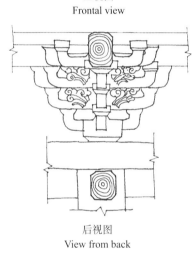

正视图
Frontal view

后视图
View from back

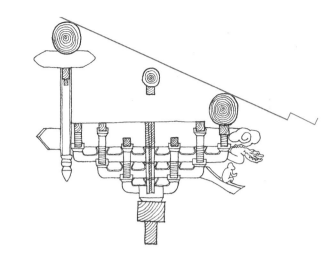

侧视图
Side view

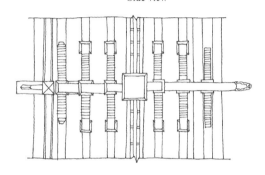

仰视图
View from below

大殿正立面当心间平身科大样图
Bracket set between front central-bay columns of main hall

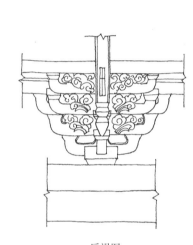

正视图
Frontal view

后视图
View from back

斗栱细部纹样图　Decoration of bracket set

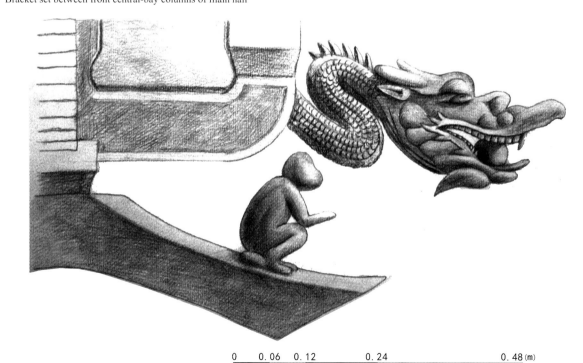

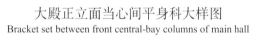

0　0.06　0.12　　0.24　　　　0.48(m)

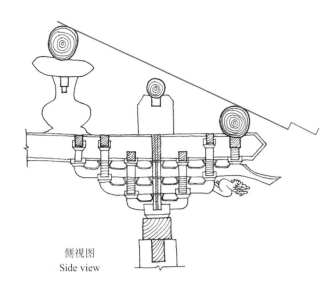
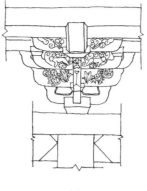
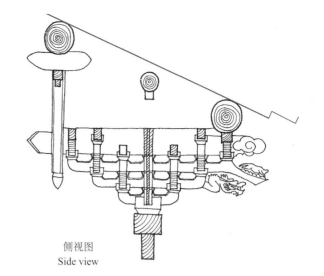
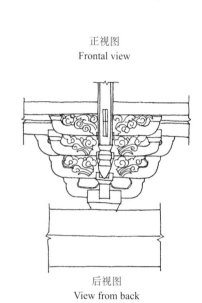

侧视图 Side view　　正视图 Frontal view　　侧视图 Side view　　正视图 Frontal view

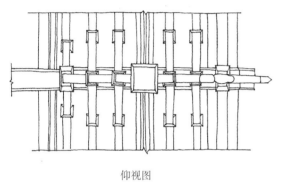
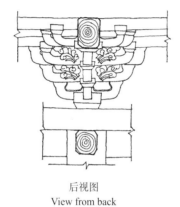
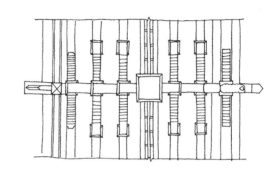

仰视图 View from below　　后视图 View from back　　仰视图 View from below　　后视图 View from back

大殿正立面梢间柱头科大样图
Bracket set atop second-to-last-bay front eaves columns of main hall

大殿正立面当心间平身科大样图
Bracket set between front central-bay columns of main hall

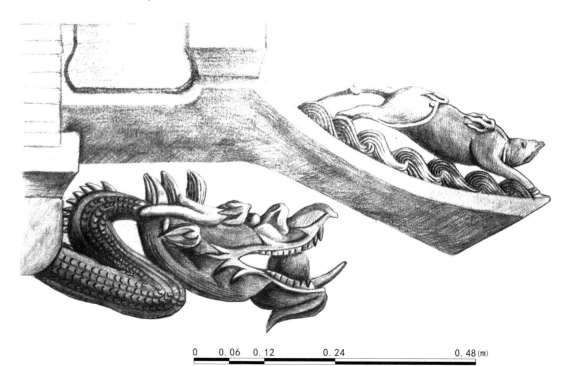

斗栱细部纹样图　Decoration of bracket set

0　0.06　0.12　0.24　0.48 (m)

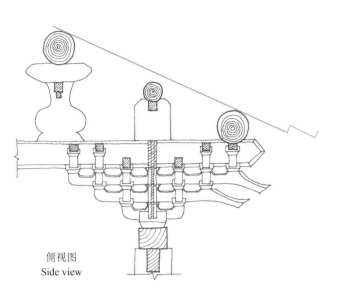
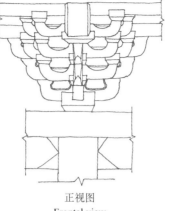
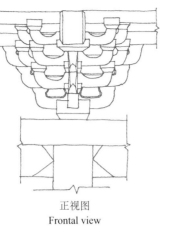
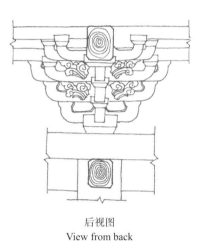

侧视图 Side view   正视图 Frontal view   侧视图 Side view   正视图 Frontal view

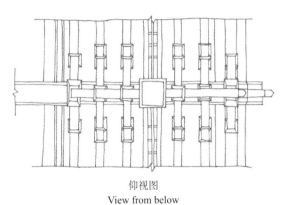
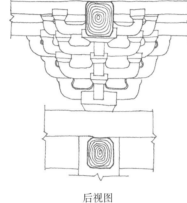
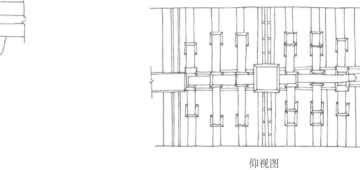

仰视图 View from below   后视图 View from back   仰视图 View from below   后视图 View from back

大殿背立面柱头科大样图
Bracket set atop rear columns of main hall

大殿山面柱头科大样图
Bracket set atop gable-side columns of main hall

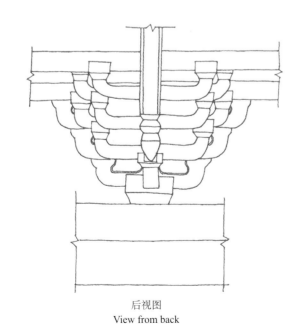
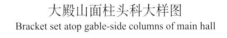
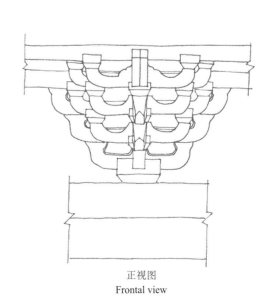
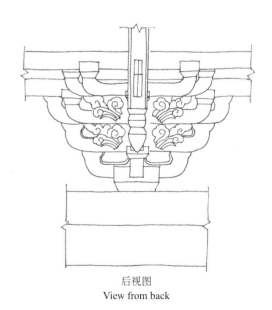

正视图 Frontal view   后视图 View from back   正视图 Frontal view   后视图 View from back

大殿背立面平身科大样图
Bracket set between rear columns of main hall

大殿山面平身科大样图
Bracket set between gable-side columns of main hall

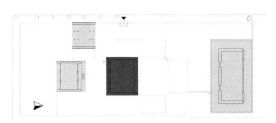

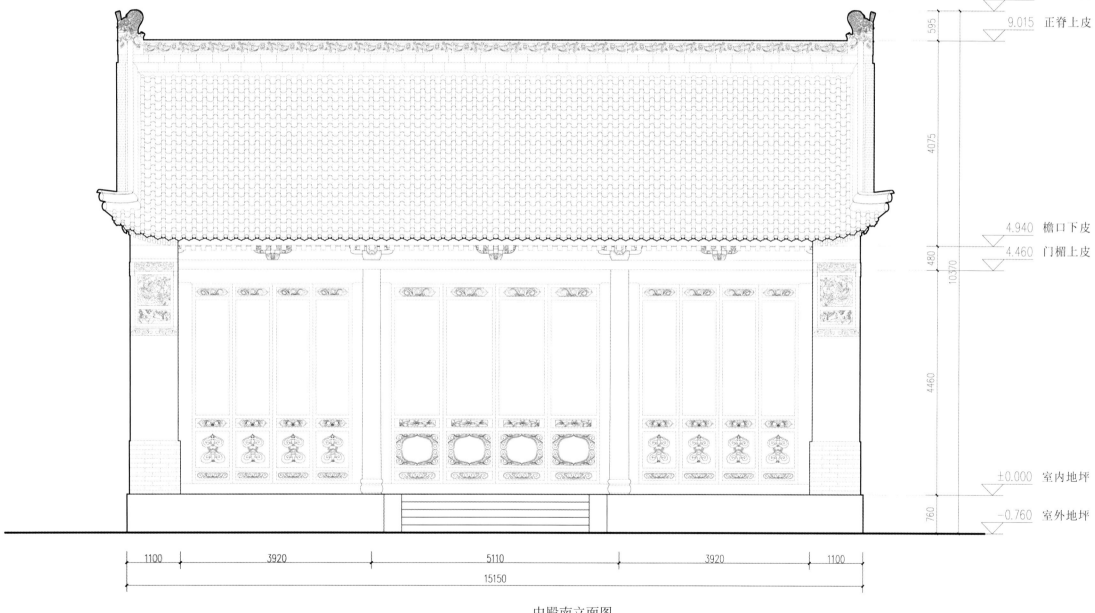

中殿南立面图
South elevation of main hall

户县东岳庙（化羊庙）

The Offering Hall of Dongyue Temple (Huayang Temple) in Hu county

Location: Huayang Valley at the northern foot of the Qin Mountains near Xi'an, Shaanxi province

Construction Date: Ming dynasty

Protection Level: Shaanxi Province Protected Site

地　　址：陕西秦岭北麓化羊峪峪口

年　　代：明代

保护级别：陕西省文物保护单位

概述

化羊庙位于秦岭北麓、化羊峪峪口内，地属西安市户县庞光镇大王村，距西安市区约13公里。

化羊庙，又名『东岳行祠』『泰岳行祠』，实为东岳庙。

化羊峪是一条南北通行秦岭的峪道，峪内有谷水流经化羊庙东侧。化羊庙建筑群坐南朝北，依山势而上，自北端山坡下的头天门至南端最高处的正殿，绵延五百余米。

化羊庙的创建时间以及创建时的组成与规模现在已无法确知，根据庙内现存的三通古碑与地方史志可知化羊庙建筑群原是坐东朝西，明永乐年间火灾后，于宣德元年（1426年）至景泰二年（1451年）进行了大规模的重建和改建，建筑群的主轴线由东西向转为南北向，其南北中轴线上的主要建筑也应是创建于这一时期。新中国成立时化羊庙建筑群保存尚完整，在新中国成立后的三十余年中陆续遭到破坏，现状建筑群由头天门、戏楼、二天门、山门、献殿、正殿、东西侧殿以及两个附属院落组成。除头天门、戏楼、献殿之外，均为20世纪80年代新建。头天门和戏楼建于清道光年间，山门建于清但时间不详。献殿年代最早，应是在明宣德元年至景泰二年（1426—1451年）间创建的。

一 原为鄠县，现简写为户县。化羊峪古称华阳峪，『化羊』应是通用已久的同音俗名。

二 一是元至元十九年（1282年）的『阿难答秦王令旨』碑（蒙汉文），原立于正殿前，现藏户县文庙；二是明景泰三年（1452年）的『重修古迹东岳庙记』碑，现立于献殿前西侧；三是明嘉靖十一年（1532年）的『西安府户县化羊峪补修东岳庙记』碑，现立于献殿前东侧。

三 主要是清乾隆四十二年（1777年）的《鄠县新志》》1933年的《鄠县县志》。

Introduction

Huayang Temple is situated at the northern foot of the Qin Mountains in Shaanxi province and nestled in the Huayang Valley after which it is named. The site, thirteen kilometers away from the sub-provincial city of Xi'an, is located in Dawang village in Hu county, Pangguang township. Huayang Temple is also known as Dongyue xingci or Taiyue xingci, two names that refer to its use as a temporary shrine dedicated to Mount Tai, the East Mountain of the Five Great Mountains or literally, the Five Peaks. Thus it is also called Dongyuemiao (Temple to the East Peak) of Hu country.

Huayang Valley serves as a walkable corridor connecting the north and south foothills of the Qin Mountains. A stream runs inside the valley east of the temple. The architecture of Huayang Temple is aligned along a central axis that runs through the main entrance in the north. The layout follows the ascending terrain of the mountain and, starting from Toutian (First Heaven) Gate at the mountain foot, ends after more than five hundred meters at the main hall, the temple's highest point.

Today we know neither the exact date of construction nor the original layout of the temple. But three extant stone tablets and local records suggest that the temple was originally oriented westwards. The orientation was changed during the large-scale repair and alteration (1426-1451) after a fire that broke out during the reign of the Ming emperor Yongle (1402-1424). We may assume that the important buildings along the main axis were also erected at that time. At the beginning of the Peoples' Republic of China, the temple architecture was still intact, but in the next three decades, it gradually degenerated. Today still extant are Toutian Gate, a stage building (*xilou*), Ertian (Second Heaven) Gate, the front or main temple gate (*shanmen*), the offering hall (*xiandian*), the main hall, east- and west-side buildings, and two annexed courtyards. Toutian Gate and the stage building were erected during the reign of emperor Daoguang of Qing (1821-1850). The front gate (*shanmen*) is also a Qing-period structure although its exact date of construction remains unclear. The offering hall is the oldest building of the complex, and probably dates to the mid-fifteenth-century reconstruction. All the other buildings are modern constructions from the 1980s.

图2 1995年版《户县文物志》中的「东岳行祠图」

图1 户县东岳庙（化羊庙）献殿

Fig.1 The Offering Hall of Dongyue Temple (HuayangTemple) in Hu County
Fig.2 The "Dongyue–xingci–Tu" in *Cultural relics chronicle of Hu County*, 1995

Survey and Mapping Information

Responsible Department: Department of Architectural History (Classes of 2010 and 2011), School of Architecture, Xi'an University of Architecture and Technology

Team Members: YUE Yanmin, ZHANG Wenbo, CUI Zhaorui, GU Ruichao, LAI Qibin, CHEN Siliang, MENG Yu, TIAN Mingming, LOU Yang, QI Haochen, LI Hui

Supervisors: LIN Yuan

Editor of Text: CHEN Siliang

Digital Modeling: CHEN Siliang

Editors of Drawings: CHEN Siliang, MENG Yu, WEN Juan

Survey Time: April 2012

户县东岳庙（化羊庙）测绘的人员名单

测　　绘：西安建筑科技大学建筑学院建筑历史2010、2011级研究生

岳岩敏　张文波　崔兆瑞　谷瑞超　赖祺彬　陈斯亮　孟　玉　田明明

楼　洋　齐昊晨　李　慧

指导教师：林　源

文献搜集与整理：陈斯亮

数字模型制作：陈斯亮

图纸绘制与整理：陈斯亮　孟　玉　文　娟

测绘时间：2012年4月

参考文献 References

[1] 阿难答.阿难答秦王令旨（碑记）.元至元十九年（1282年）.

[2] 董德昭.重修古迹东岳庙记（碑记）.明景泰三年（1452年）.

[3] 王九思.西安府户县化羊峪补修东岳庙记（碑记）.明嘉靖十一年（1532年）.

[4] 汪以诚.鄂县新志[M].清乾隆四十二年刻本（1777年）.

[5] 强云诚、赵葆真.云县县志[M].西安酉山书局铅印本.1933.

[6] 户县文物志编纂委员会编.户县文物志[M].西安：陕西人民教育出版社.1995.

[7] 林源、裘琳娟、陈斯亮.西安户县化羊庙献殿研究[J].文物建筑（第7辑）.2014.

图6 户县化羊庙献殿后檐柱头科斗栱

图4 户县东岳庙献殿前檐梢间平身科斗栱

图5 户县东岳庙献殿前檐柱头科斗栱

图3 户县东岳庙献殿前檐西北角科斗栱

Fig.3 Front eaves bracket set atop corner column at north-west, offering Hall of Dongyue Temple in Hu County
Fig.4 Front eaves bracket set atop corner column at north-west, Offering Hall of Dongyue Temple
Fig.5 Bracket set atop front eaves column offering Hall of Dongyue Temple in Hu County
Fig.6 Bracket set atop back eaves column offering Hall of Huayang Temple in Hu County

图9　户县东岳庙献殿西山墙外檐斗栱

图8　户县东岳庙献殿平梁部分构架

图7　户县东岳庙献殿内部梁架

Fig.7　Interior framework of offering Hall of Dongyue Temple in Hu County
Fig.8　Structure of flat beam, offering Hall of Dongyue Temple in Hu County
Fig.9　Exterior bracket atop western gable wall, offering Hall of Dongyue Temple in Hu County

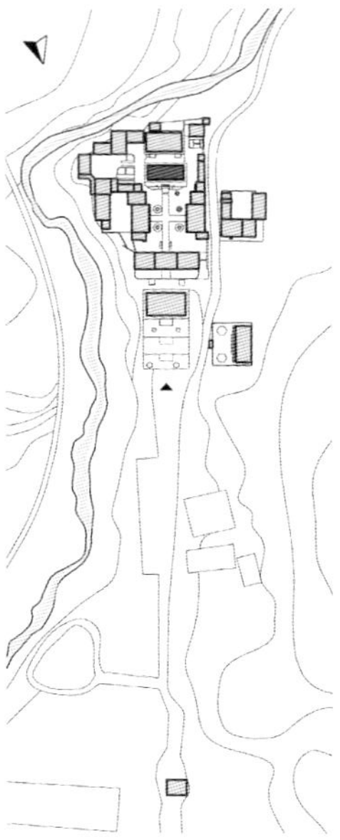

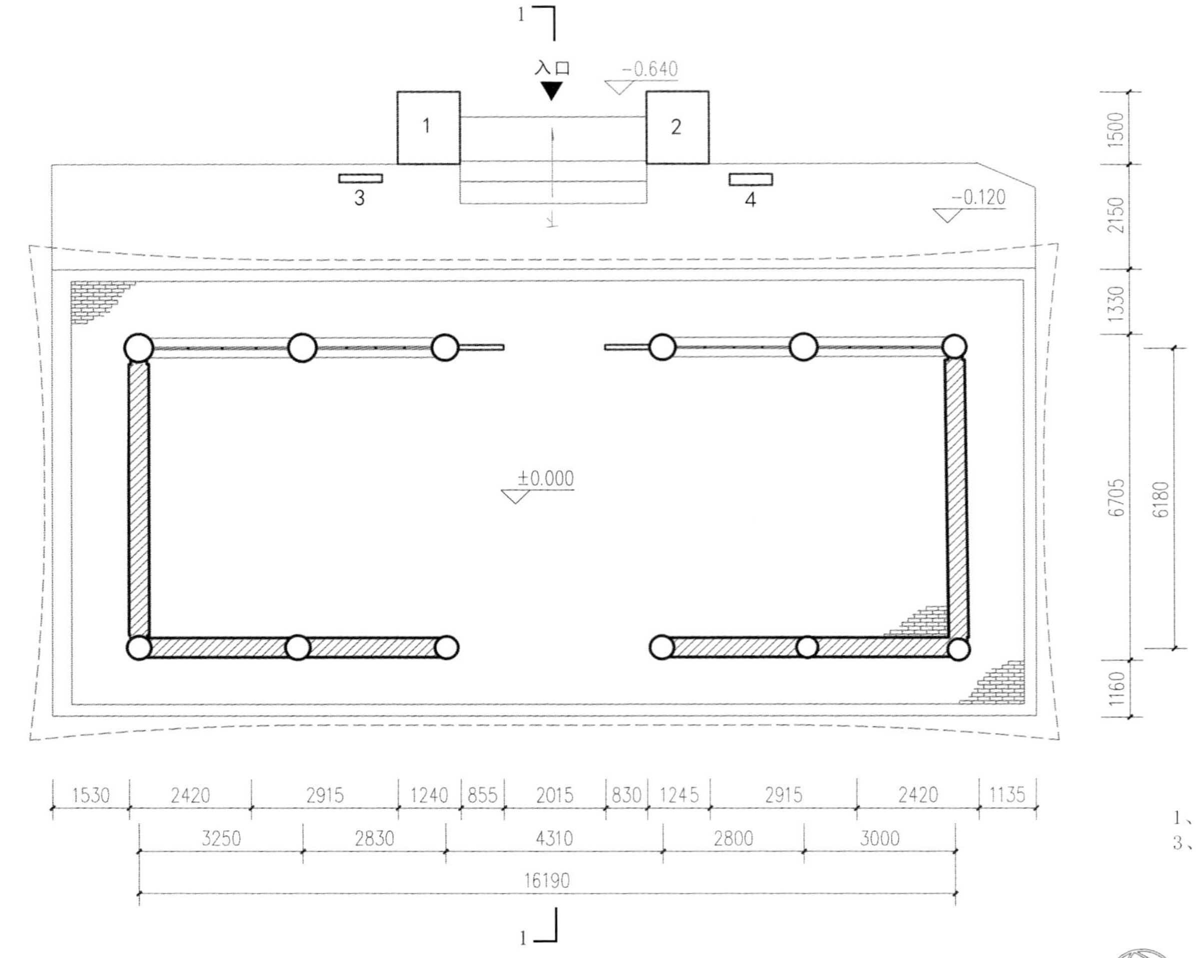

1、2 石狮子
3、4 碑

献殿平面图
Plan of offering hall

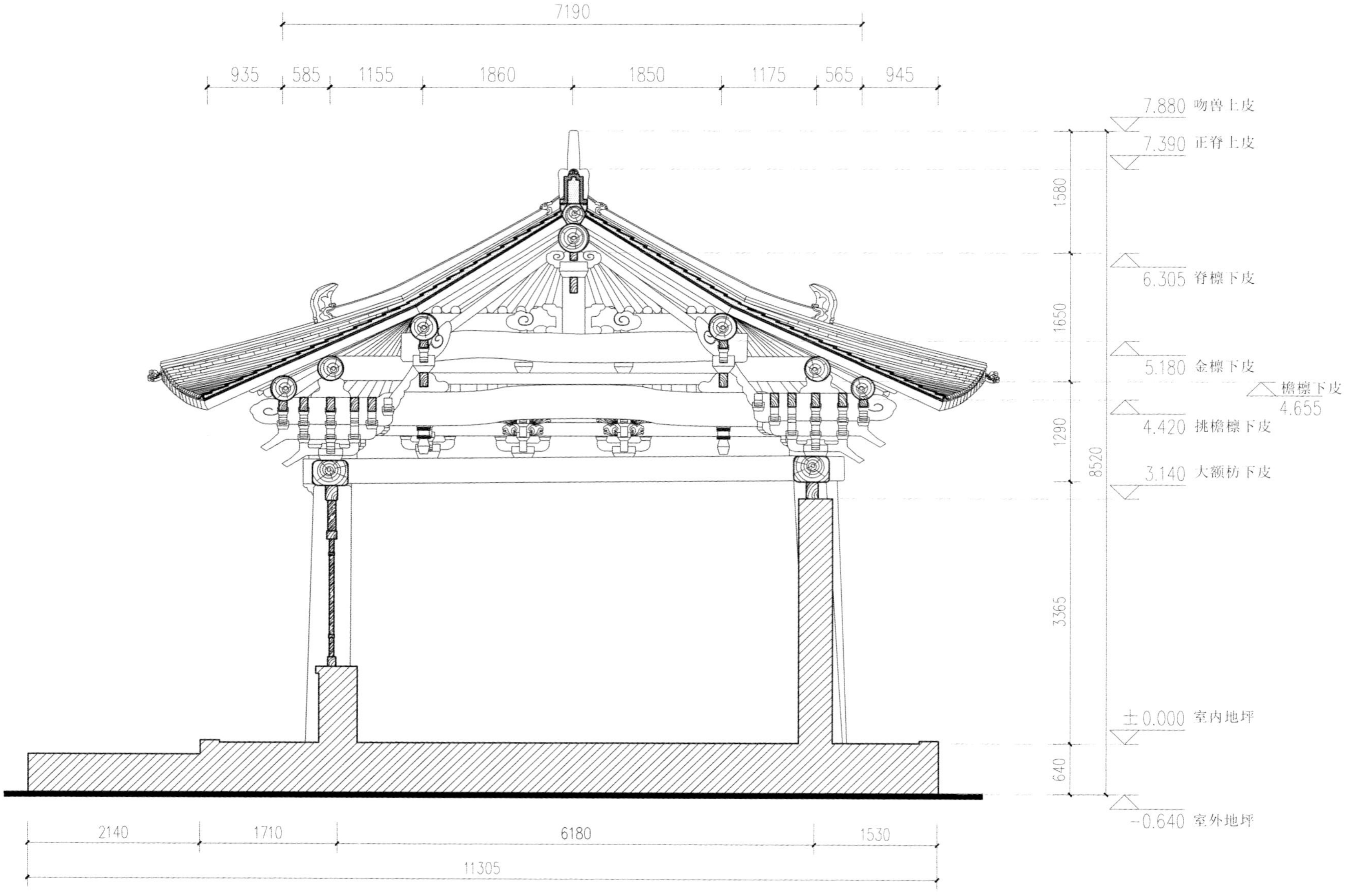

献殿 1-1 剖面图
Section 1-1 of offering hall

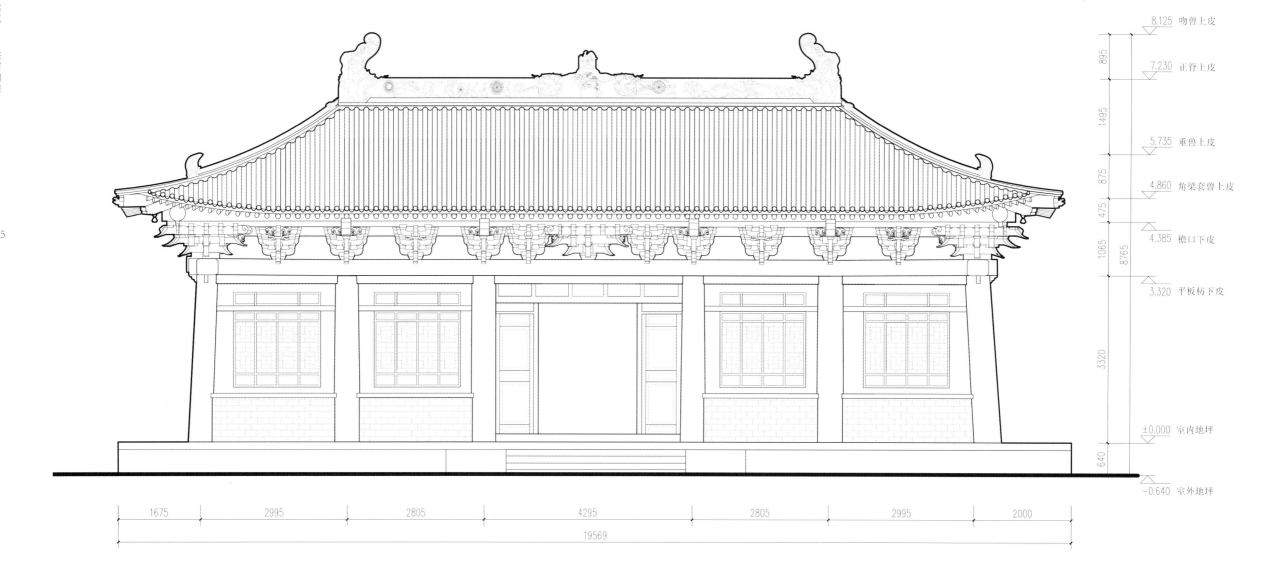

献殿北立面图
North elevation of offering hall

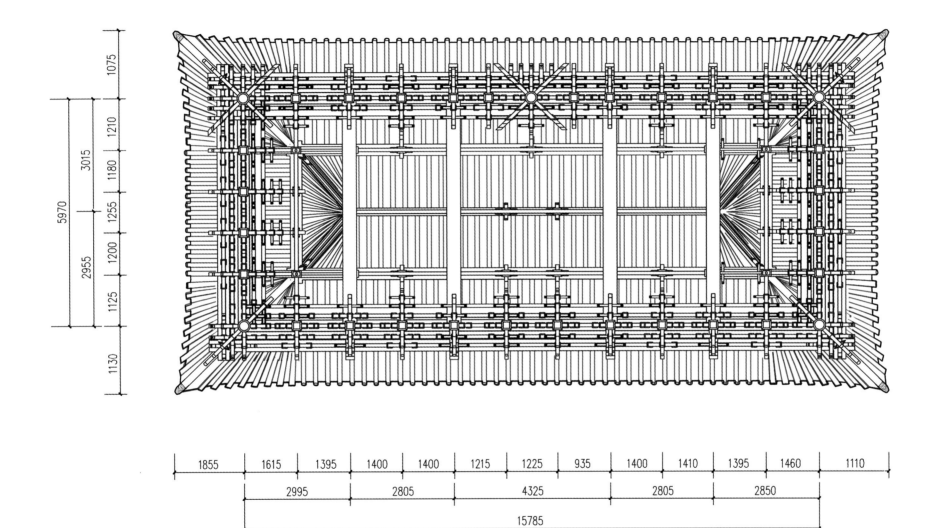

献殿梁架仰视图
Plan of framework of offering hall as seen from below

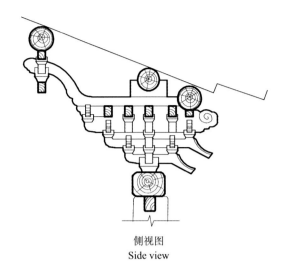
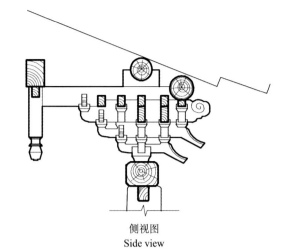
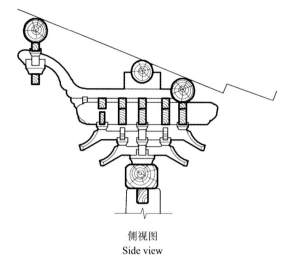
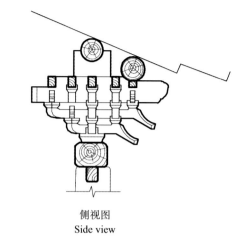

侧视图
Side view

侧视图
Side view

侧视图
Side view

侧视图
Side view

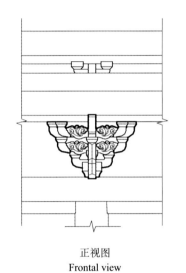
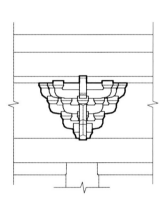
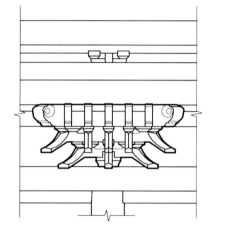
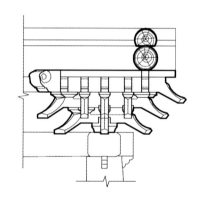

正视图
Frontal view

正视图
Frontal view

正视图
Frontal view

正视图
Frontal view

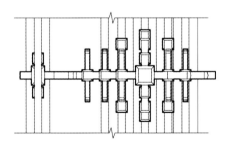
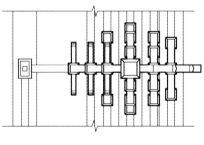
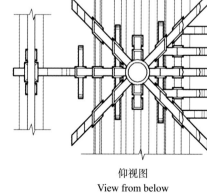

仰视图
View from below

仰视图
View from below

仰视图
View from below

仰视图
View from below

献殿后檐当心间平身科大样图
Bracket set between central-bay rear eaves columns of offering hall

献殿后檐梢间平身科大样图
Bracket set between central-to-last-bay rear eaves columns of offering hall

献殿前檐当心间平身科大样图
Bracket set between central-bay front eaves columns of offering hall

献殿前檐角科大样图
Bracket set atop front eaves corner columns of main hall

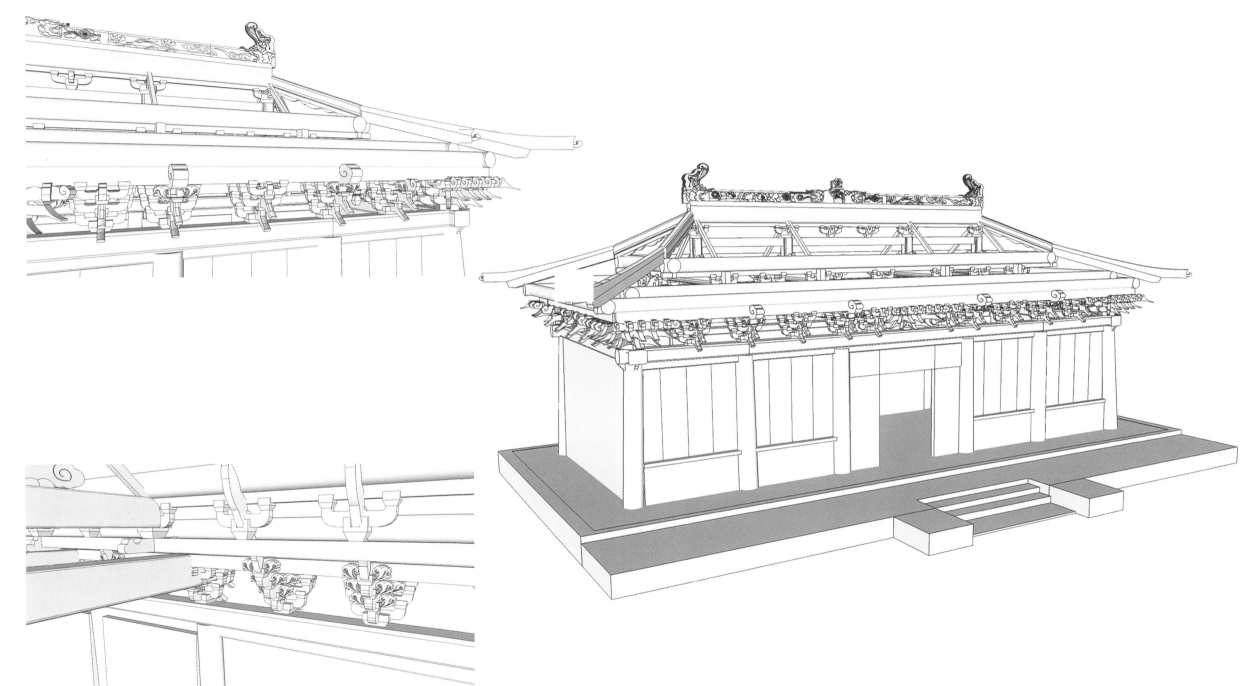

献殿模型
Reconstruction of offering hall

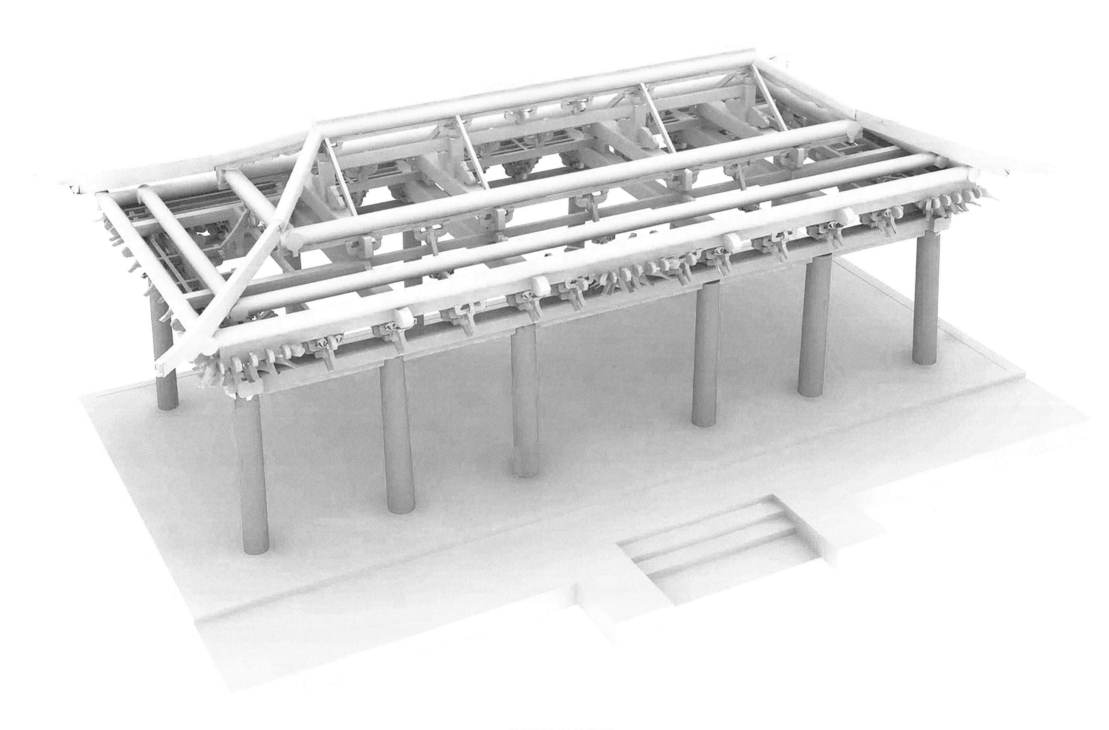

献殿框架结构模型
Structured model of offering hall

三原城隍庙
City God Temple of Sanyuan

Location: Qu'an Street in Sanyuan, Shaanxi province
Construction Date: Ming Dynasty
Protection Level: National Priority Protected Site (fifth batch)

地　　址：陕西三原县城渠岸街
年　　代：明代
保护级别：全国重点文物保护单位（第五批）

Introduction

Originally built in 1375, the City (Chenghuang) God Temple is situated in the middle part of Qu'an Street in the county city of Sanyuan. It is one of the City God temples with the largest and most intact layout in China.

The temple consists of four courtyards aligned one after the other. Along the main axis stand, from south to north, a stone-carved screen wall (1550), a timber-framed archway (*pailou*; with a plaque saying "Xianyou weiling zhaoying ci" [The Temple of the Prestigious, Benevolent, Righteous, Clairvoyant, Bright, and Responsive]), a gatehouse (*menlou*), a second timber-framed archway (*pailou*; with a plaque saying "*zhijiang zaizi*" [the god comes and leaves through here]), a stone archway (*pailou*; with a plaque saying "*mingling baozhang*" [the bright spirit protects]), a stage building (1757), a third timber-framed archway (*pailou*; with a plaque saying "*mingling dianyou*" [the bright spirit blesses]; built in 1582 but repaired between 1831 and 1861), an offering hall (*xiandian*; 1375), and the main hall (1375). Behind the main hall stand Mingyin (Pious Offering) Pavilion (1552) and a resting hall (*qindian*; 1486). The offering hall is connected to the roof of the main hall by a shared gutter and flanked by a drum tower and a bell tower (both built in 1375). The temple underwent repair and alteration on several occasions.

概述

城隍庙位于三原县城渠岸街中段，始建于明洪武八年（1375年），是我国保存至今的规模最为宏大、格局最为完整的城隍庙建筑群之一。

整个建筑群包括前后四进院落，中轴线上的主要建筑由南至北依次为砖雕照壁（建于明嘉靖二十九年，1550年）、木牌坊（额题『显佑威灵昭应祠』）、门楼、『陟降在兹』木牌坊、『明灵奠佑』木牌坊（建于明万历十年，1582年）、戏楼（建于清乾隆二十二年，1757年）、『明灵保障』石牌坊、献殿和正殿（建于明洪武八年，1376年），正殿后为明禋亭（建于明嘉靖三十一年，1552年）和寝殿（建于明成化二十二年，1486年）。献殿和正殿为勾连搭形式。献殿前左右两侧分立钟楼和鼓楼（均建于明洪武八年，1376年）。自建成至清代，曾多次进行维修、重修及增建。

Fig.1 Screen wall and timber archway of City God Temple of Sanyuan
Fig.2 "Zhijiang zaizi" timber archway of City God Temple of Sanyuan
Fig.3 "Mingling baozhang" stone archway of City God Temple of Sanyuan
Fig.4 "Mingling baozhang" stone archway of City God Temple of Sanyuan

图3 三原城隍庙『明灵保障』石牌坊

图2 三原城隍庙『陟降在兹』木牌坊

图4 三原城隍庙『明灵保障』石牌坊雕饰纹样

图1 三原城隍庙入口照壁和木牌坊

Survey and Mapping Information

Responsible Department: Department of Architecture (Class of 2005), School of Architecture, Xi'an University of Architecture and Technology

Team Members: YU Lulu, NIU Tengfei, WANG Yangyang, WANG Qing, WU Yang, LI Rui, YANG Ming, GUO Biao, ZHANG Hengyan, REN Bingyu, WEN Linqi, XIE Han, XUE Fei, HUANG Yahui, ZHANG Qian, WU Chao, CHENG Yibo, YAN Weiyang, SHI Yuli, ZHANG Nan, JIN Xueli, ZHOU Jin, ZHAO Ziwei, HAO Xin, WANG Yujing, FENG Wenfeng, LIU Xiaoyan, ZHANG Tao, LI Jiaxin, LIN Wenchao, WU Shuyun, XU Fei, GAO Xinyi, BEI Ning, WEI Lin, MIAO Xuan, SHANG Chan, SHI Minmin, TANG Tang, DOU Wei, LI Xiaoyi, HAN Meng, GUO Di

Supervisors: LIN Yuan

Editors of Drawings: XIA Nan, SHEN Peiyu, HUANG Sida, LI Shuangshuang, LI Wanru, LI Zhen, TONG Mengfei, LEI Honglu, WEN Wujuan

Survey Time: October 2008

三原城隍庙测绘的人员名单

测绘：西安建筑科技大学建筑学院建筑学2005级

于路路　牛腾飞　王杨扬　王青　吴杨　李瑞　杨铭　郭彪
张恒言　任丙玉　文琳琪　谢涵　薛斐　黄雅慧　张千吴　吴超
程奕博　颜威扬　石宇立　张楠　金雪丽　周瑾　赵紫薇　郝欣
王玉婧　冯文峰　颜潇衍　刘潇衍　张涛　李佳欣　林文超　武舒韵　徐飞
高心怡　贝宁　韦琳　苗璇　商婵　石忞旻　唐瑭　窦巍
李小艺　韩濛　郭迪

指导教师：林源

图纸整理：夏楠　申佩玉　黄思达　李双双　李宛儒　李祯　仝梦菲　雷鸿鹭　汶武娟

测绘时间：2008年10月

参考文献 References

［一］三原县志编纂委员会编．三原县志·陕西地方志丛书．西安：陕西人民出版社，2000．

［二］赵立瀛主编．陕西古建筑．西安：陕西人民出版社，1992．

［三］国家文物局主编．中国文物地图集·陕西分册．西安：西安地图出版社，1998．

图6 三原城隍庙"明灵奠佑"木牌坊

图5 三原城隍庙戏楼

Fig.5 Stage building of City God Temple of Sanyuan
Fig.6 "*Mingling dianyou*" timber archway of City God Temple of Sanyuan

图9 三原城隍庙鼓楼二层屋面

图8 三原城隍庙鼓楼一层角科斗栱

图7 三原城隍庙鼓楼

图10 三原城隍庙大殿

Fig.7 Drum tower of City God Temple of Sanyuan
Fig.8 Bracket set atop corner column, drum tower of City God Temple of Sanyuan
Fig.9 Second-floor roof ridge of drum tower of City God Temple of Sanyuan
Fig.10 Main hall of City God Temple of Sanyuan

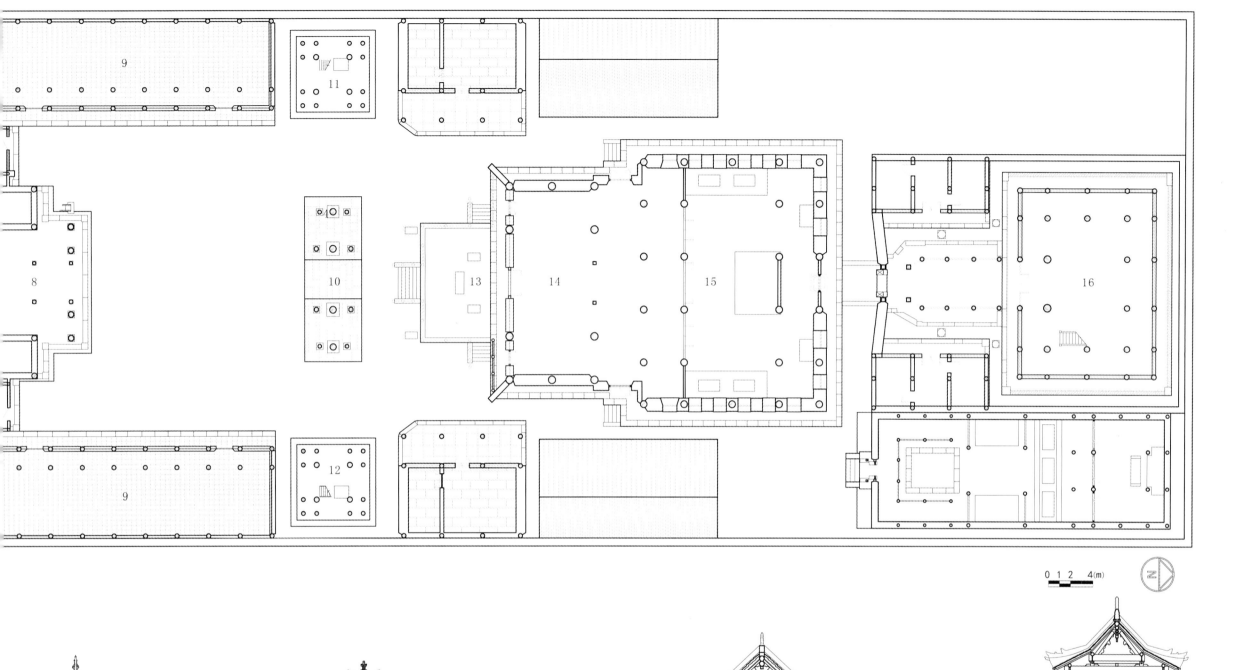
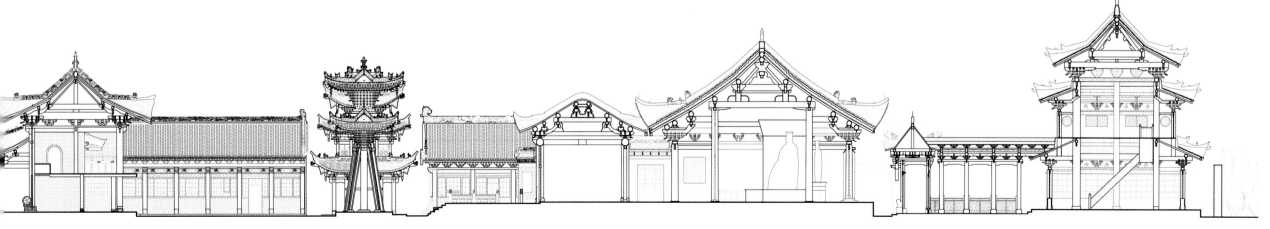

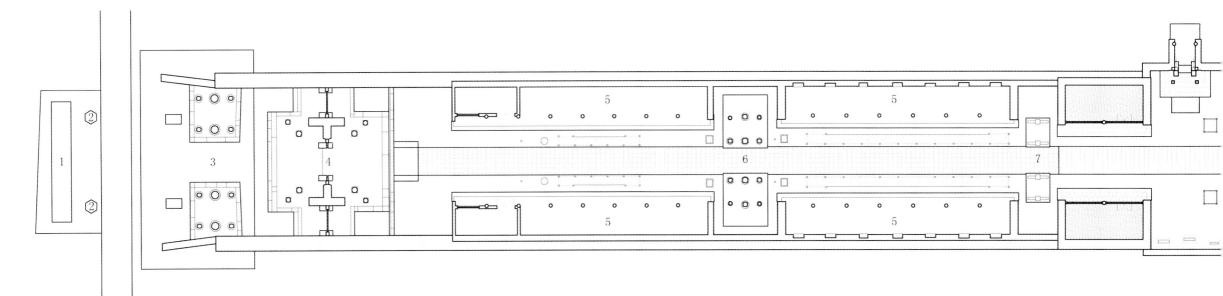

总平面图
Site plan

1. 照壁 Screen Wall
2. 铁番竿 Iron flagpoles
3. 牌坊 Archway
4. 门楼 Gatehouse
5. 东西碑廊 East-and west-said stele corridor
6. "陟降在兹" 木牌坊 *Zhijiang zaizi* timber archway
7. "明灵保障" 石牌坊 *Mingling baozhang* stone archway
8. 戏楼 Stage building
9. 东西配殿 East-and west-side halls
10. "明灵奠佑" 木牌坊 *Mingling dianyou* timber archway
11. 钟楼 Bell tower
12. 鼓楼 Drum tower
13. 月台 Front platform
14. 献殿 Offering hall
15. 正殿 Main hall
16. 财神殿 Caishen Hall

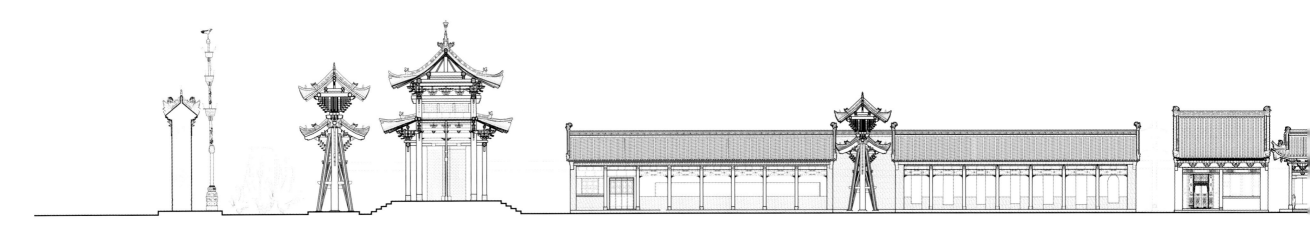

院落整体纵剖面图（西视）
Longitudinal section through courtyards (view from the west)

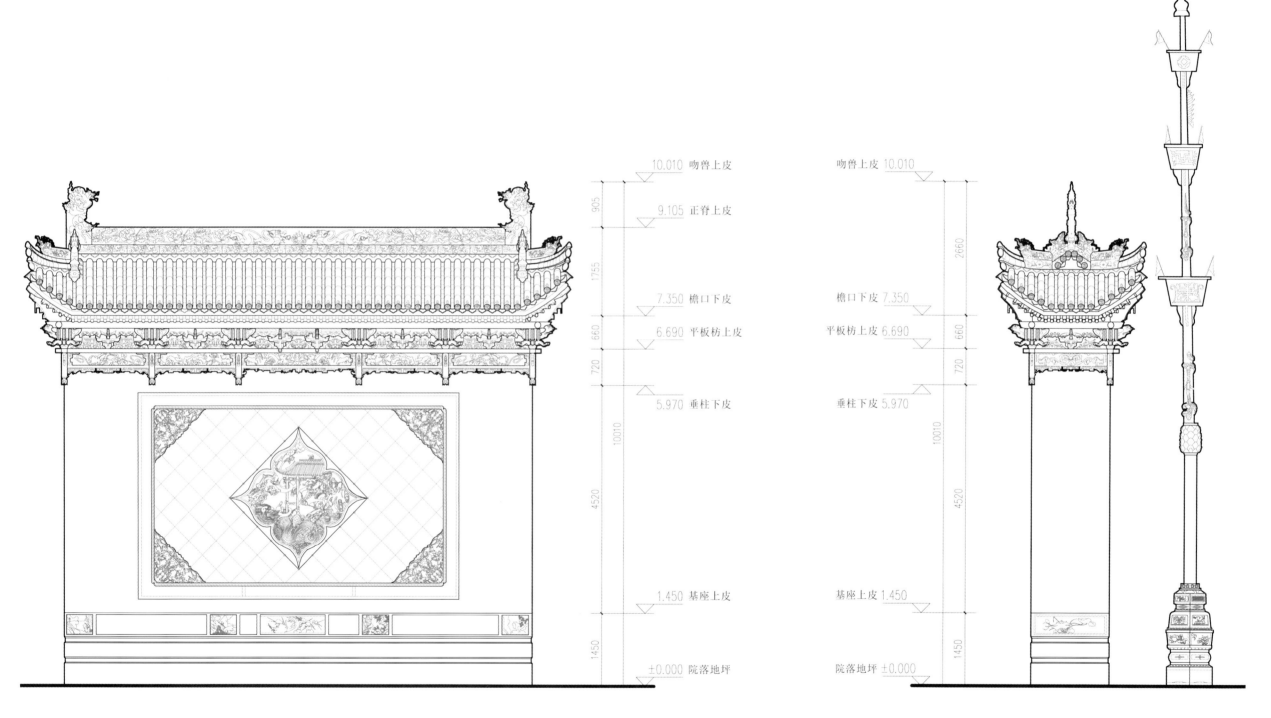

照壁北立面图
North elevation of screen wall

照壁东立面图
East elevation of screen wall

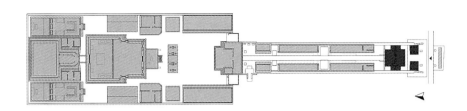

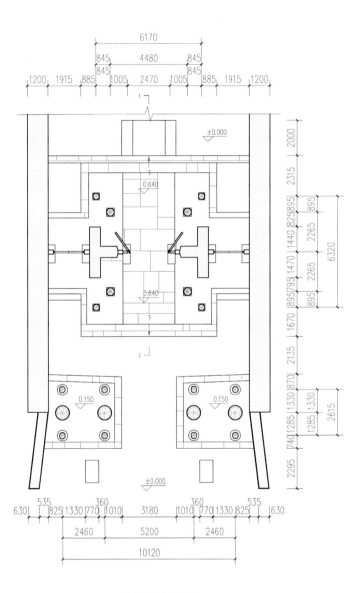

门楼平面图
Plan of gatehouse

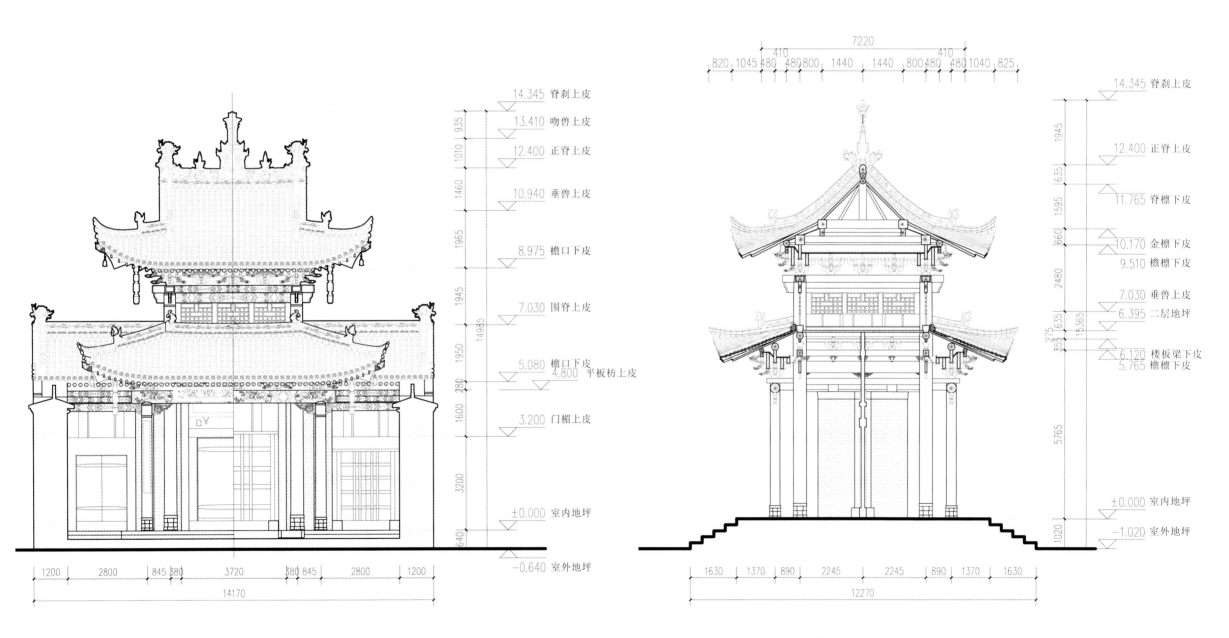

门楼南–北立面图
South-north elevation of gatehouse

门楼 1-1 剖面图
Section 1-1 of gatehouse

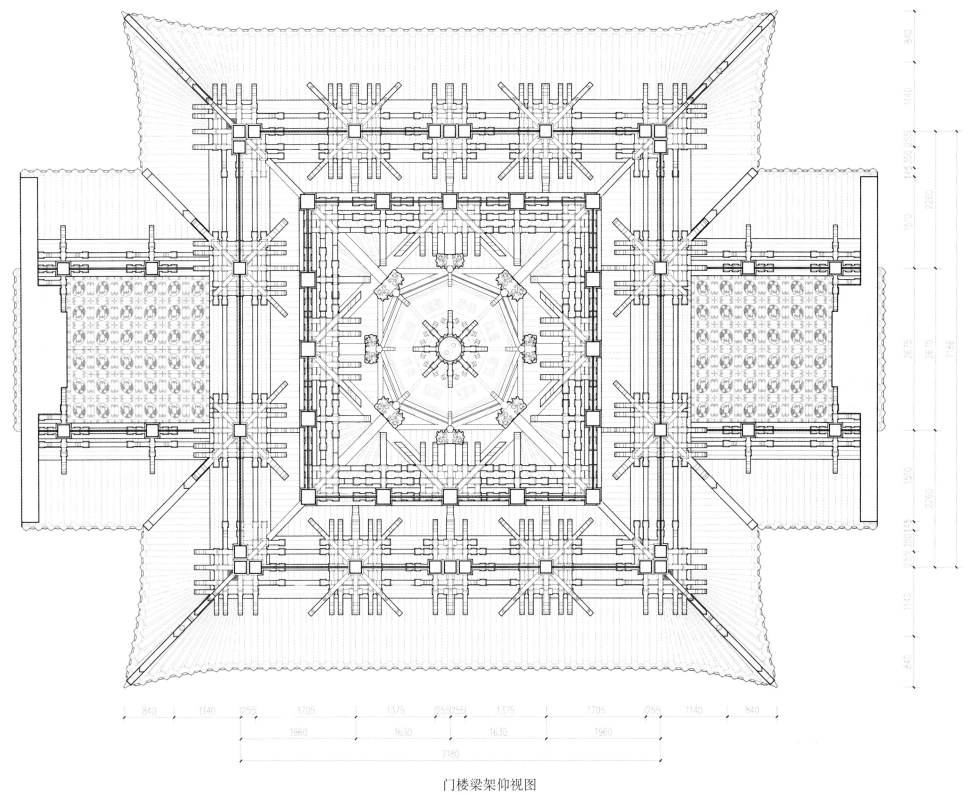

门楼梁架仰视图
Plan of framework of gatehouse as seen form below

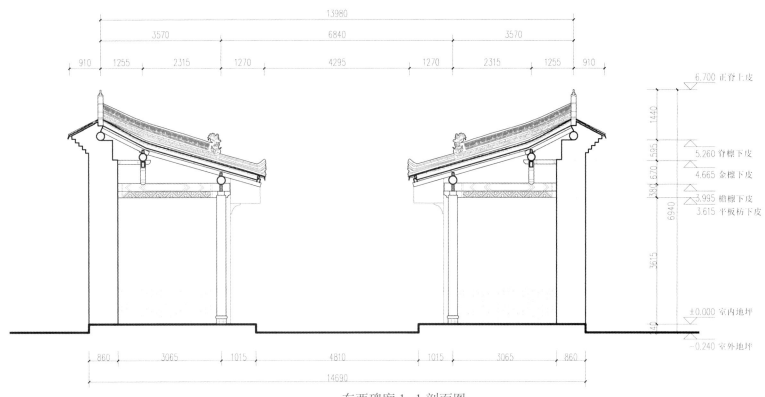

东西碑廊 1-1 剖面图
Cross-section of east-and west-side stele corridor

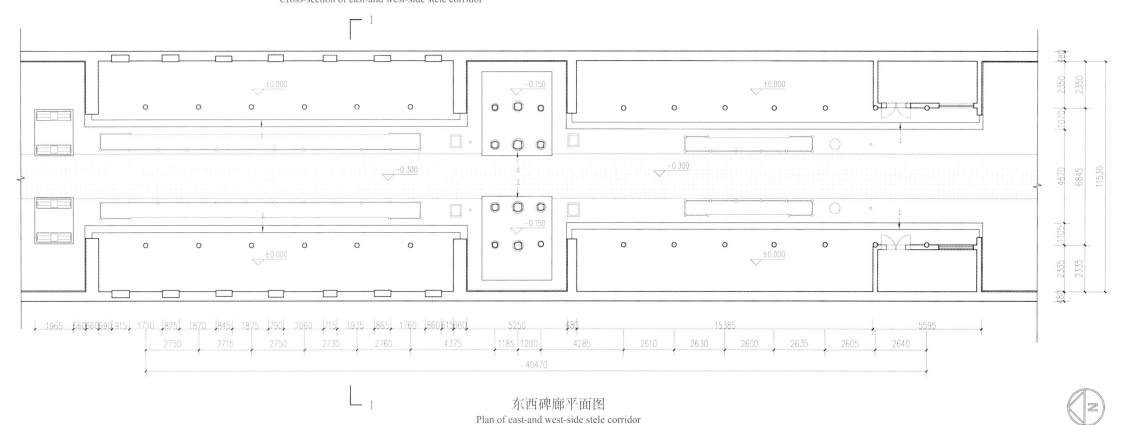

东西碑廊平面图
Plan of east-and west-side stele corridor

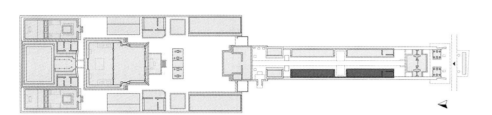

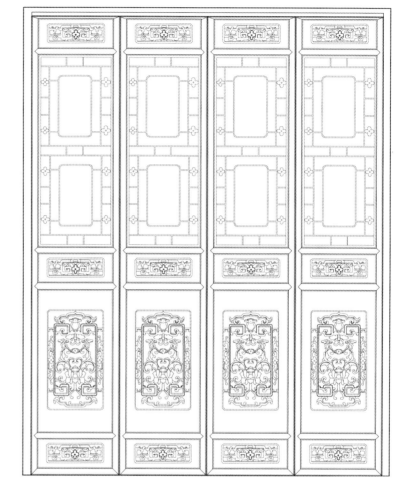

碑廊门窗大样图
Doors and windows of east-and west-side stele corridor

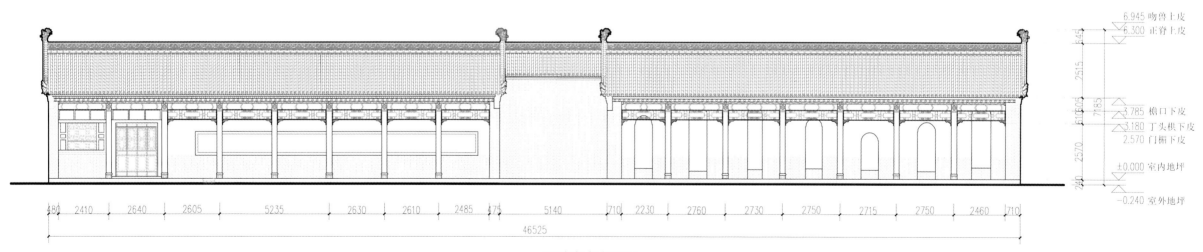

西碑廊东立面图
East elevation of west- side stele corridor

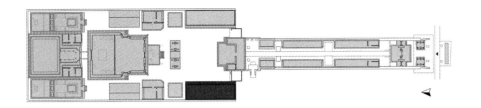

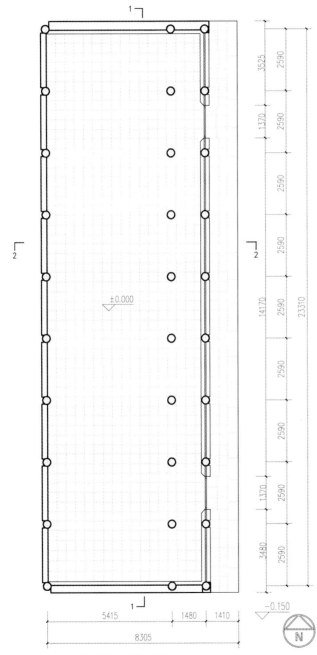

西配殿 1 平面图
Plan of west-side hall 1

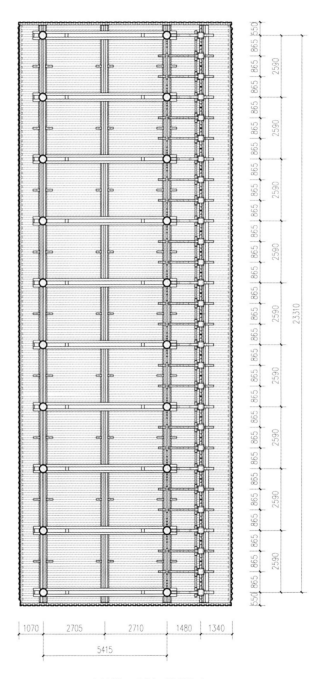

西配殿 1 梁架仰视图
Plan of framework of west-side hall 1 as seen from below

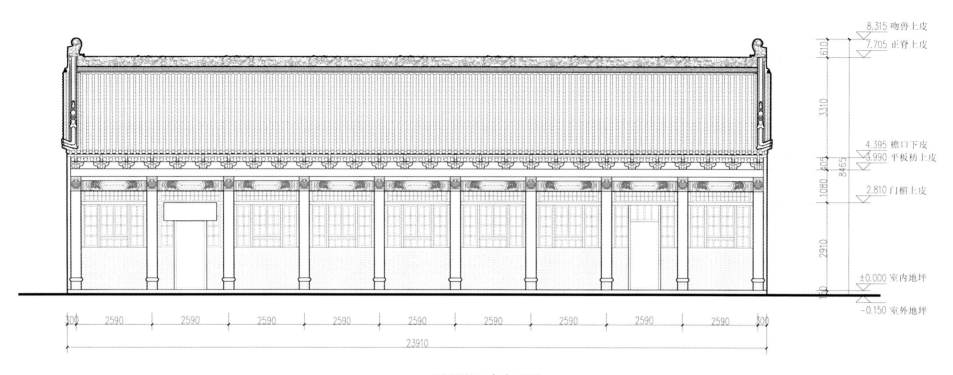

西配殿 1 东立面图
East elevation of west-side hall 1

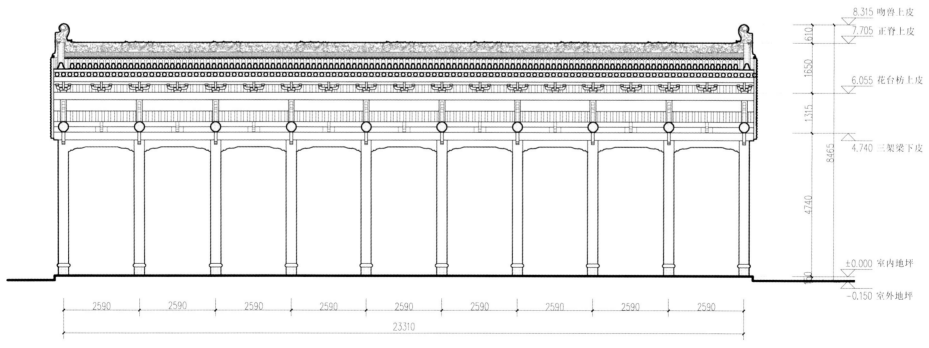

西配殿 1 1-1 剖面图
Section 1-1 of west side hall 1

西配殿 1 北山墙立面图
Elevation of northern gable wall of west-side hall 1

西配殿 1 2—2 剖面图
Section 2-2 of west-side hall 1

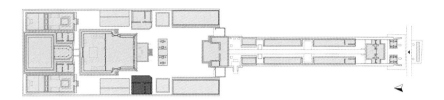

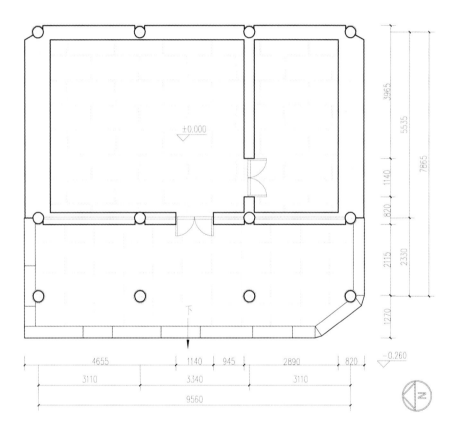

西配殿2 平面图
Plan of of west-side hall 2

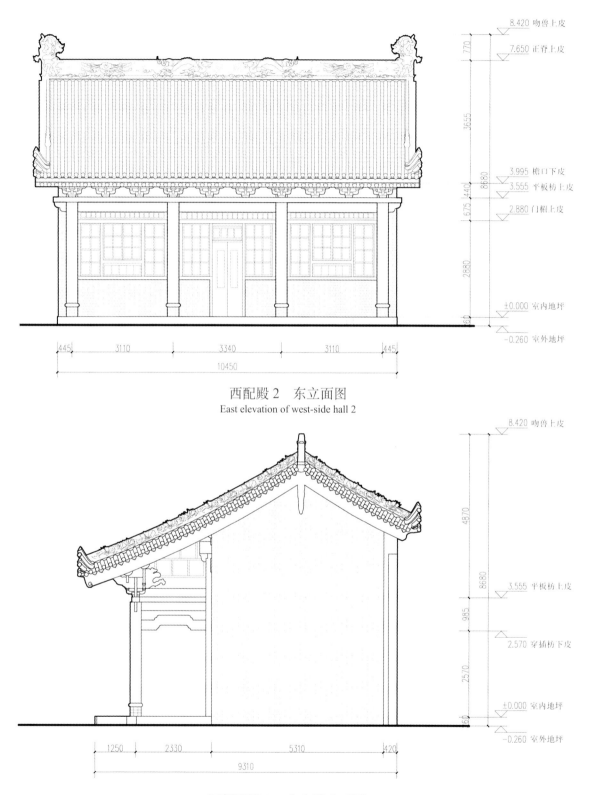

西配殿2 东立面图
East elevation of west-side hall 2

西侧配殿2 南山墙立面图
Elevation of southern gable wall of west-side hall 2

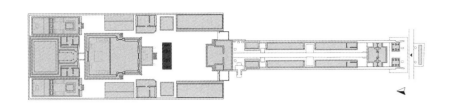
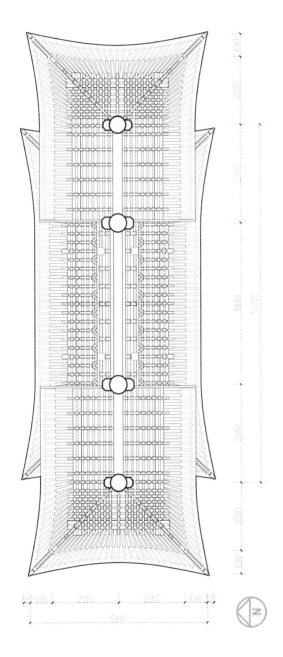
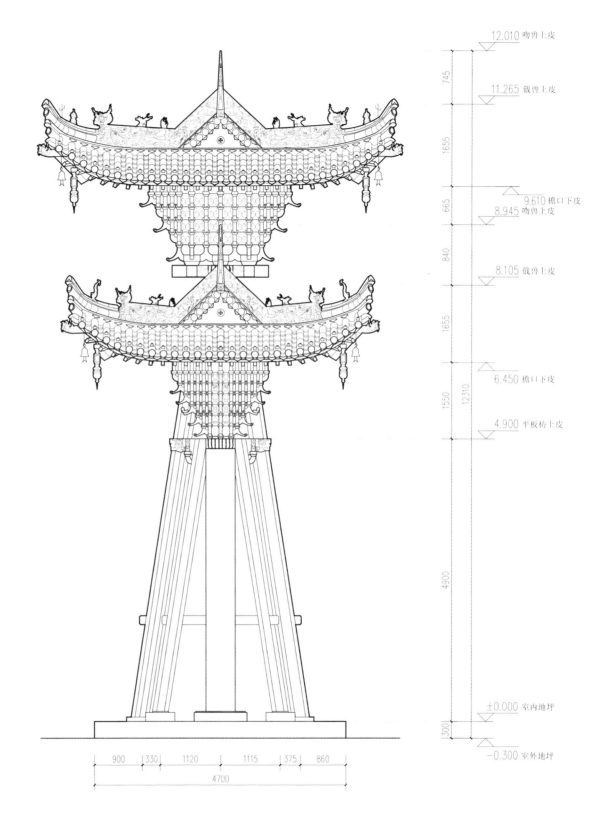

"明灵奠佑"木牌坊梁架仰视图
Plan of framework of *"mingling dianyou"* timber archway as seen from below

"明灵奠佑"木牌坊西立面图
West elevation of *"mingling dianyou"* timber archway

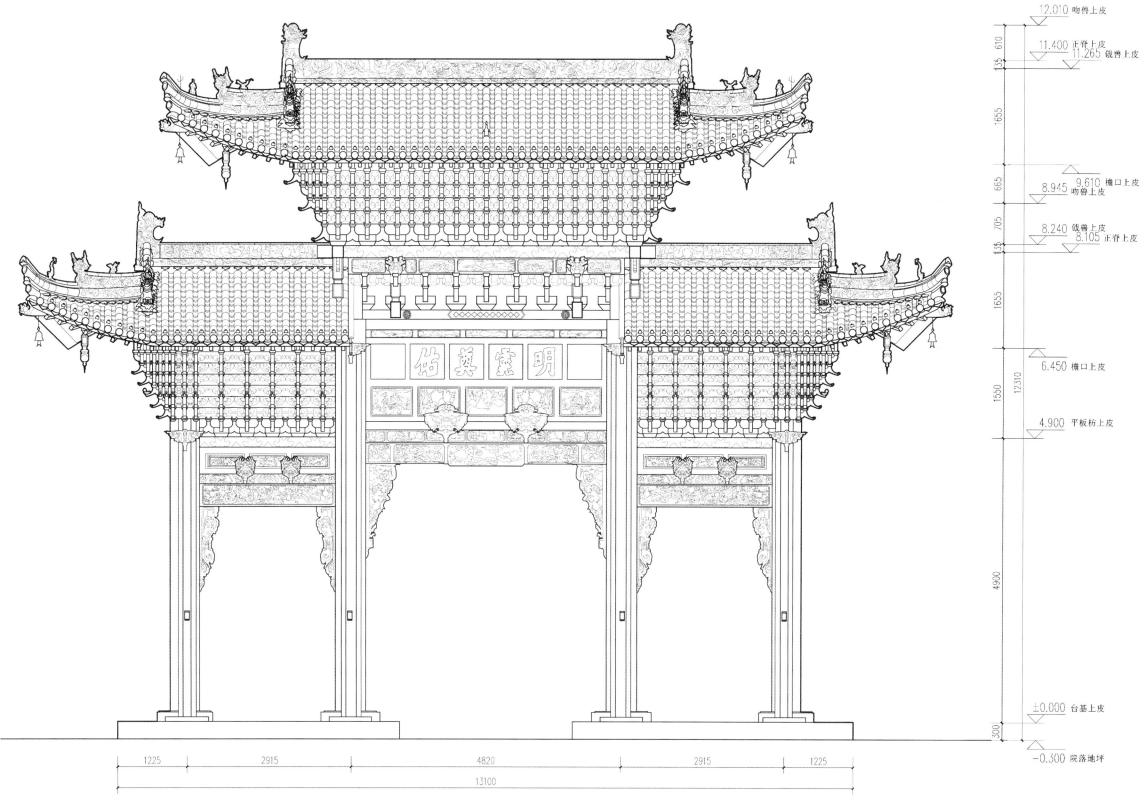

"明灵奠佑"木牌坊南立面图
South elevation of *"mingling dianyou"* timber archway

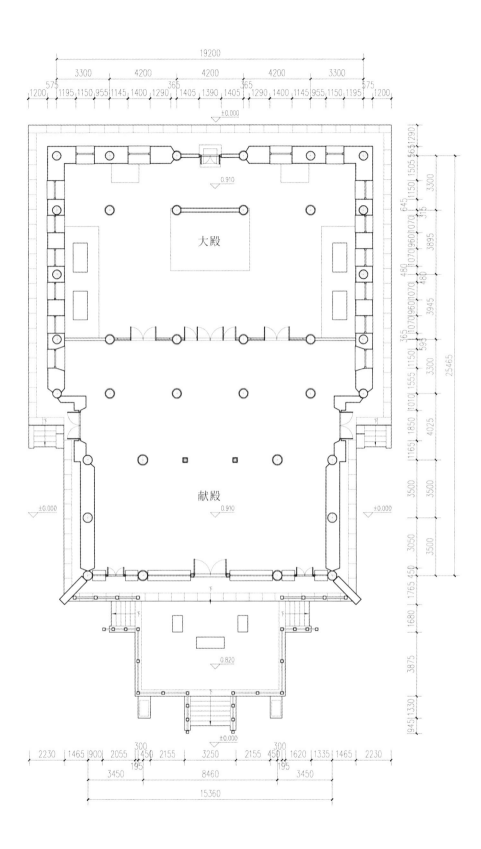

大殿与献殿平面图
Plan of main hall and offering hall

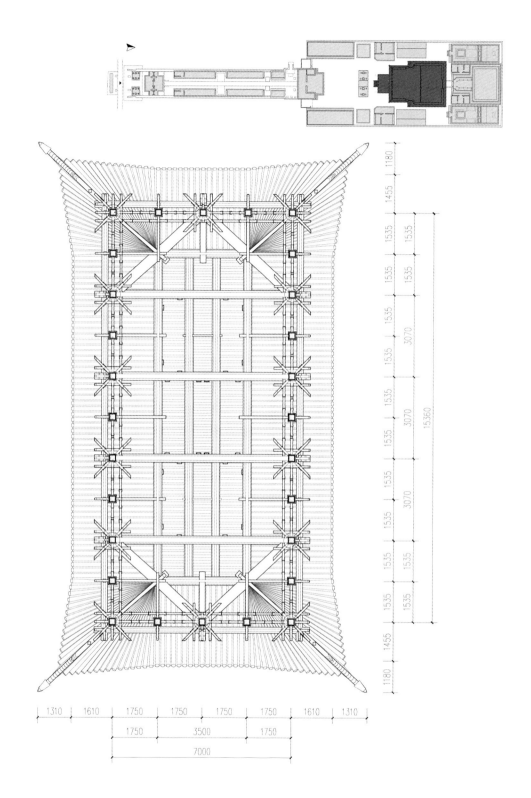

献殿梁架仰视图
Plan of framework of offering hall as seen from below

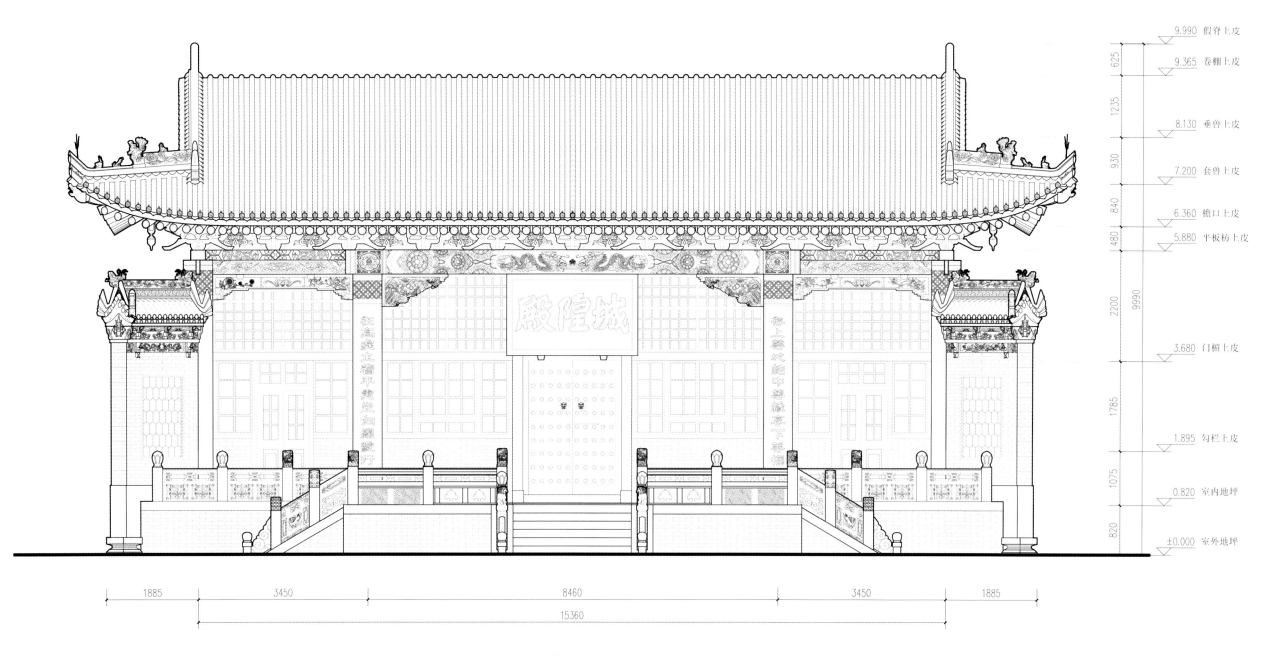

献殿南立面图
South elevation of offering hall

大殿梁架仰视图
Plan of framework of main hall as seen from below

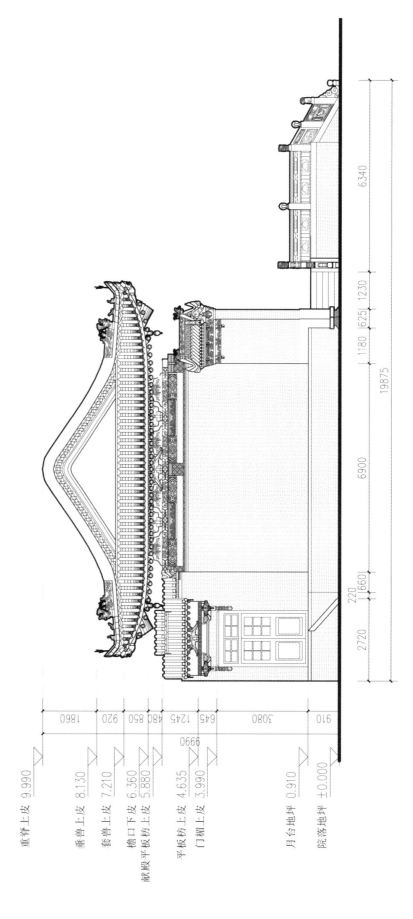

献殿东立面图
East elevation of offering hall

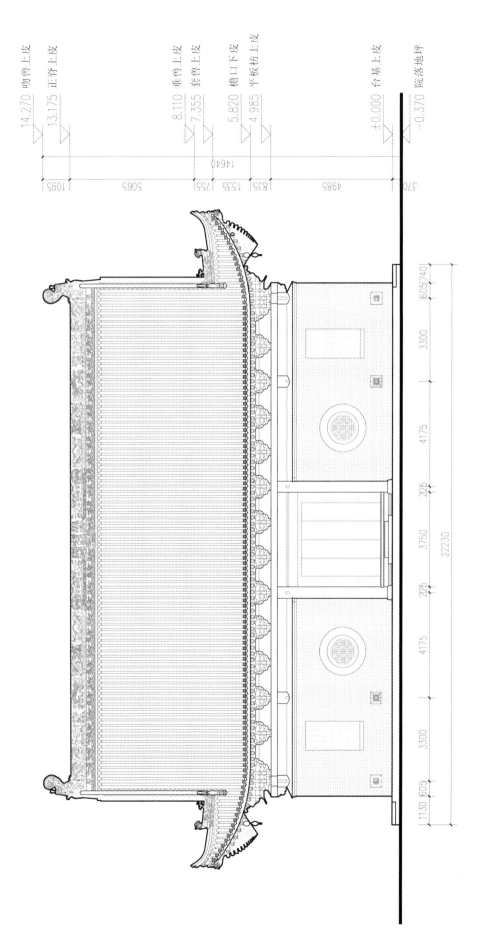

大殿北立面图
North elevation of offering hall

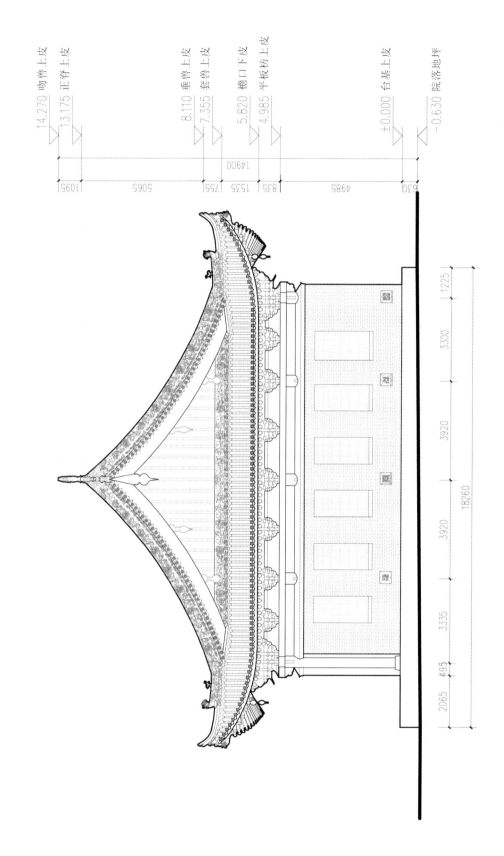

大殿东立面图
East elevation of main hall

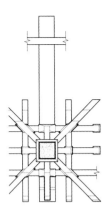

仰视图
View from below

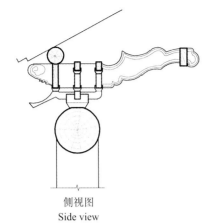

侧视图
Side view

正视图
Frontal view

献殿侧面柱头科大样图
Bracket sets atop columns, gable side of offering hall

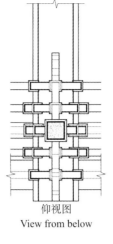

仰视图
View from below

侧视图
Side view

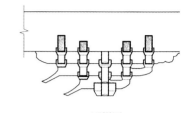

正视图
Frontal view

大殿柱头科大样图
Bracket sets atop columns, of main hall

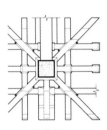

仰视图
View from below

侧视图
Side view

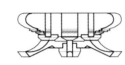

正视图
Frontal view

献殿侧面中柱头科大样图
Bracket sets atop central column, gable side of offering hall

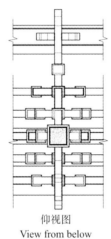

仰视图
View from below

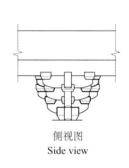

侧视图
Side view

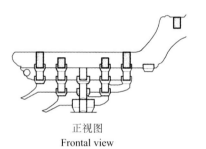

正视图
Frontal view

大殿平身科大样图
Intercolumnar bracket sets of main hall

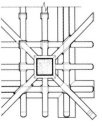

仰视图
View from below

侧视图
Side view

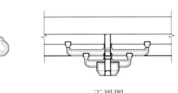

正视图
Frontal view

献殿平身科大样图
Intercolumnar bracket sets of offering hall

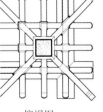

仰视图
View from below

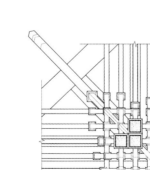

正视图
Frontal view

献殿角科大样图
Corner bracket sets of offering hall

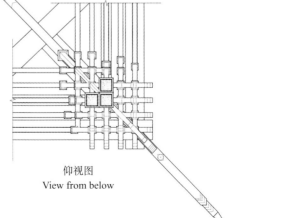

仰视图
View from below

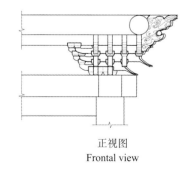

正视图
Frontal view

大殿角科大样图
Corner bracket sets of main hall

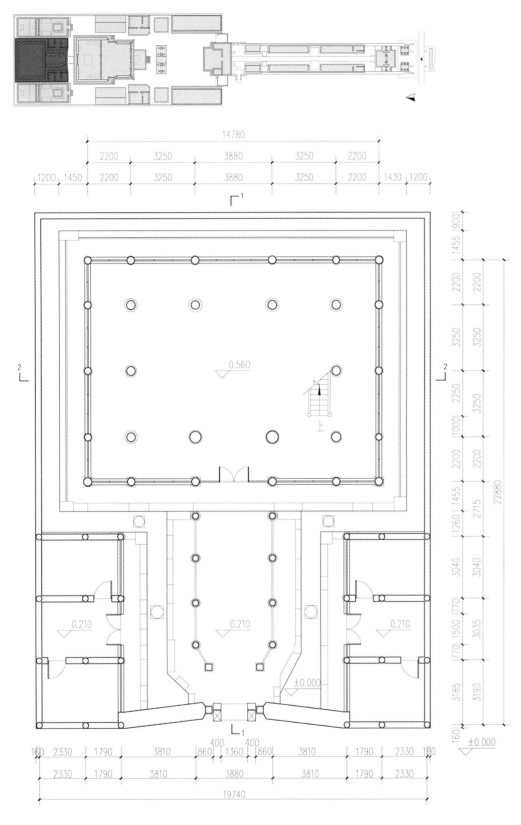

寝殿一层平面图
Plan of first floor of resting hall

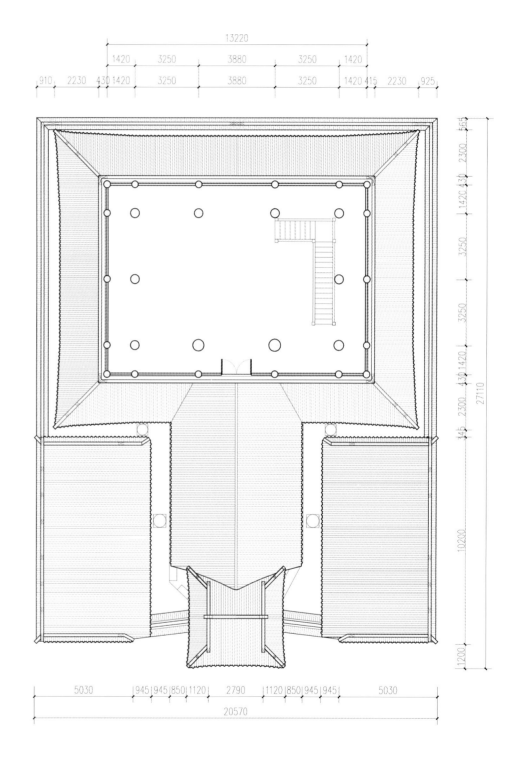

寝殿二层平面图
Plan of second floor of resting hall

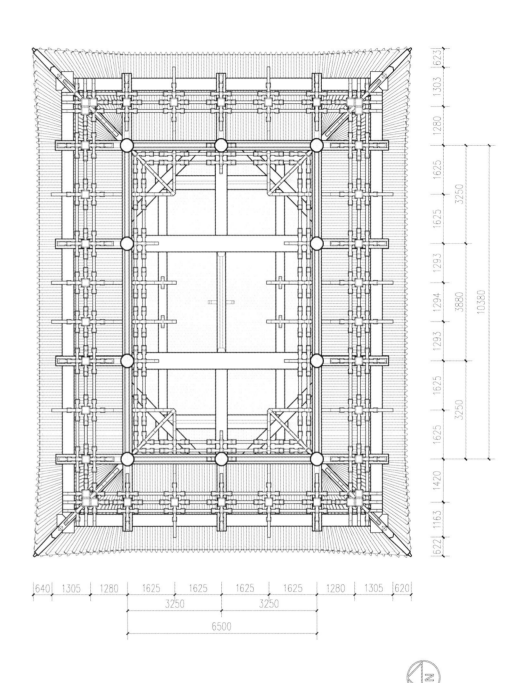

寝殿一层梁架仰视图
Plan of first-floor framework of resting hall as seen from below

寝殿二层梁架仰视图
Plan of second-floor framework of resting hall as seen from below

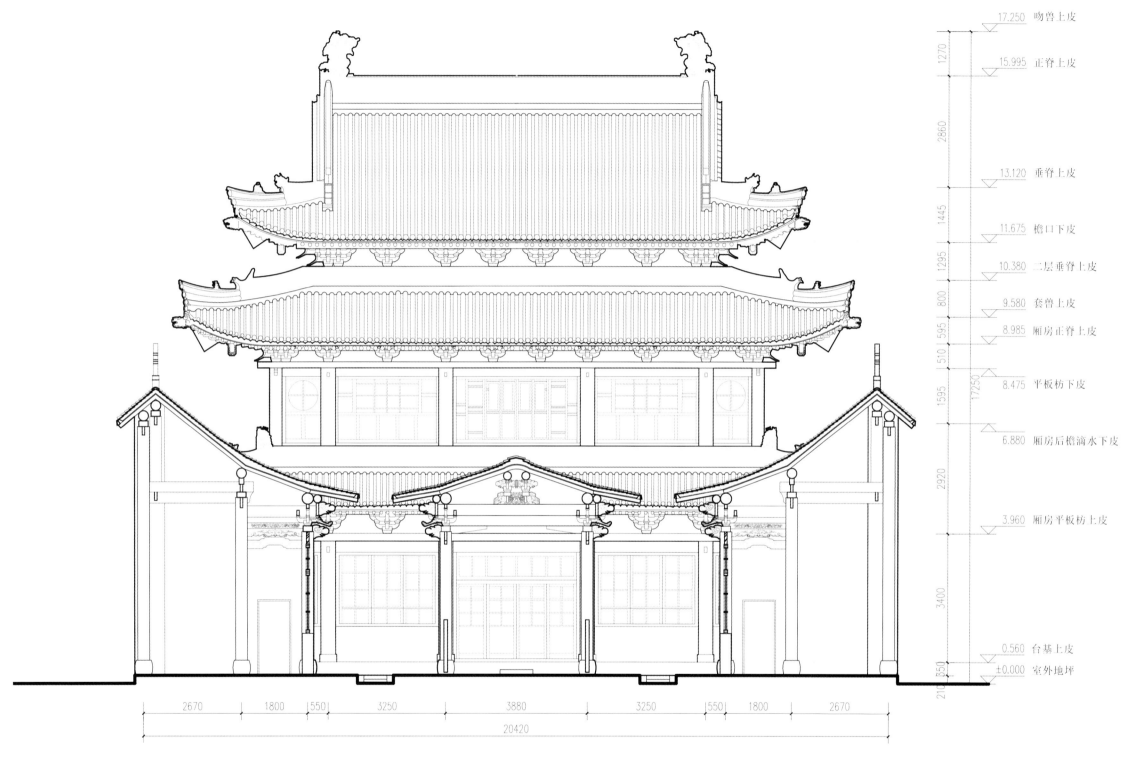

寝殿院落南立面图
South elevation of courtyard with resting hall

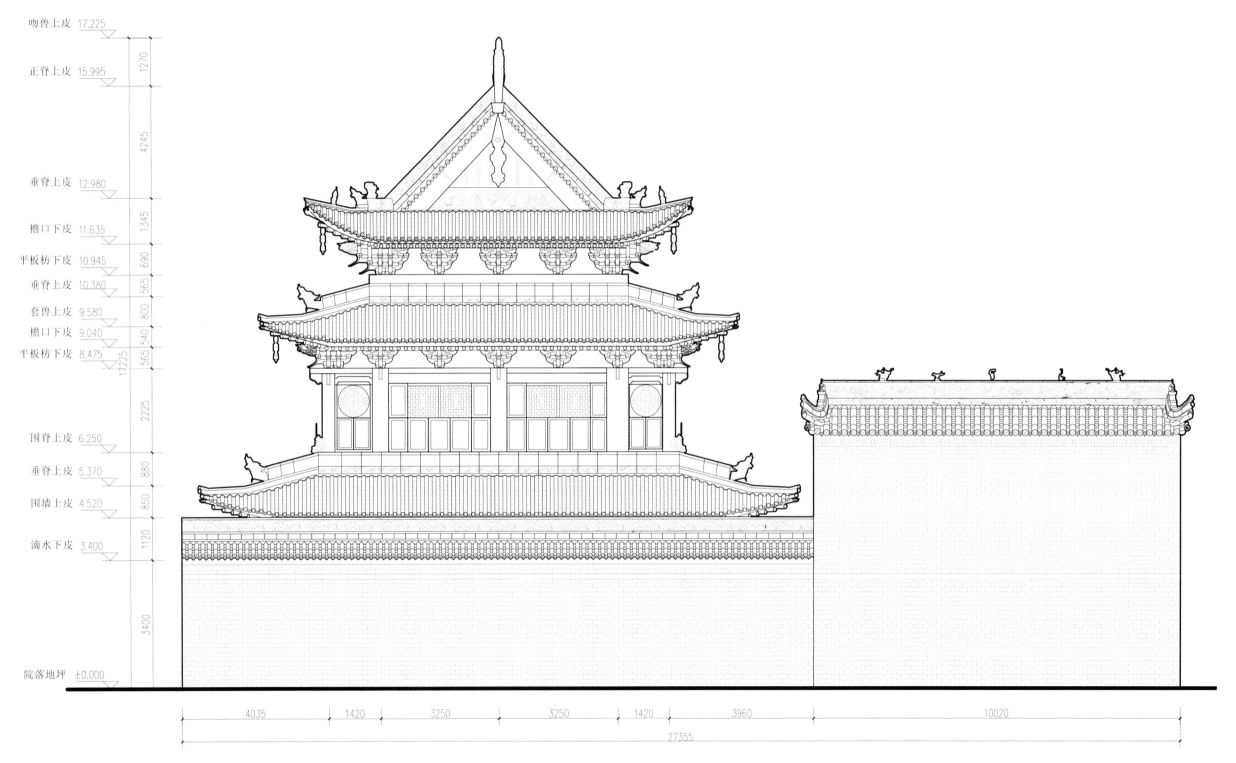

寝殿东立面图
East elevation of resting hall

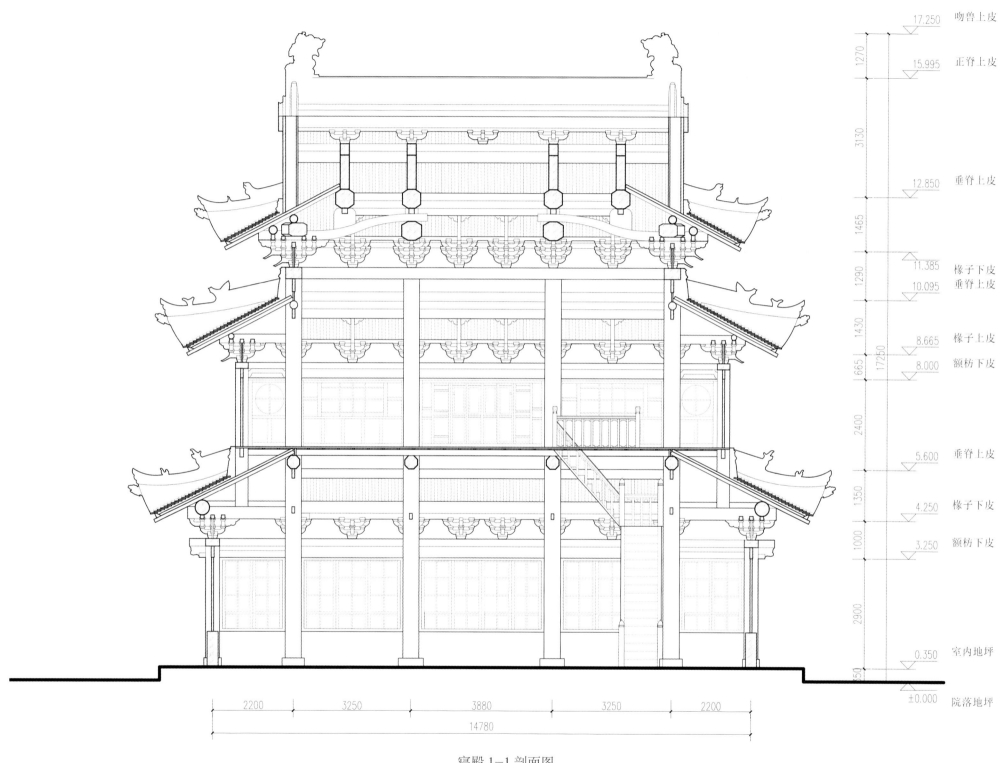

寝殿 1-1 剖面图
Section 1-1 of resting hall

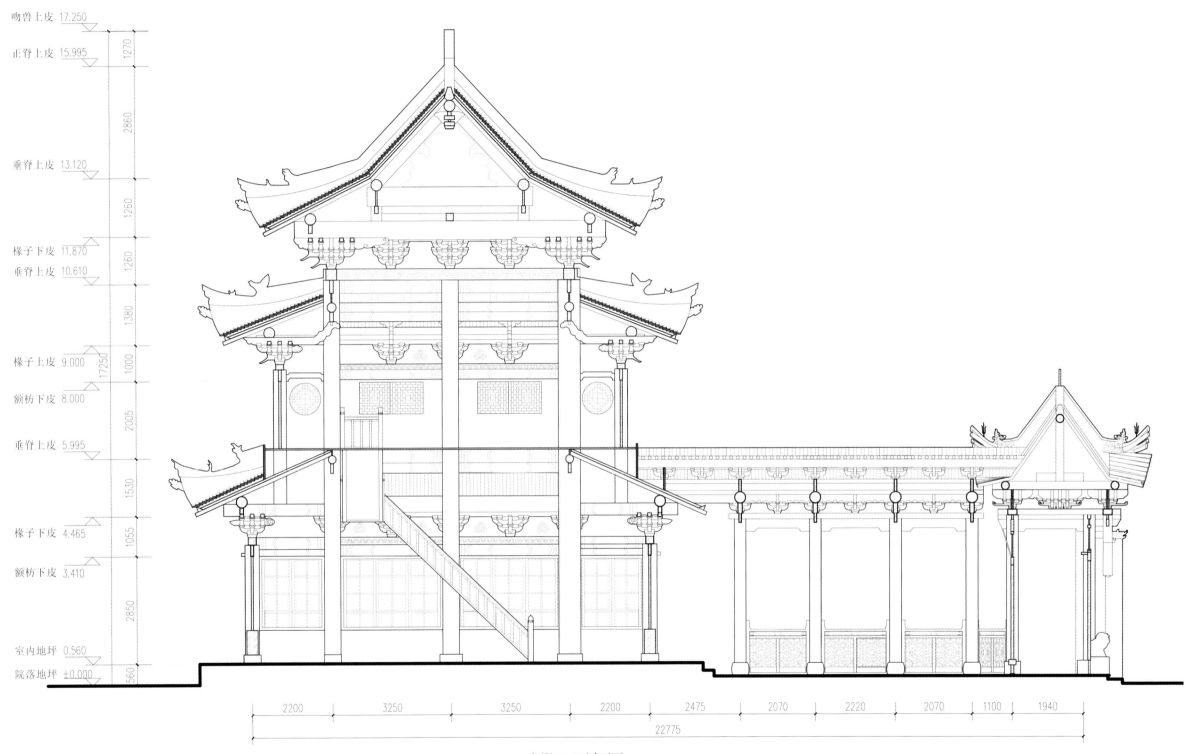

寝殿 2-2 剖面图
Section 2-2 of resting hall

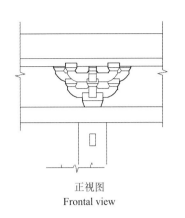 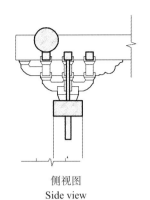 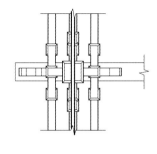 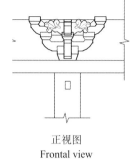 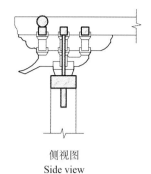 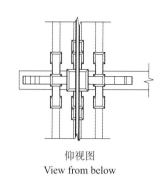

| 正视图 | 侧视图 | 仰视图 | 正视图 | 侧视图 | 仰视图 |
| Frontal view | Side view | View from below | Frontal view | Side view | View from below |

寝殿一层柱头科大样图
Bracket sets atop first-floor columns of resting hall

寝殿二层柱头科大样图
Bracket sets atop second-floor columns of resting hall

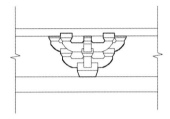 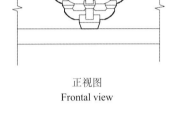  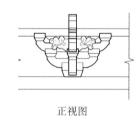 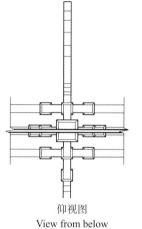

| 正视图 | 侧视图 | 仰视图 | 正视图 | 侧视图 | 仰视图 |
| Frontal view | Side view | View from below | Frontal view | Side view | View from below |

寝殿一层平身科大样图
Bracket set between first-floor columns of resting hall

寝殿二层平身科大样图
Bracket set between second-floor columns of resting hall

 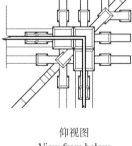 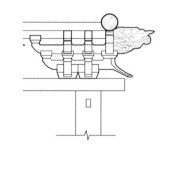 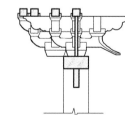 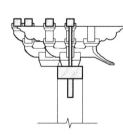 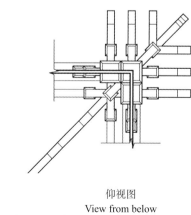

| 正视图 | 侧视图 | 仰视图 | 正视图 | 侧视图 | 仰视图 |
| Frontal view | Side view | View from below | Frontal view | Side view | View from below |

寝殿一层角科大样图
First-floor corner bracket sets of resting hall

寝殿二层角科大样图
Second-floor corner bracket sets of resting hall

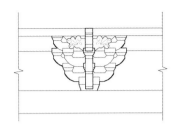
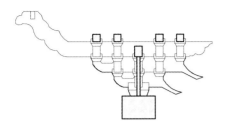
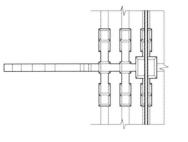

正视图
Frontal view

侧视图
Side view

仰视图
View from below

寝殿三层平身科大样图
Bracket set between third-floor columns of of resting hall

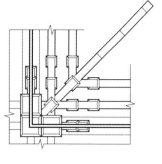

正视图
Frontal view

仰视图
View from below

寝殿三层角科大样图
Third-floor corner bracket sets of resting hall

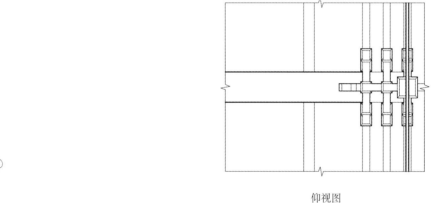
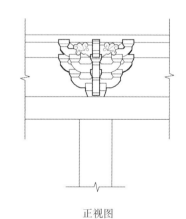

仰视图
View from below

正视图
Frontal view

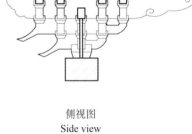

正视图
Frontal view

侧视图
Side view

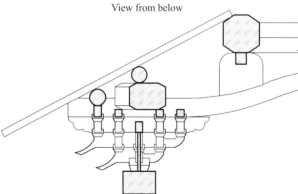
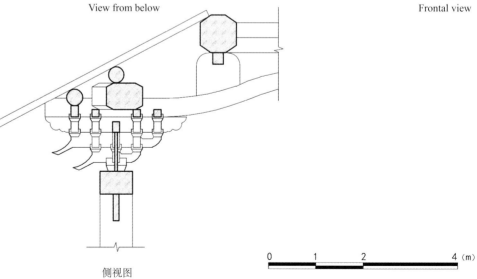

后视图
View from back

仰视图
View from below

寝殿三层平身科大样图
Bracket set between third-floor columns of of resting hall

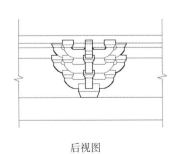
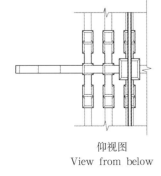

侧视图
Side view

寝殿三层柱头科大样图
Bracket set atop third-floor columns of resting hall

泾阳文庙
Confucian Temple in Jingyang

Location: Wenmiao Street in Jingyang, Shaanxi province

Construction Date: Ming and Qing dynasties

Protection Level: Shaanxi Province Protected Site

地　　址：陕西泾阳县文庙街

始建年代：明—清

保护级别：陕西省文物保护单位

Introduction

The Confucian Temple in the historical county city of Jingyang, Jinggan township, is situated on Wenmiao Street and flanked in the north and south by Beijigong Street and Nanhuan Street respectively. The date of construction is unclear, but a Song-dynasty stone stele (*Chongxiu Wenmiao beiji*) records repair in 1090 which suggests that at least some buildings were already in place before the late eleventh century. Following the catastrophic earthquake that destroyed the temple during the reign of emperor Jiajing of Ming (r. 1522-1566), the county magistrate Dai Zhong initiated reconstruction soon afterwards. The complex underwent further repair in 1576, 1632, 1764, between 1796 and 1820, and between 1821 and 1850. In 1865, the county magistrate Huang Fushen raised money for the renovation of Dacheng Hall, which was repaired again two decades later thanks to a donation of 40,000 taels of silver provided by the female patron Zhou Wu from Anwubao. Since then, Jinyang Confucian Temple has since retained many of its historical features until the present day.

In the early years of the Peoples' Republic of China, the temple served as a school and afterwards as a grain supply center and a seed company. Since 1980, the site has been protected at the county level and since 1992 April 20th, at the provincial level. The County Cultural Heritage Administration Commission has used the site as its headquarter office since 1985. Today, it also serves as a county museum.

The Confucian Temple in Jinyang is recognized for its grand scale and intact layout. Today, many buildings are still aligned symmetrically along the central axis including the Ten-thousand-foot Palatial Wall (Wanren gongqiang), the main entrance gate, Pan Pond, Ji Gate, Yue (Music) House, the east- and west-side buildings and Dacheng Hall. The site covers an area of 5289 m sq. with a built-up area of 1531 m sq.

概述

泾阳县文庙位于泾干镇老县城文庙街，南临南环路，北界北极宫大街，其始建年代待考，据宋刻《重修文庙碑记》中载有元祐五年（1090年）重修情况，可知北宋中期以前已经存在。明嘉靖年间（1522—1566年）曾毁于地震，由时任知县钟岱发起重修；万历四年（1576年）、崇祯五年（1632年）、清乾隆二十九年（1764年）及嘉庆、道光年间均有修葺。同治四年（1865年）知县黄傅绅筹修大成殿，光绪十一年（1885年）安吴堡吴周氏捐银四万两重加修葺，遂成现状。

中华人民共和国成立之初，文庙一度用作学校，之后改为粮站、种子公司，1980年公布为县级文物保护单位，1992年4月20日升级为第三批陕西省文物保护单位。1985年县文物管理委员会迁入办公，现为县博物馆所在地。

泾阳文庙规模宏大，建制完整，现存建筑有万仞宫墙、泮池、戟门、乐房、东西庑和大成殿等，按南北中轴线对称排列，共占地5289平方米，建筑面积1531平方米。

图1 泾阳文庙戟门
图2 泾阳文庙大成殿
图3 泾阳文庙大成殿前廊

Fig.1 Ji Gate of Confucian Temple of Jingyang
Fig.2 Dacheng Hall of Confucian Temple of Jingyang
Fig.3 Front gallery of Dacheng Hall, Confucian Temple of Jingyang

Survey and Mapping Information

Responsible Department: Department of Architecture (Class of 2006), School of Architecture, Xi'an University of Architecture and Technology

Team Members: ZHAO Chunxiao, LAI Jialong, YU Jianwei, CAO Jialing, TANG Feng, LI Huimin, REN Wenling, YAN Wei, ZHANG Xiao, XING Qian, LIANG Yan

Supervisors: LIN Yuan

Editors of Drawings: XIA Nan, SHEN Peiyu, HUANG Sida, LI Wanru, WEN Wujuan

Survey Time: October 2008

泾阳文庙测绘的人员名单

测　绘：西安建筑科技大学建筑学院建筑学2006级研究生

赵春晓　来嘉隆　于健伟　曹佳玲　唐枫　李惠敏　任文玲　严巍

指导教师：林源

图纸整理：夏楠　申佩玉　黄思达　李宛儒　文娟

张骁　邢倩　梁燕

测绘时间：2008年10月

References 参考文献

[一] 泾阳县志编纂委员会编. 泾阳县志. 西安：陕西人民出版社，2001.

[二] 林源主编. 泾水之阳——陕西泾阳历史建筑测绘图志. 西安：三秦出版社，2016.

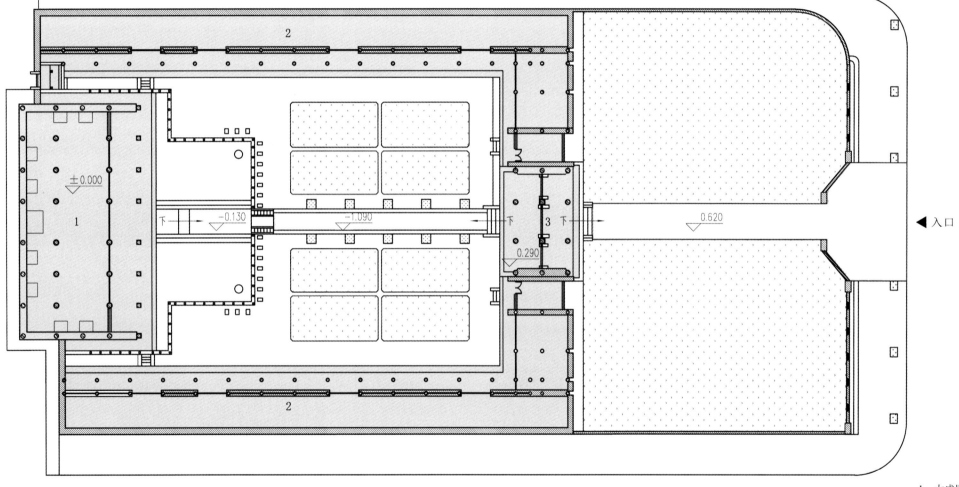

泾阳文庙总平面图
Site plan of Confucian Temple of Jingyang

1　大成殿　Dacheng Hall
2　两庑　East-and west-side buildings
3　戟门　Ji Gate

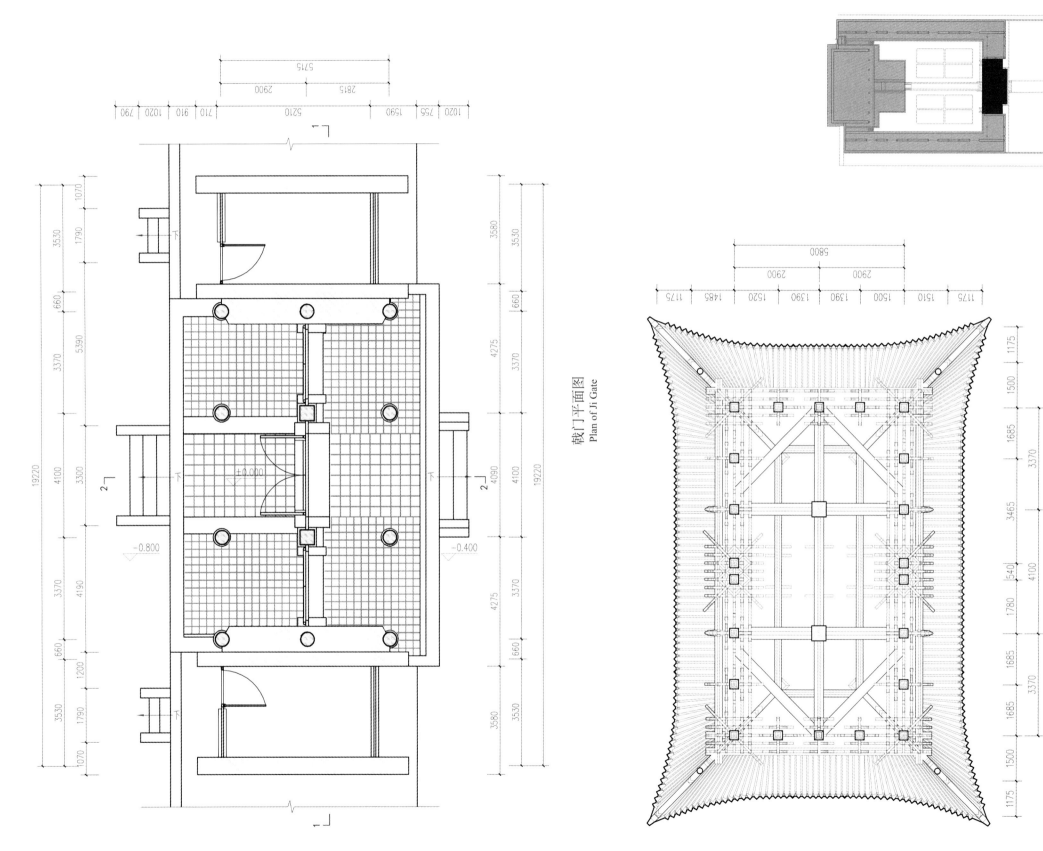

戟门平面图
Plan of Ji Gate

戟门梁架仰视图
Framework of Ji Gate as seen from below

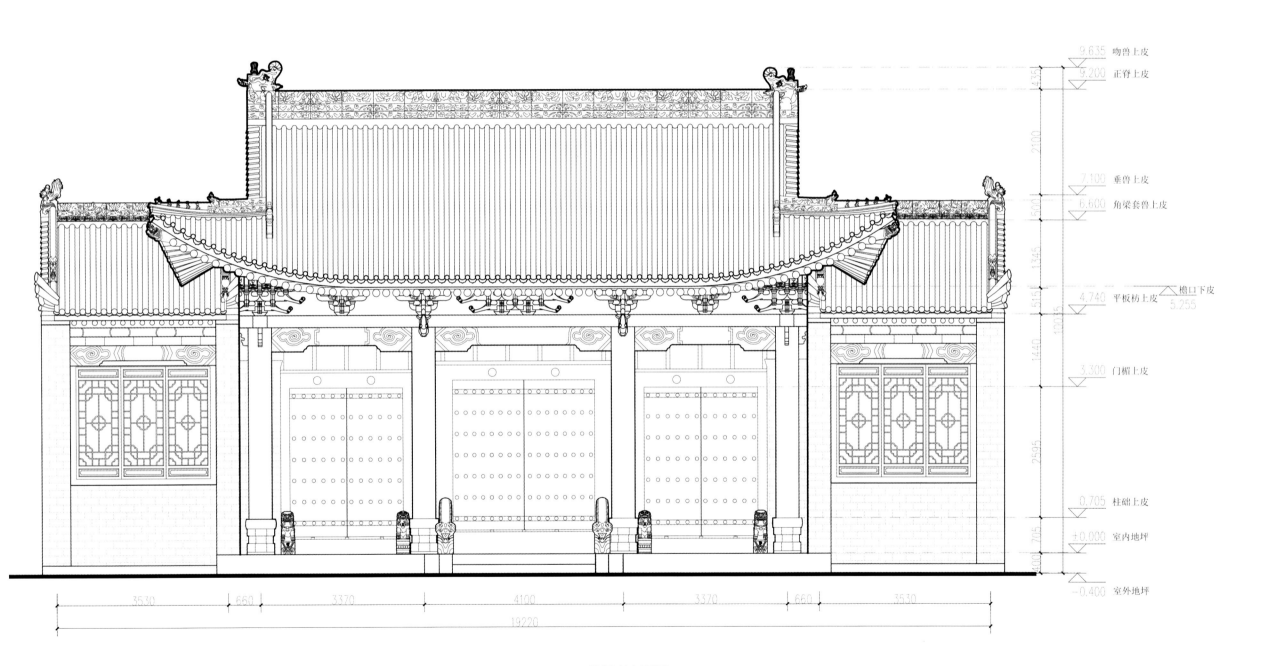

戟门南立面图
South elevation of Ji Gate

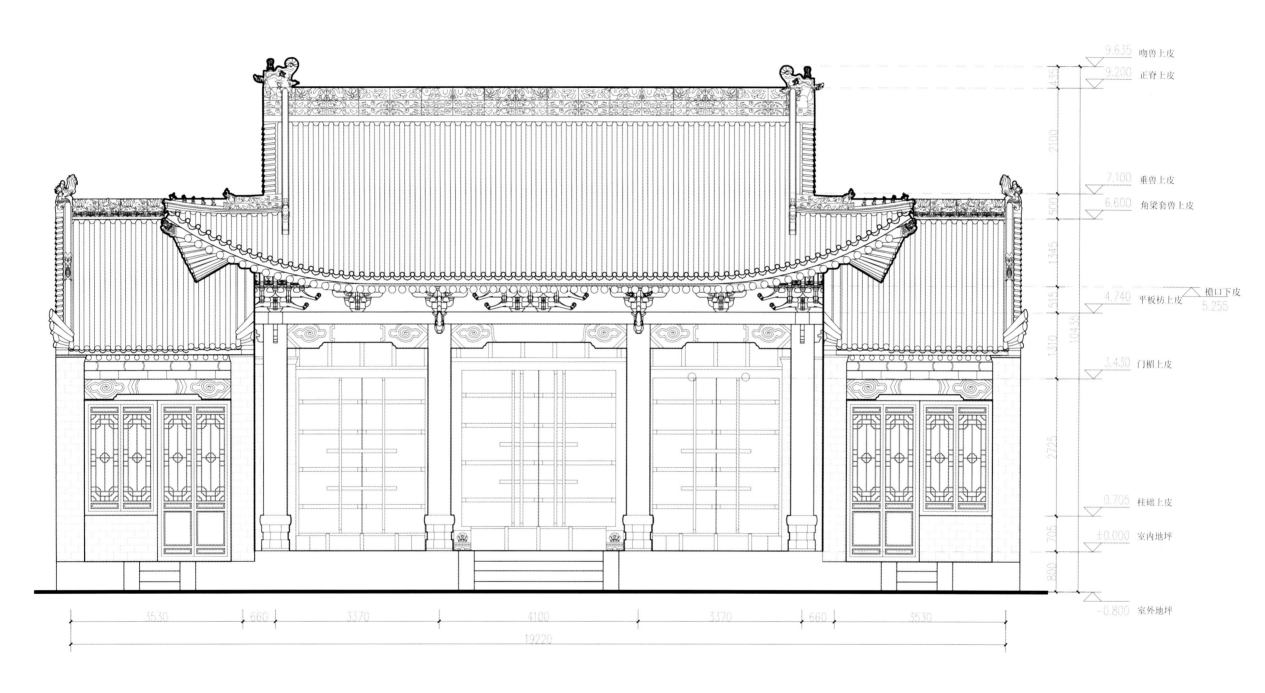

戟门北立面图
North elevation of Ji Gate

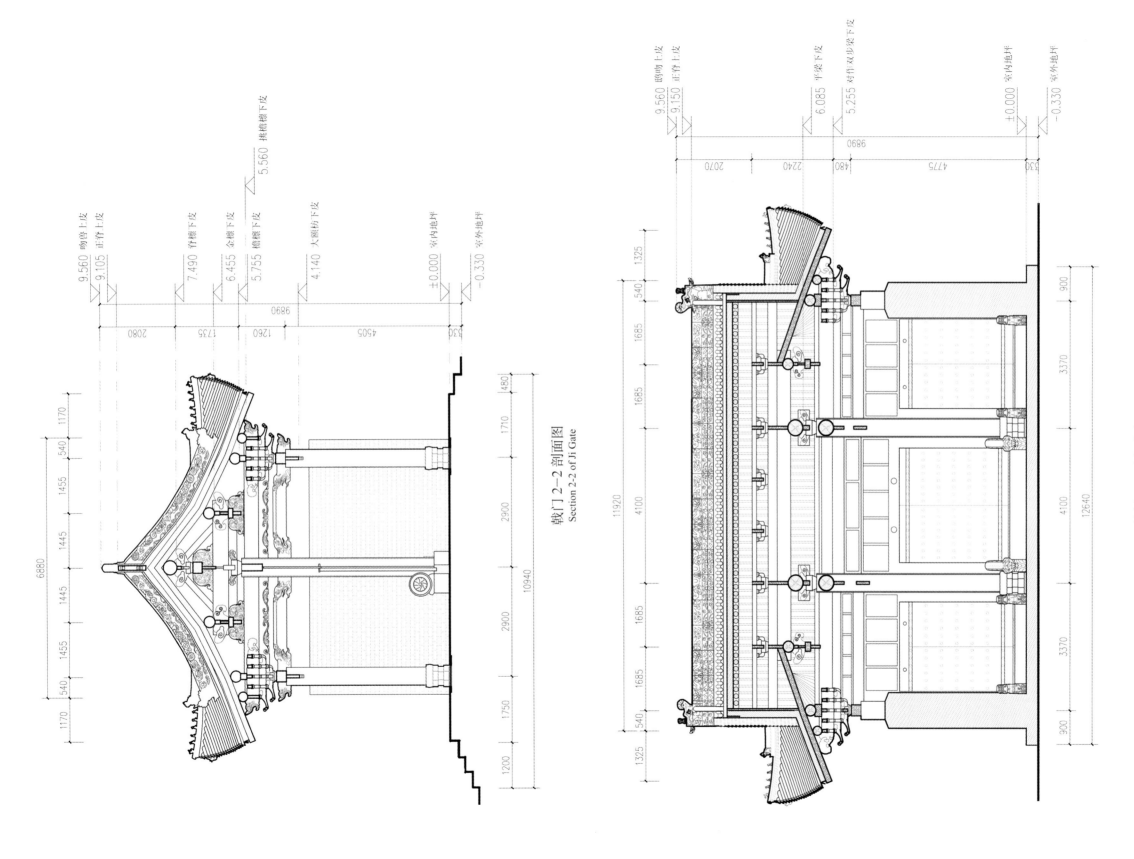

戟门 2-2 剖面图
Section 2-2 of Ji Gate

戟门 1-1 剖面图
Section 1-1 of Ji Gate

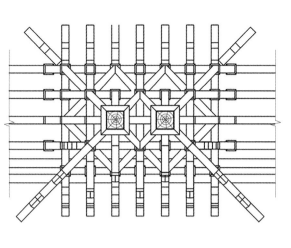

仰视图
View from below

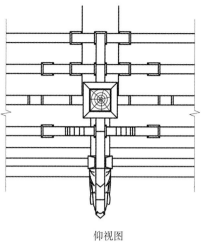

仰视图
View from below

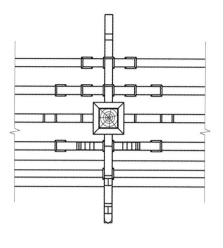

仰视图
View from below

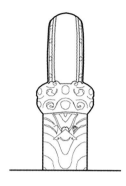

正视图
Frontal view

正视图（当心间）
Frontal view (central bay)

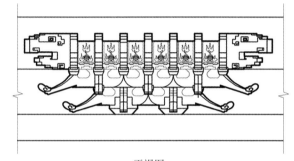

正视图
Frontal view

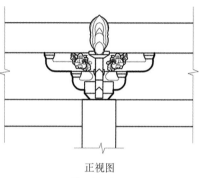

正视图
Frontal view

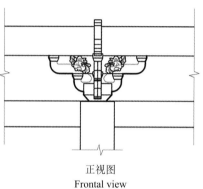

正视图
Frontal view

背视图
View from the back

正视图（次间）
Frontal view (side bay)

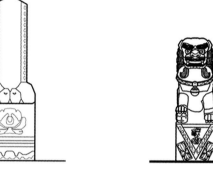

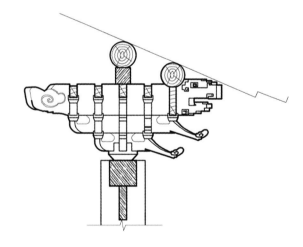

侧视图
Side view

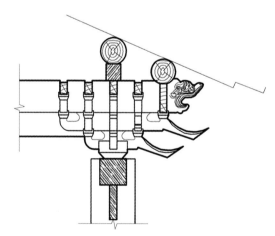

侧视图
Side view

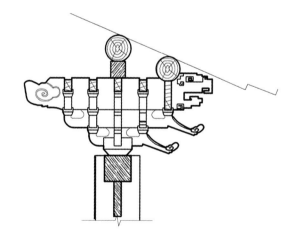

侧视图
Side view

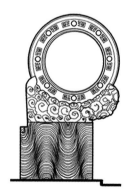

侧视图
Side view

侧视图
Side view

戟门当心间平身科大样图
Bracketing between central-bay columns of Ji Gate

戟门柱头科大样图
Bracket sets atop column of Ji Gate

戟门次间平身科大样图
Bracket set between side-bay columns of Ji Gate

戟门门枕石大样图
Cushion stone of Ji Gate

戟门石狮大样图
Stone lion of Ji Gate

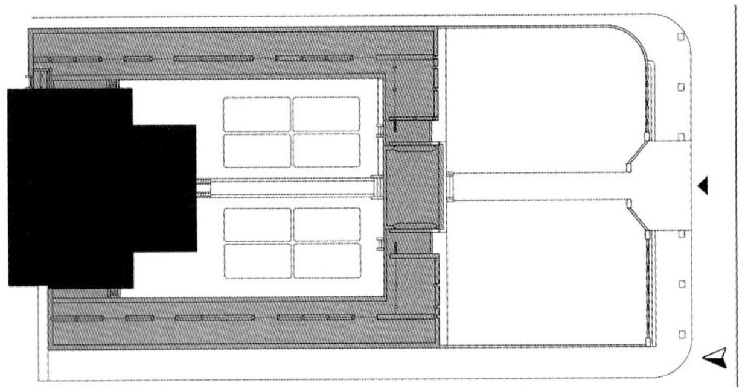

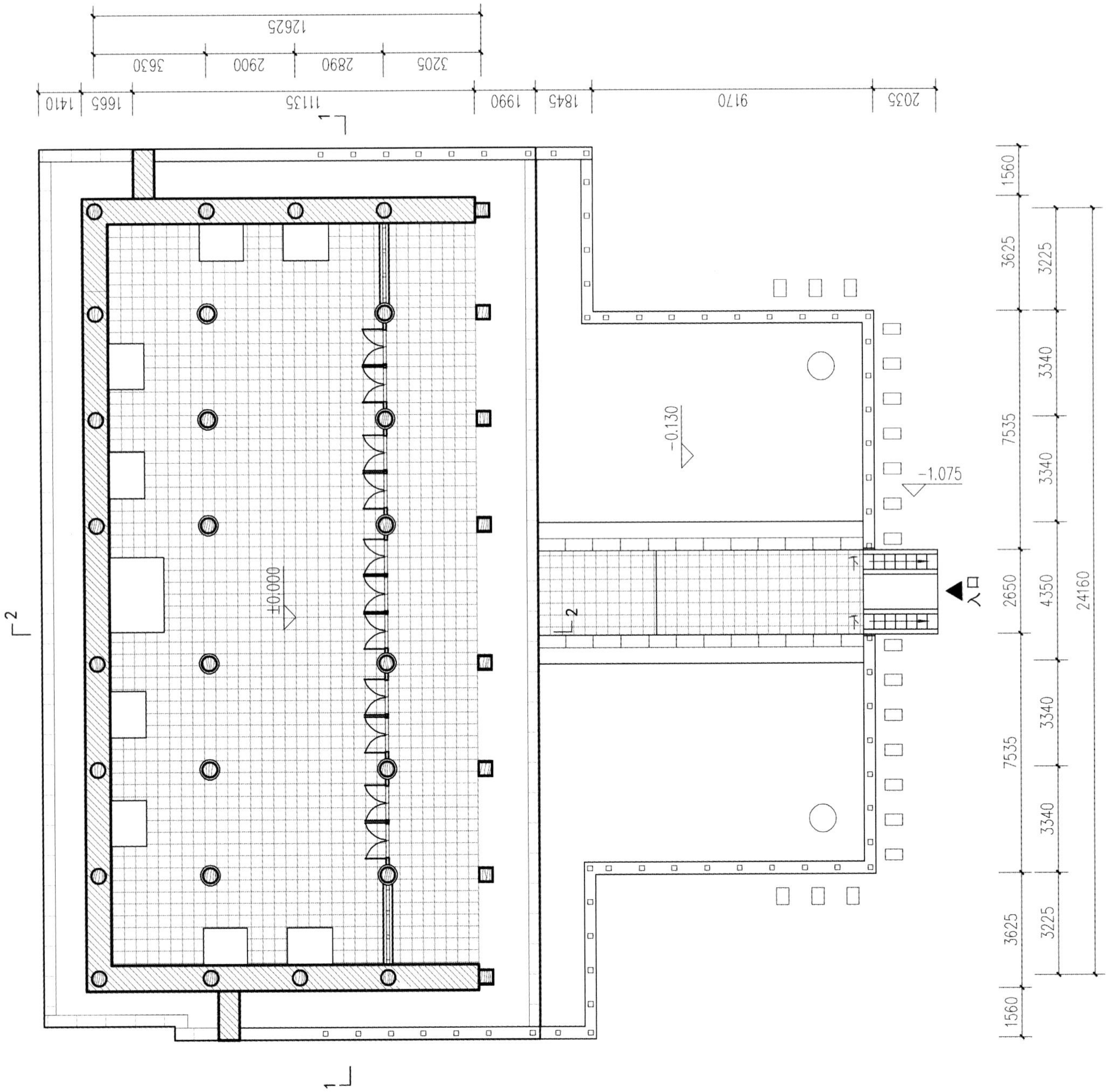

大成殿平面图
Plan of Dacheng Hall

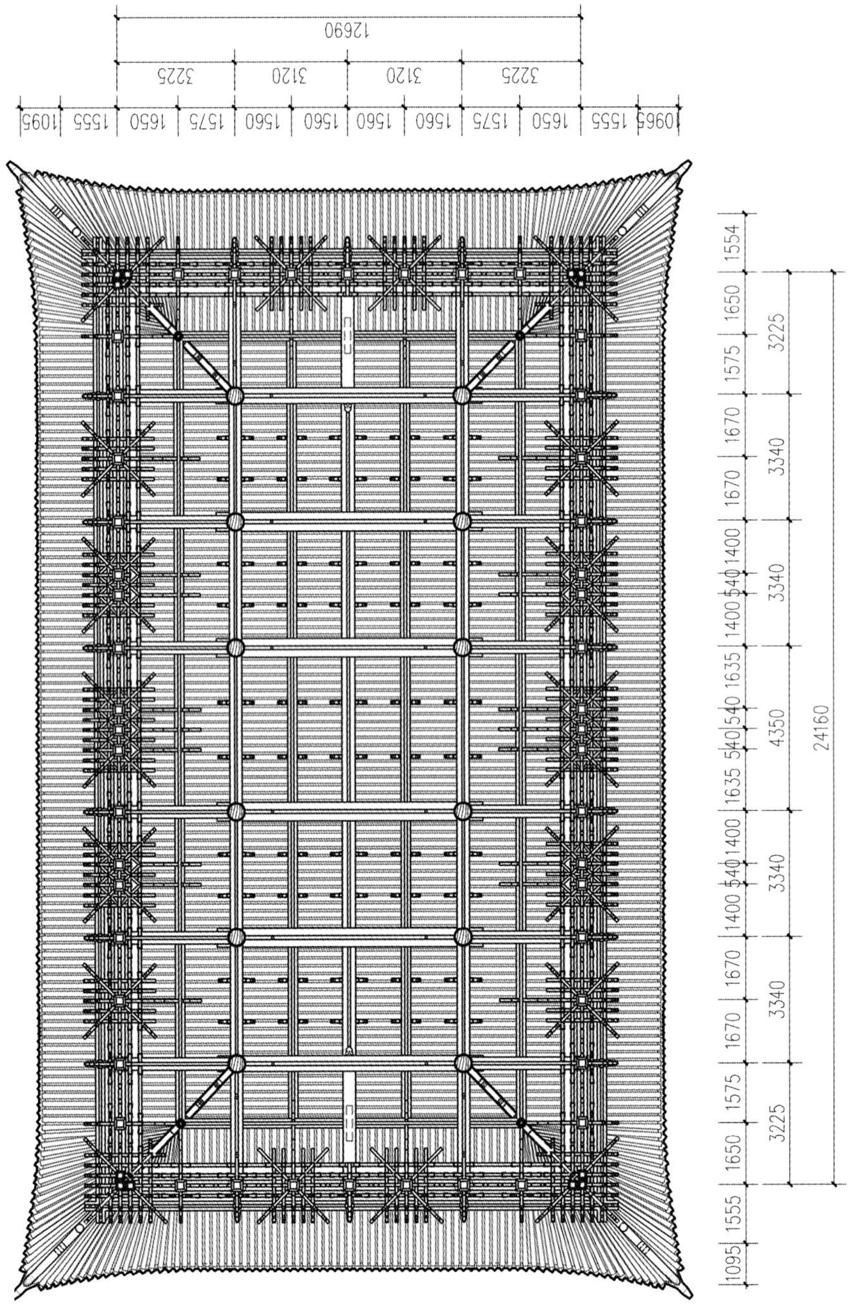

大成殿梁架仰视图
Plan of framework of Dacheng Hall as seen from below

156

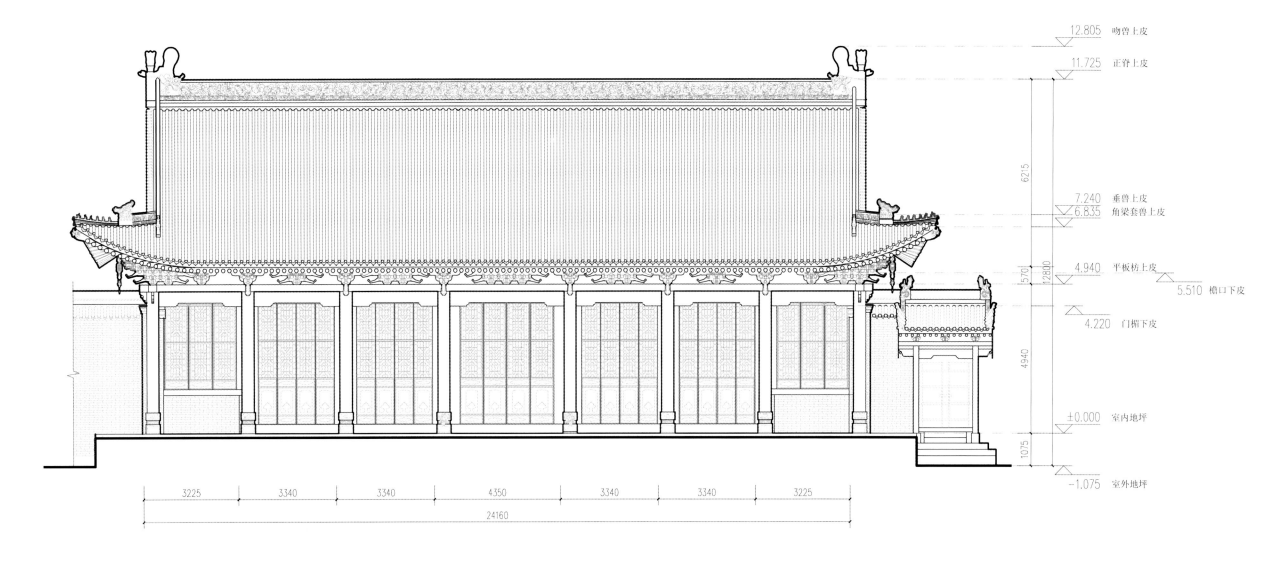

大成殿南立面图
South elevation of Dacheng Hall

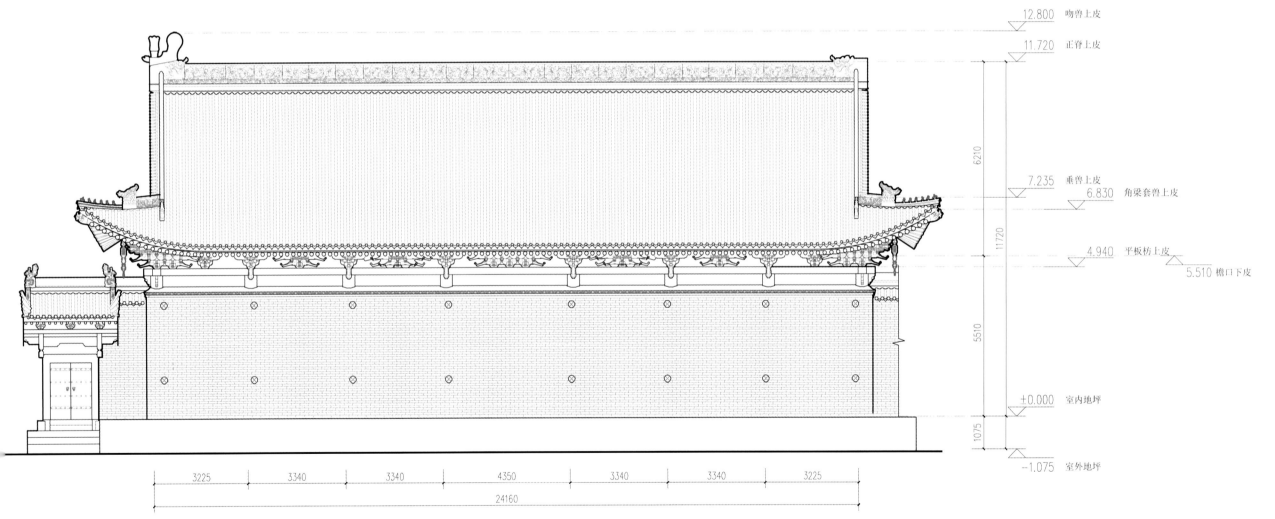

大成殿北立面图
North elevation of Dacheng Hall

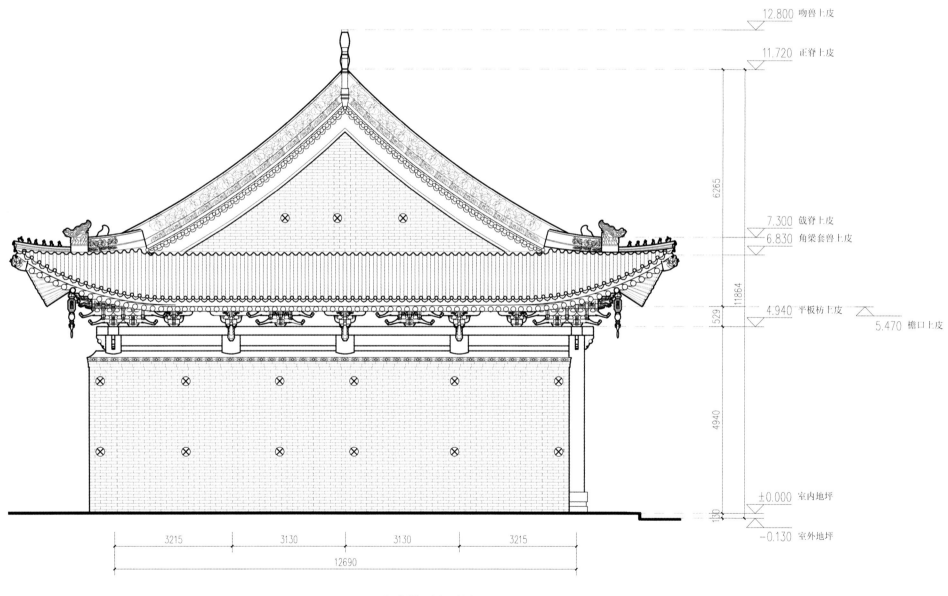

大成殿西立面图
West elevation of Dacheng Hall

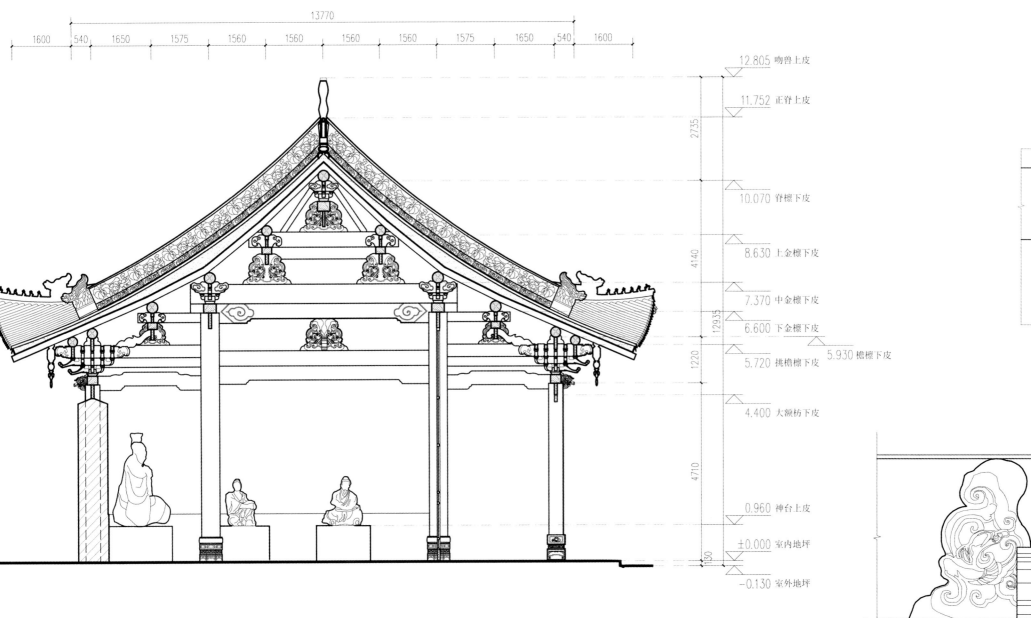

大成殿 2-2 剖面图
Section 2-2 Dacheng Hall

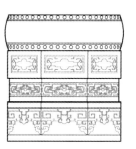

大成殿金柱柱础大样图
Interior column base of Dacheng Hall

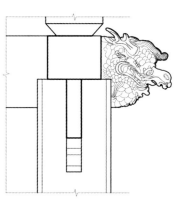

大成殿梁头大样图
Beam head of Dacheng Hall

大成殿驼峰大样图
Camel's-hump-shaped brace of Dacheng Hall

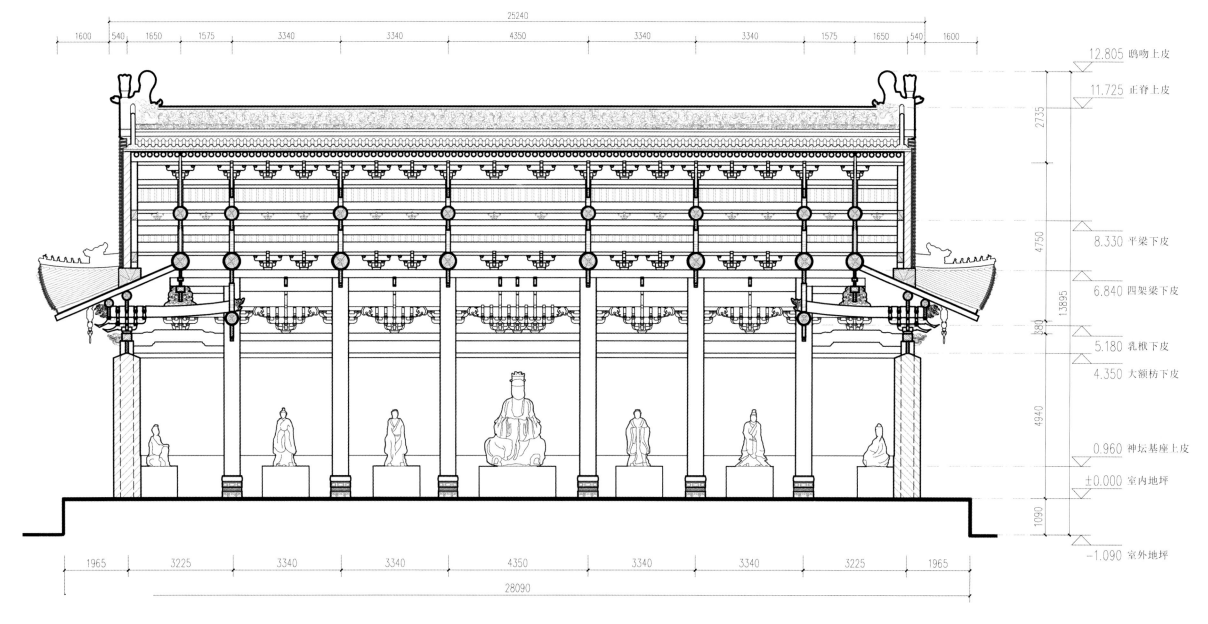

大成殿 1-1 剖面图
Section 1-1 of Dacheng Hall

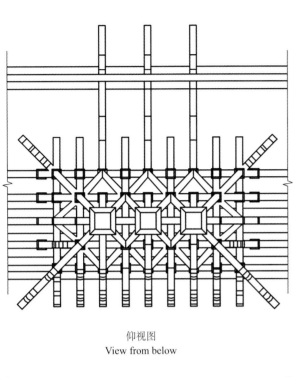
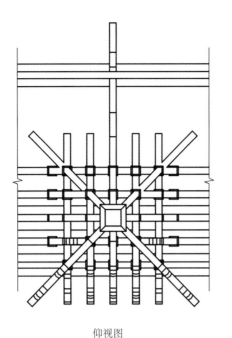
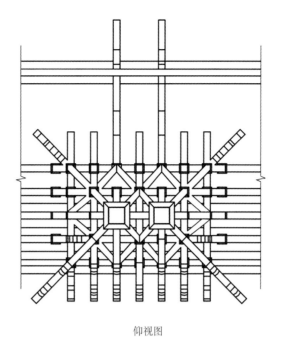
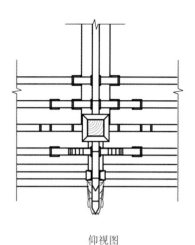

仰视图　　　　　　　　　　　仰视图　　　　　　　　　　　仰视图　　　　　　　　　　　仰视图
View from below　　　　　　View from below　　　　　　View from below　　　　　　View from below

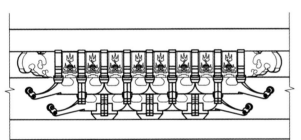
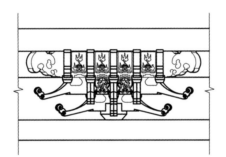
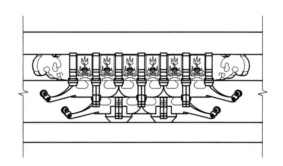
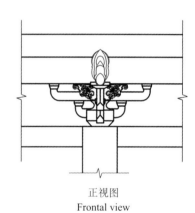

正视图　　　　　　　　　　　正视图　　　　　　　　　　　正视图　　　　　　　　　　　正视图
Frontal view　　　　　　　　Frontal view　　　　　　　　Frontal view　　　　　　　　Frontal view

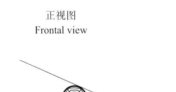
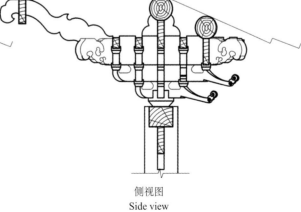

侧视图　　　　　　　　　　　侧视图　　　　　　　　　　　侧视图　　　　　　　　　　　侧视图
Side view　　　　　　　　　Side view　　　　　　　　　Side view　　　　　　　　　Side view

大成殿当心间平身科大样图　　大成殿梢间平身科大样图　　　大成殿次间平身科大样图　　　大成殿柱头科大样图
Bracketing between central-bay　Bracketing between second-to-last-　Bracketing between side-bay　　Bracketing set atop column
columns of Dacheng Hall　　　bay columns of Dacheng Hall　　columns of Dacheng Hall　　　of Dacheng Hall

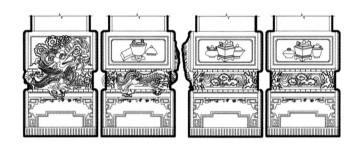

柱1柱础展开大样图（南－东/西－北）
Unfolded view of base of column 1 (south-east-west-north)

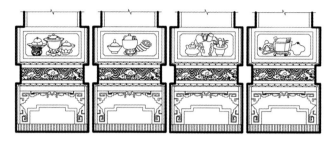

柱2柱础展开大样图（南－东－西－北）
Unfolded view of base of column 2 (south-east-west-north)

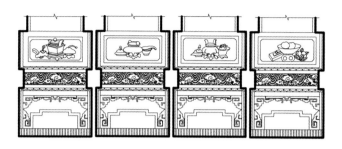

柱3柱础展开大样图（南－东－西－北）
Unfolded view of base of column 3 (south-east-west-north)

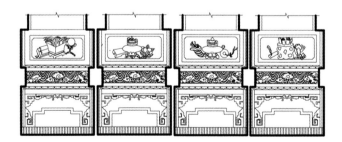

柱4柱础展开大样图（南－东－西－北）
Unfolded view of base of column 4 (south-east-west-north)

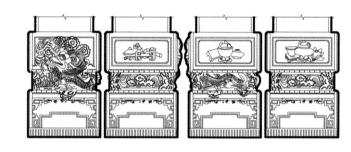

柱5柱础展开大样图（南－东－西－北）
Unfolded view of base of column 5 (south-east-west-north)

柱6柱础展开大样图（南－东－西－北）
Unfolded view of base of column 6 (south-east-west-north)

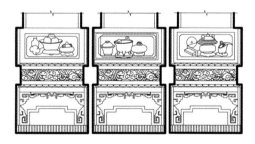

柱7柱础展开大样图（南－东／西－北）
Unfolded view of base of column 7 (south-east-west-north)

柱8柱础展开大样图（南－东／西－北）
Unfolded view of base of column 8 (south-east-west-north)

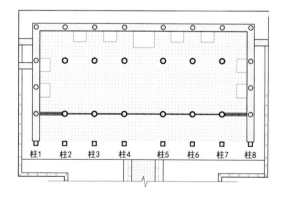

大成殿柱础索引图
Placement of column bases of Dacheng Hall

韩城文庙
Confucian Temple in Hancheng

Location: Dongxue Alley in the historical district of Hancheng, Shaanxi

Construction Date: Ming dynasty

Protection Level: National Priority Protected Site (fifth batch)

地　　址：陕西韩城老城区东学巷

年　　代：明代

保护级别：全国重点文物保护单位（第五批）

Introduction

The Confucian Temple of Hancheng is located in Dongxue Alley in the historical district of the town. It is the largest extant Confucian Temple and among the largest Ming architecture complexes in Shaanxi province to date.

Built in 1371 on the site of a former Yuan-dynasty temple, the grand layout we see today is the result of continuous repair and alteration conducted under the Ming emperors Tianshun (r. 1457-1464), Chenghua (r. 1465-1487) and Wanli (r. 1573-1620) and the Qing emperor Qianlong (r. 1735-1796). With its main entrance facing south, the complex consists of four courtyards aligned one after the other along the almost 200-m-long axis and covers an area of over 8,000 m sq. The Confucian Temple is situated opposite of the City God Temple of Hancheng and separated by an east-west oriented road.

There is a courtyard in front of the temple, enclosed in on the north by a timber-framed *pailou* standing on Dongxue Alley and in the south by a glazed-tile five-dragon screen wall and Lingxing Gate, the outer temple gate. Erected between 1573 and 1620 during the reign of Ming emperor Wanli, Lingxing Gate is a three-bay wooden archway (using six columns) with overhanging gable roof (*xuanshan*). The six columns rise above the roof. The area between Lingxing Gate and Ji Gate forms the first temple courtyard, containing a pond, a double-arched stone bridge, Gengyi (Clothes Changing) Pavilion, Zhizhai (Fasting) Pavilion, a stele pavilion, and a centuries-old cypress tree. Behind Ji Gate lies the second temple courtyard that is enclosed by east-and west-side buildings and in the north, by Dacheng Hall. A massive, large architrave (*da'e*) is installed under the front eaves of Dacheng Hall, and the rear central-bay interior columns have been moved off-axis. The number of front and rear eaves columns is not the same. The third temple courtyard starts behind Dacheng Hall and ends at Minglun (Elucidating Ethics) Hall, where the front and rear interior columns are also displaced. The fourth courtyard finally reaches Zunjing (Respecting Scriptures) Pavilion, which was built under the Ming emperor Hongzhi (r. 1488-1505).

概述

韩城文庙位于韩城老城区东学巷，是陕西地区现存规模最大的文庙建筑群，也是陕西地区保存基本完好的一处大型明代建筑群。

韩城文庙是在元代建筑旧址上于明洪武四年（1371年）重建而成的，后经明天顺、成化、万历以及清乾隆年间历次整修、重建，形成宏大的规模。整个建筑群坐北朝南，前后四进院落，南北中轴线长度近200米，占地总面积8000余平方米。文庙建筑群以北隔一东西向道路与韩城城隍庙建筑群相对。

庙前东学巷跨街立有木牌坊，与街南的五龙琉璃照壁和文庙的第一道门（棂星门）之间连缀以围墙，形成一处文庙门前的闭合院落。棂星门建于明万历年间（1573—1620年），为六柱三间悬山顶木牌坊，六柱均为通天柱。自棂星门至戟门为第一进院落，棂星门北有泮池、双孔石桥、更衣亭、致斋亭与碑亭，院内树龄几百年的古柏郁郁苍苍。戟门以北至大成殿及东西庑为第二进院落。大成殿前檐用大额，明间的后檐金柱有移柱做法。大成殿以北至明伦堂为第三进院落，明伦堂明间的前、后檐金柱均为移柱做法。明伦堂以北至尊经阁为最后一进院落，尊经阁始建于明弘治年间（1488—1505年）。

Fig.1 Lingxing Gate of Confucian Temple of Hancheng
Fig.2 Intercolumnar bracketing of Lingxing Gate, Confucian Temple of Hancheng
Fig.3 Ji Gate of Confucian Temple of Hancheng
Fig.4 Dacheng Hall of Confucian Temple of Hancheng

图1 韩城文庙棂星门

图3 韩城文庙戟门

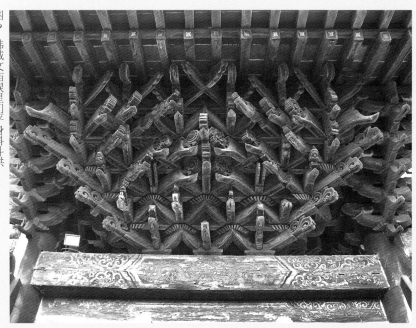

图2 韩城文庙棂星门平身科斗栱

图4 韩城文庙大成殿

Survey and Mapping Information

Responsible Department: Department of Architecture (Class of 2004), School of Architecture, Xi'an University of Architecture and Technology

Team Members: ZHU Fengchao, WU Guanyu, ZHANG Hehan, MEI Chuan, GE Xiaoman, JIN Binbin, WANG Hailiang, WANG Yu, WANG Zheng, ZHANG Minhong, GUAN Yue, LIU Linxi, LI Kun, LI Xuejiao, XUE Zhe, FAN Xiaoye, ZHAO Xiaqing, HANG Yu, HU Xiaojie, CAI Weijie, YAN Jing, ZHANG Lei, WANG Chao, ZHANG Guoli, DENG Wenqing, LIU Shoudong, YANG Liuqing, ZHAO Meng, LI Peng, GAO Xiang, WANG Ruixin

Supervisors: LIN Yuan, Kong Liming

Editors of Drawings: WANG Ruyue, WEN Juan

Survey Time: October 2007

韩城文庙测绘的人员名单

测　绘：西安建筑科技大学建筑学院建筑学2004级

朱凤超　吴冠宇　张合涵　梅　川　葛霄蔓　靳斌斌　王海亮　王　宇
王　正　张敏红　管　玥　刘临西　李　焜　李雪姣　薛　喆　范小烨
赵夏青　杭　宇　胡小洁　蔡伟洁　闫　晶　张　雷　王　超　张国莉
邓文青　刘守东　杨柳青　赵　萌　栗　鹏　高　翔　王瑞鑫

指导教师：林　源　孔黎明

图纸整理：王茹悦　文　娟

测绘时间：2007年10月

参考文献 References

[一] 赵立瀛主编. 陕西古建筑 [M]. 西安：陕西人民出版社，1992.

[二] 国家文物局主编. 中国文物地图集 [M]. 陕西分册. 西安：西安地图出版社，1998.

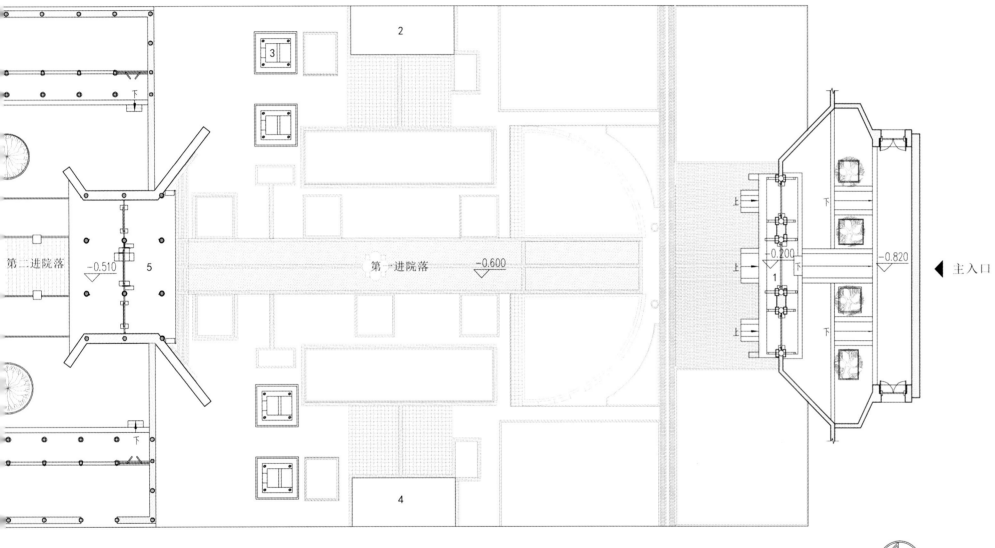

韩城文庙总平面图
Site plan of Confucian Temple of Hancheng

1 棂星门 Lingxing Gate
2 更衣亭 Gengyi Pavilion
3 碑亭 Stele pavilion
4 致斋所 Zhizhai Pavilion
5 戟门 Ji Gate
6 大成殿 Dacheng Hall
7 明伦堂 Minglun Hall
8 东厢房 Eastern wing-room
9 西厢房 Western wing-room
10 尊经阁 Zunjing Pavilion

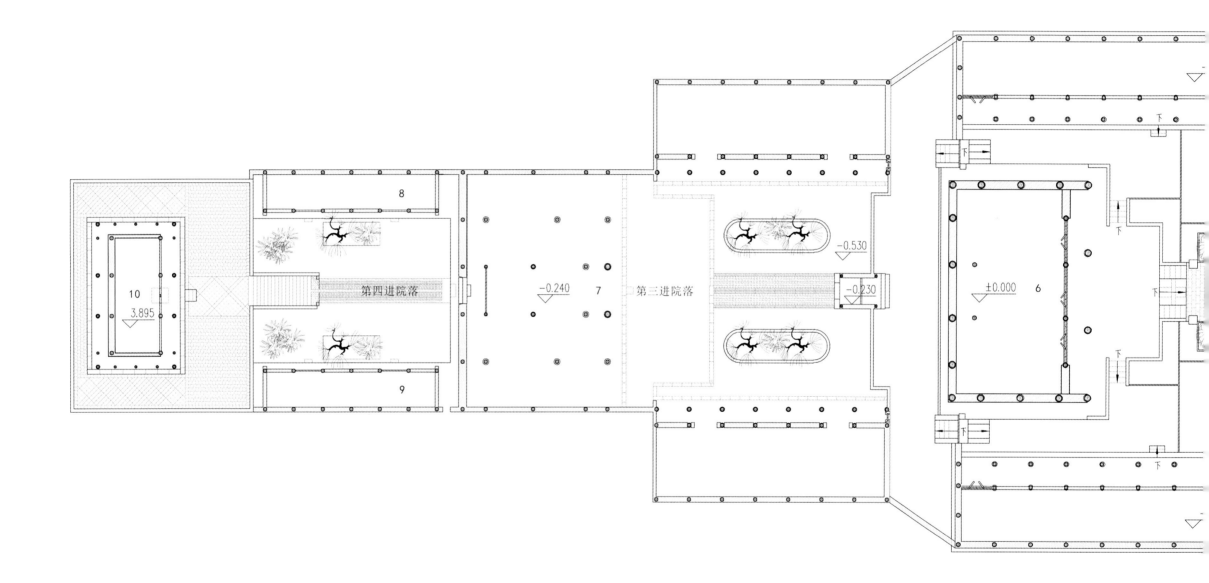

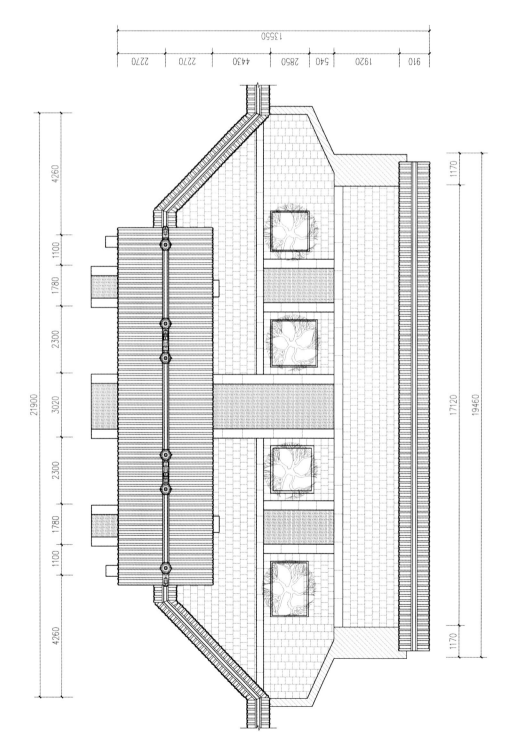

棂星门柱网平面图
Plan of column grid of Lingxing Gate

棂星门屋顶平面图
Plan of roof of Lingxing Gate

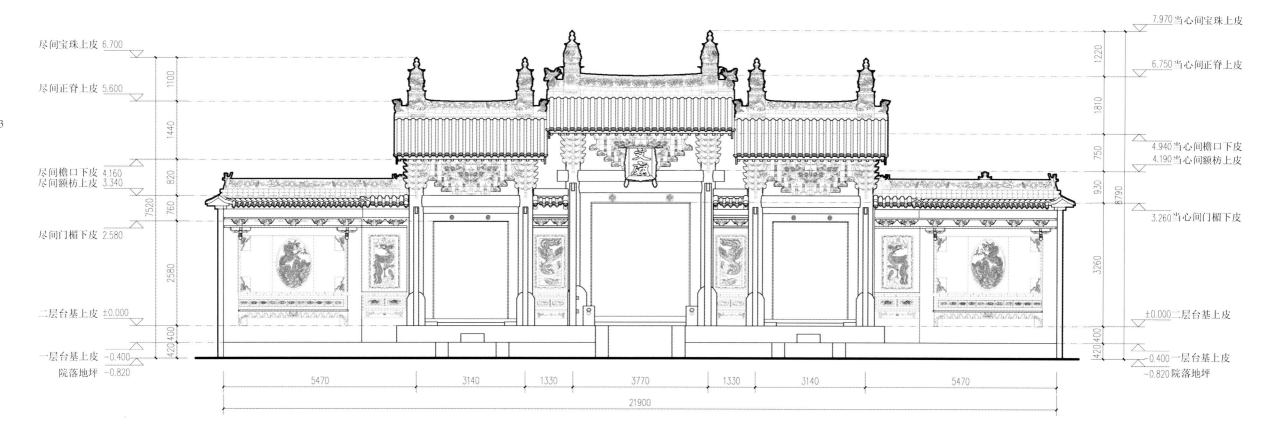

棂星门南立面图
South elevation of Lingxing Gate

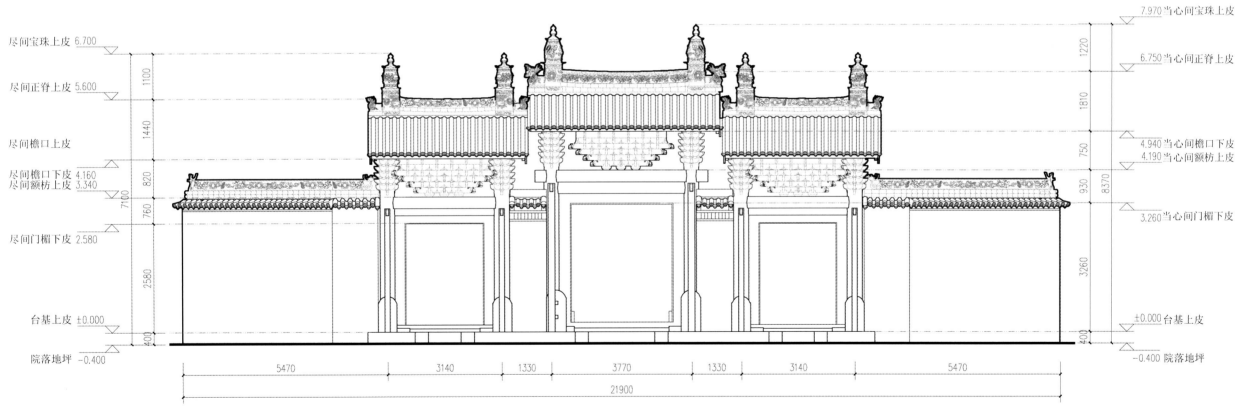

棂星门北立面图
North elevation of Lingxing Gate

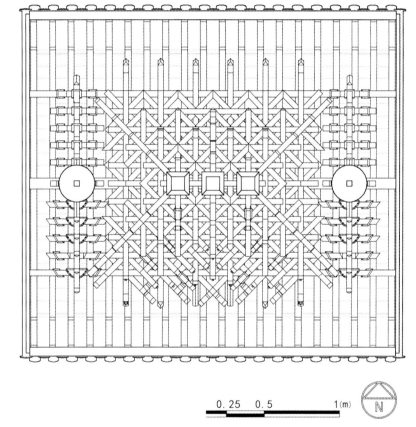

棂星门次间梁架仰视图
Plan of side-bay framework of Lingxing Gate as seen from below

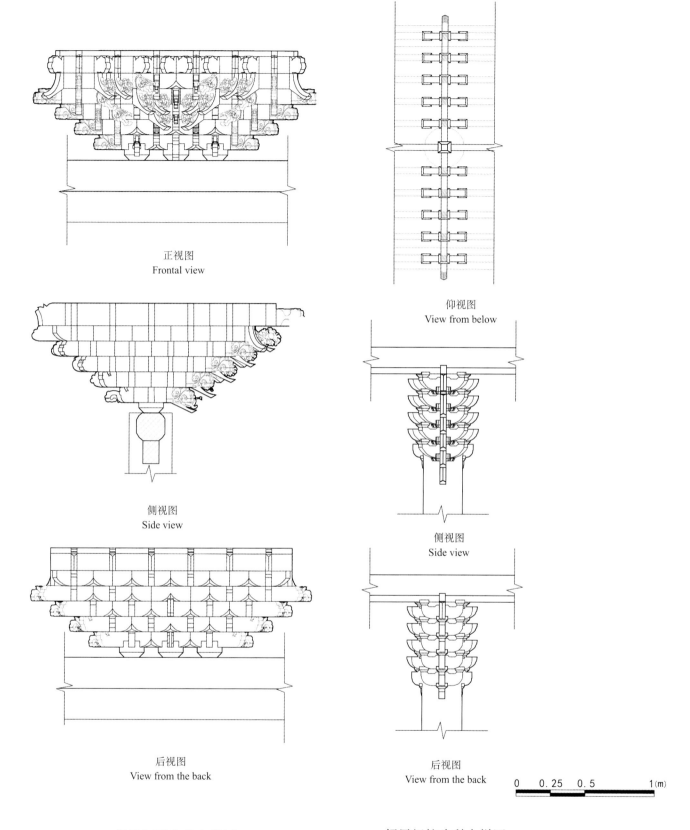

正视图
Frontal view

仰视图
View from below

侧视图
Side view

侧视图
Side view

后视图
View from the back

后视图
View from the back

棂星门平身科大样图
Bracketing between column of Lingxing Gate

棂星门柱头科大样图
Bracketing atop column of Lingxing Gate

棂星门夹间大样图
Bay between two doorways of Lingxing Gate

棂星门八字墙东侧龙纹砖雕大样图
Carved stone dragon of eastern wing wall of Lingxing Gate

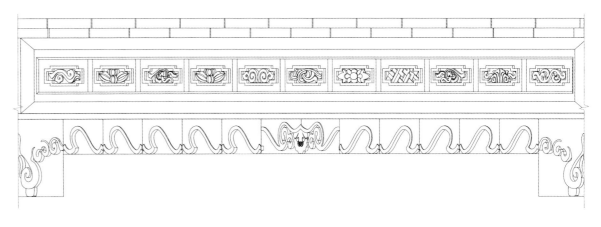

棂星门八字墙砖雕大样图
Stone carving of wing wall of Lingxing Gate

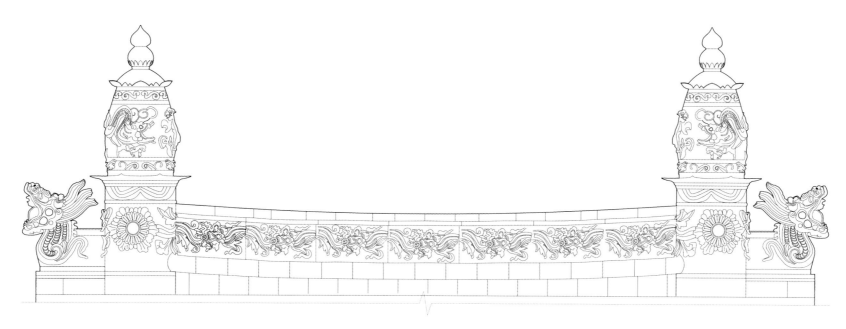

棂星门当心间屋脊北立面
North elevation of central-bay roof ridge of Lingxing Gate

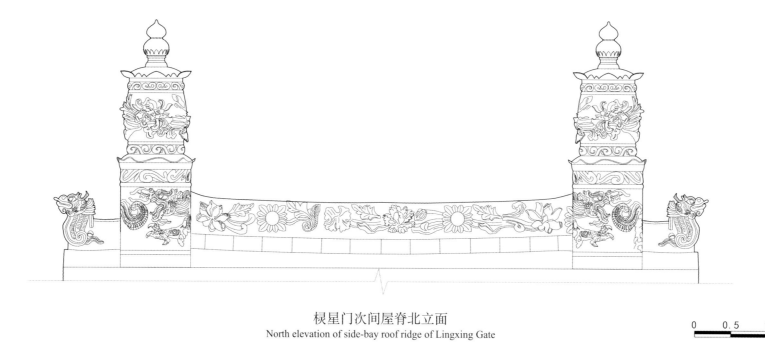

棂星门次间屋脊北立面
North elevation of side-bay roof ridge of Lingxing Gate

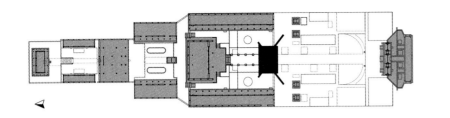

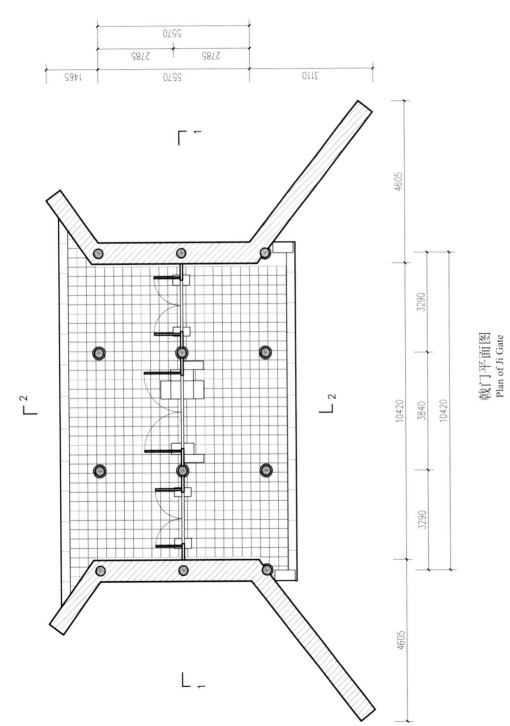

戟门平面图
Plan of Ji Gate

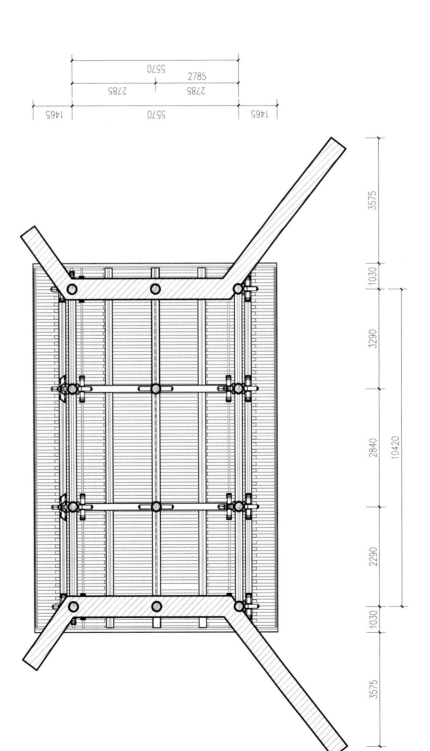

戟门梁架仰视图
Plan of framework Ji Gate as seen from below

戟门南立面图
South elevation of Ji Gate

戟门北立面图
North elevation of Ji Gate

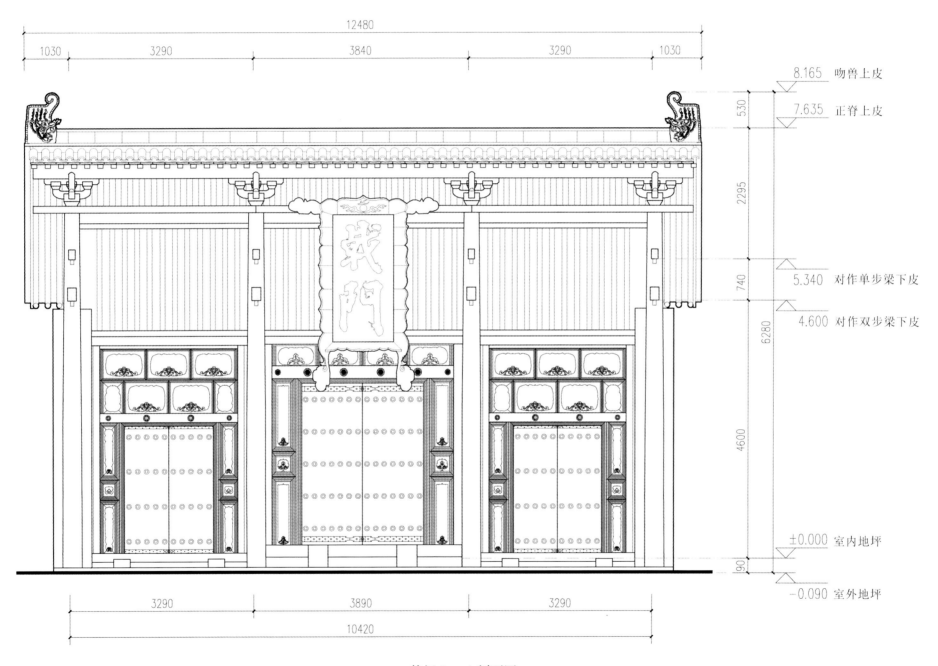

戟门 1－1 剖面图
Section 1-1 of Ji Gate

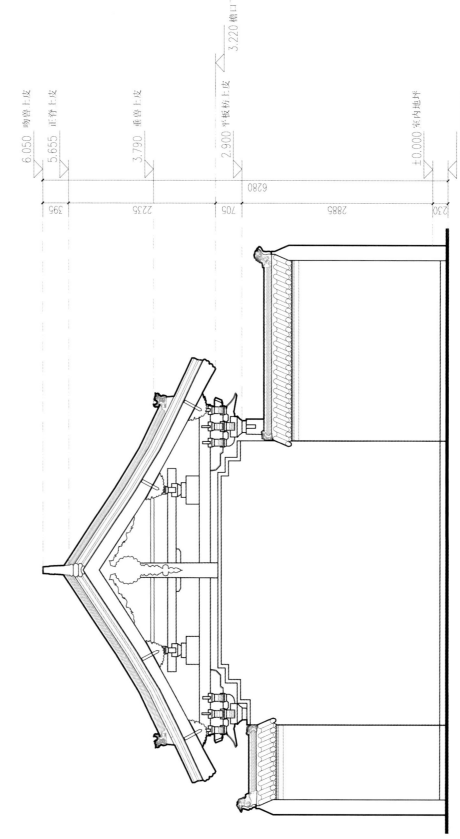

戟门 2—2 剖面图
Section 2-2 of Ji Gate

戟门西立面图
West elevation of Ji Gate

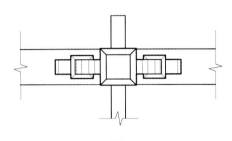

仰视图
View from below

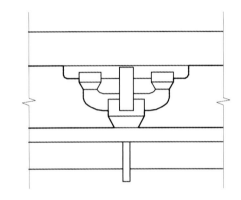

正视图
Frontal view

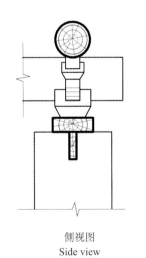

侧视图
Side view

戟门平身科大样图
Intercolumnar bracket set of Ji Gate

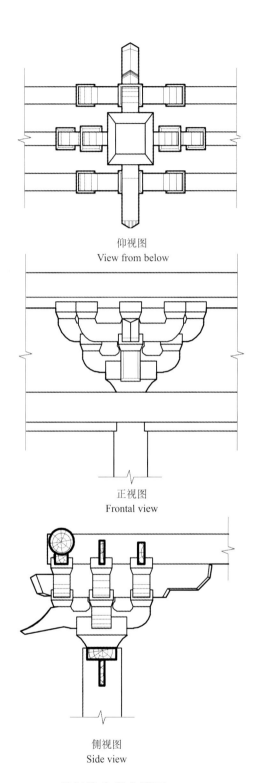

仰视图
View from below

正视图
Frontal view

侧视图
Side view

戟门柱头科大样图
Column-top bracket set of Ji Gate

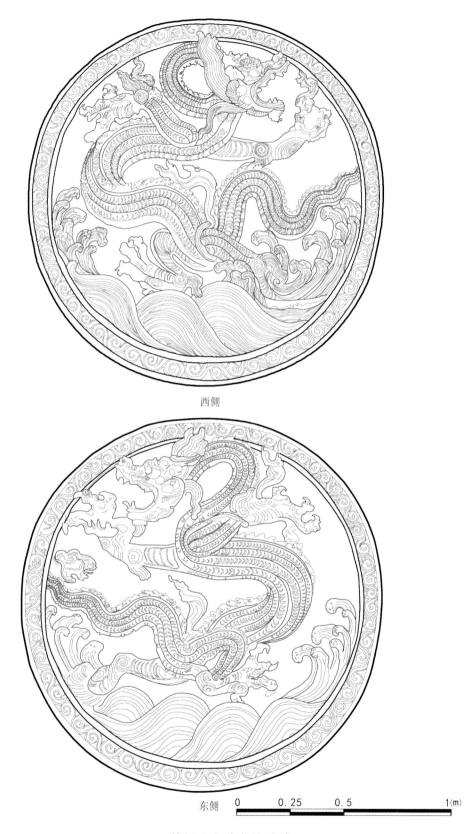

西侧

东侧

戟门八字墙龙纹砖雕
Carved stone dragon of wing wall of Ji Gate

戟门北八字墙吻兽
Ridge ornament of northern wing wall of Ji Gate

戟门南八字墙外侧吻兽
Ridge ornament positioned at the outer end of the southern wing wall of Ji Gate

戟门南八字墙里侧吻兽
Ridge ornament positioned at the inner end of the southern wing wall of Ji Gate

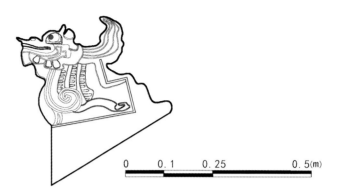
戟门垂兽
Diagonal ridge ornament of Ji Gate

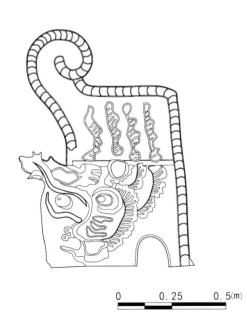
戟门正脊吻兽
Principal ridge ornament of Ji Gate

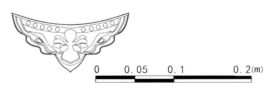
戟门瓦当
Eave-end tile of Ji Gate

戟门滴水
Drip tile of Ji Gate

透视图
Perspective view

侧视图
Side view

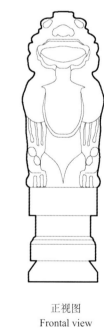
正视图
Frontal view

戟门石狮子
Stone lion of Ji Gate

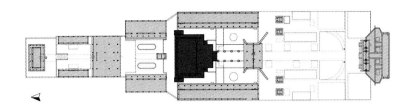
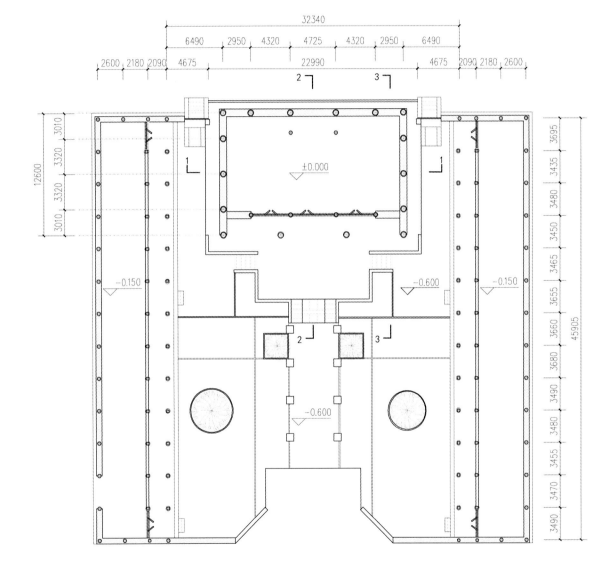
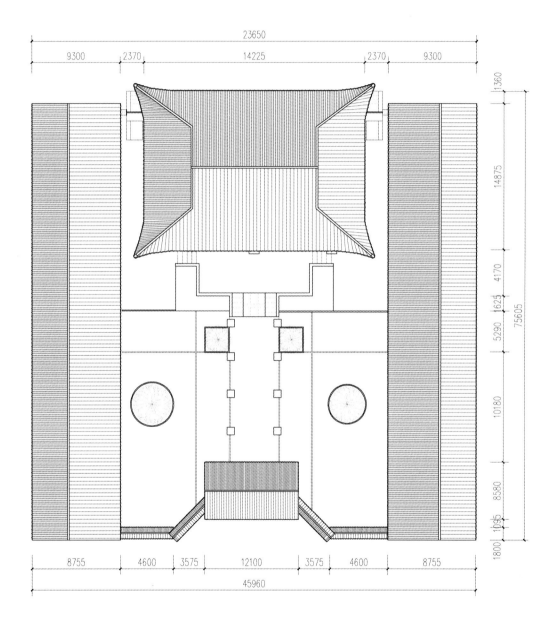

大成殿院落平面图
Plan of courtyard with Dacheng Hall

大成殿院落屋顶平面图
Plan of roofs of courtyard with Dacheng Hall

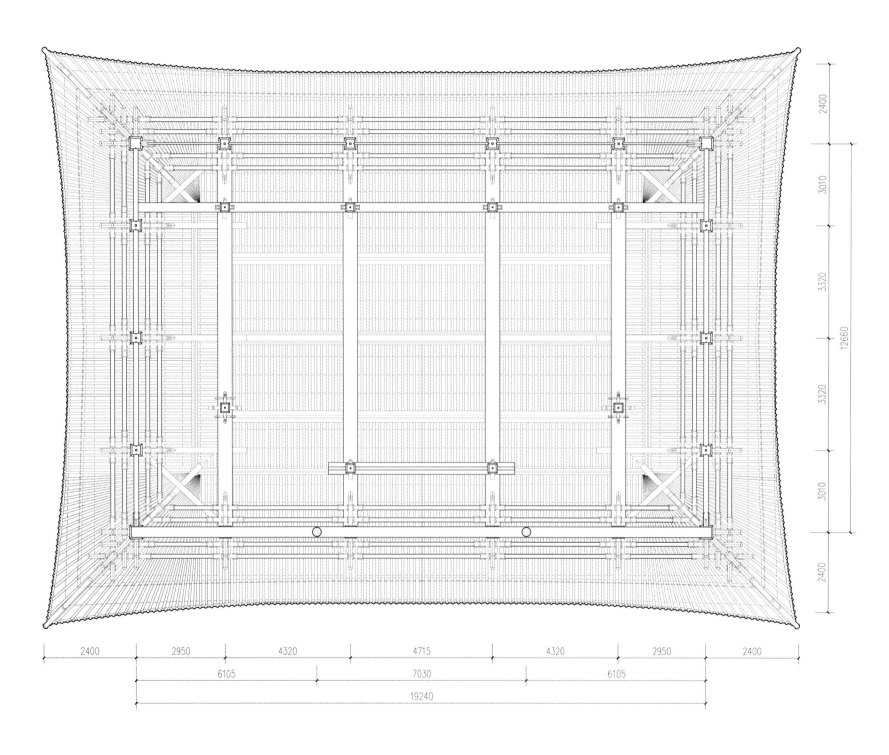

大成殿梁架仰视图
Plan of framework of Dacheng Hall as seen from below

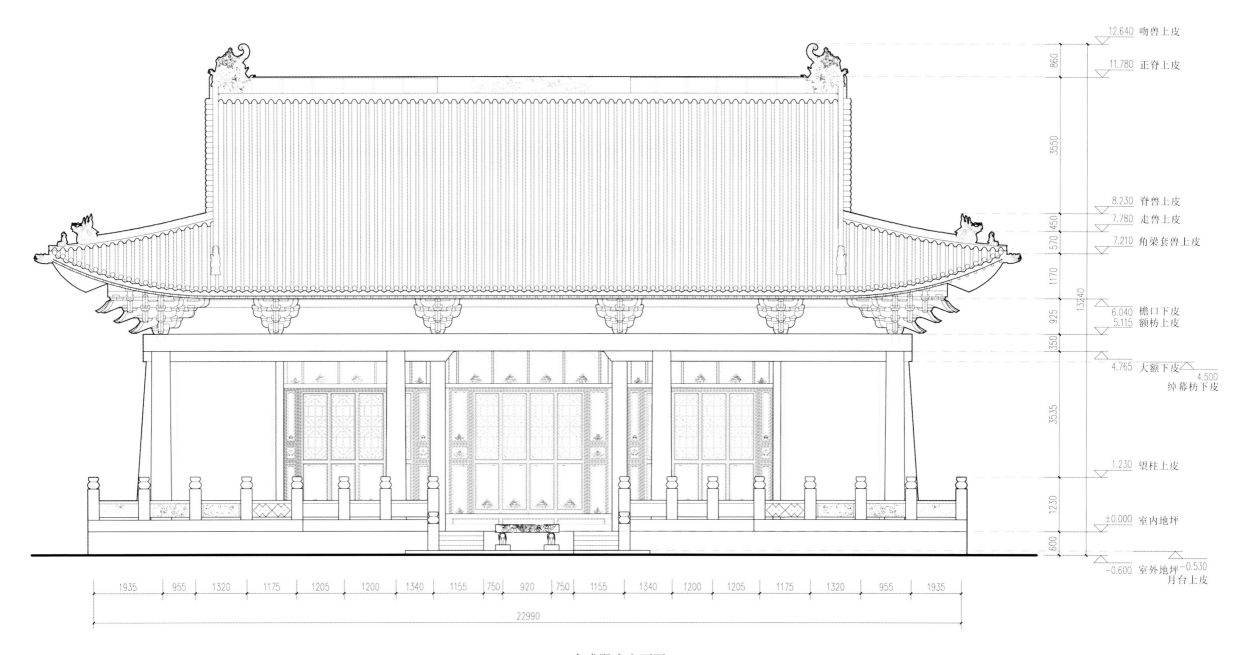

大成殿南立面图
South elevation of Dacheng Hall

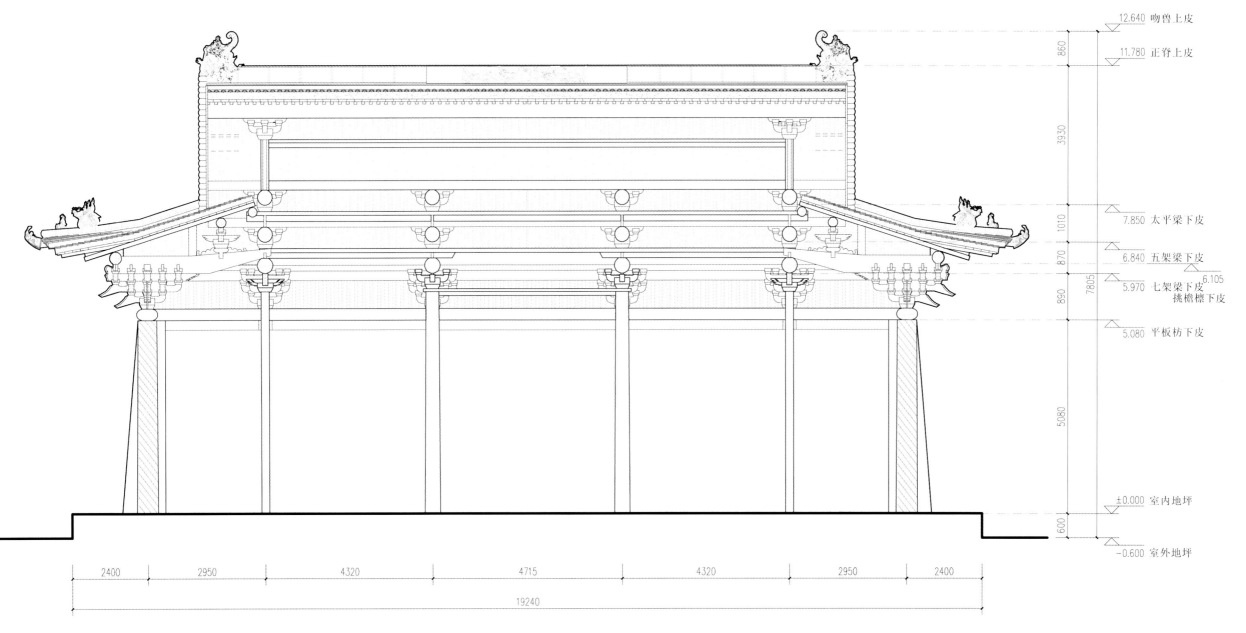

大成殿 1-1 剖面图
Section 1-1 of Dacheng Hall

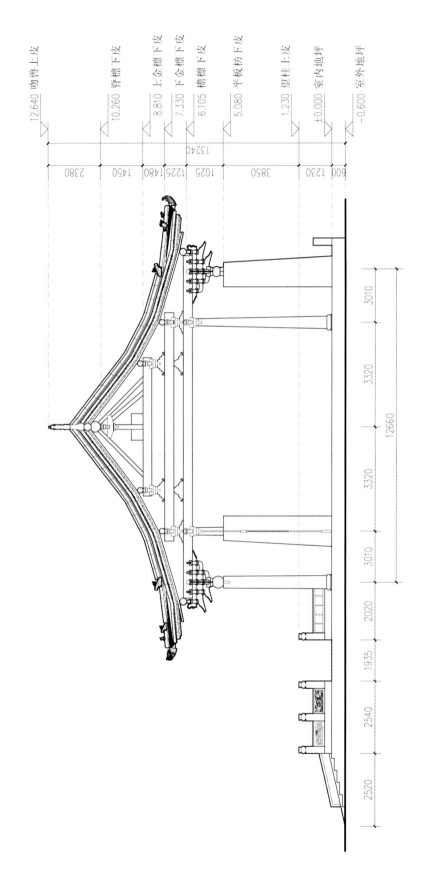

大成殿 2-2 剖面图
Section 2-2 of Dacheng Hall

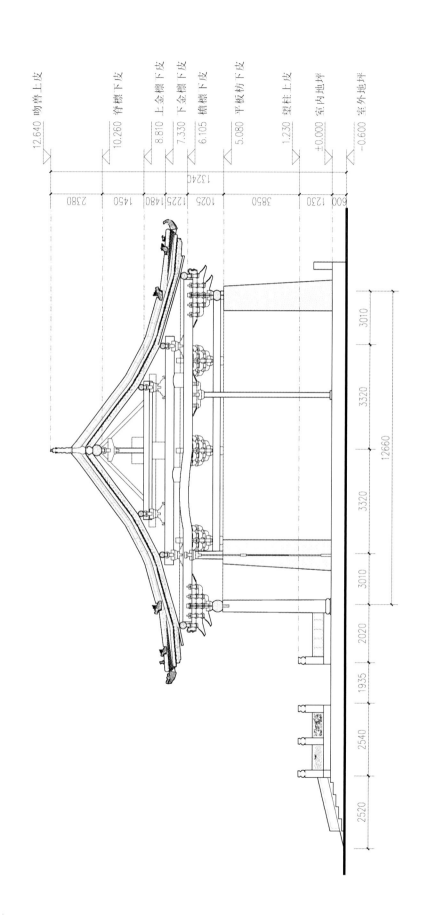

大成殿 3-3 剖面图
Section 3-3 of Dacheng Hall

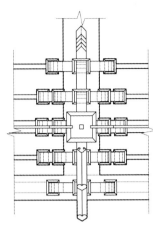

仰视图
View from below

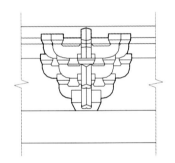

正视图
Frontal view

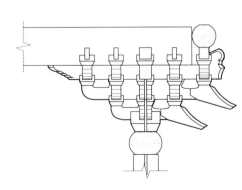

侧视图
Side view

大成殿平身科大样图
Intercolumnar bracket set of Dacheng Hall

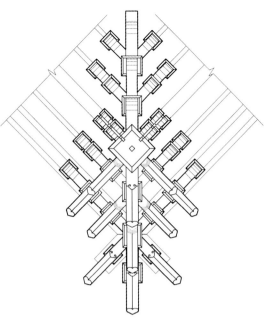

仰视图
View from below

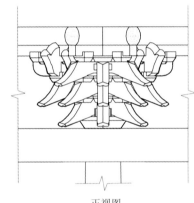

正视图
Frontal view

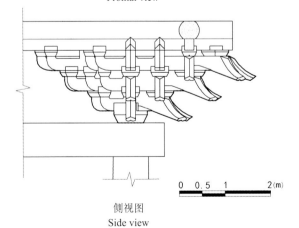

侧视图
Side view

大成殿角科大样图
Corner bracket set of Dacheng Hall

大成殿室内牌匾大样图
Plaque installed inside Dacheng Hall

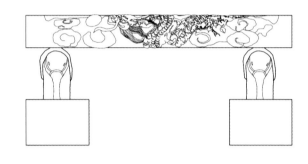

南立面图
South elevation

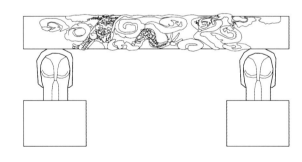

北立面图
North elevation

大成殿陛面雕龙石柱图
Stone columns with dragon carving, podium of Dacheng Hall

大成殿陛面龙纹浮雕图
Dragon-shaped relief, podium of Dacheng Hall

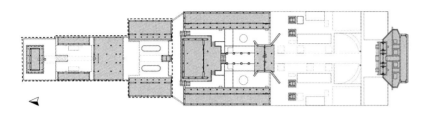
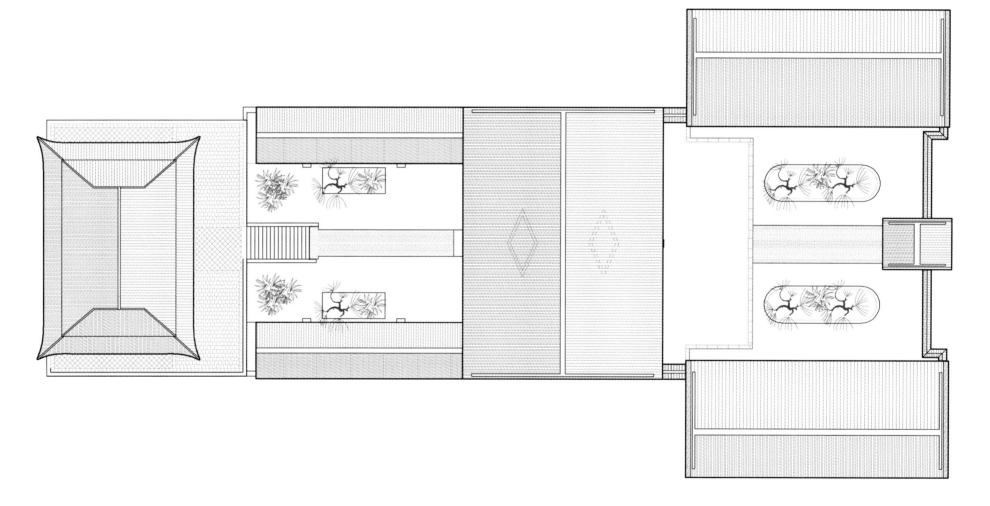

第三、第四进院落屋顶平面图
Plan of roofs of the third and fourth courtyards

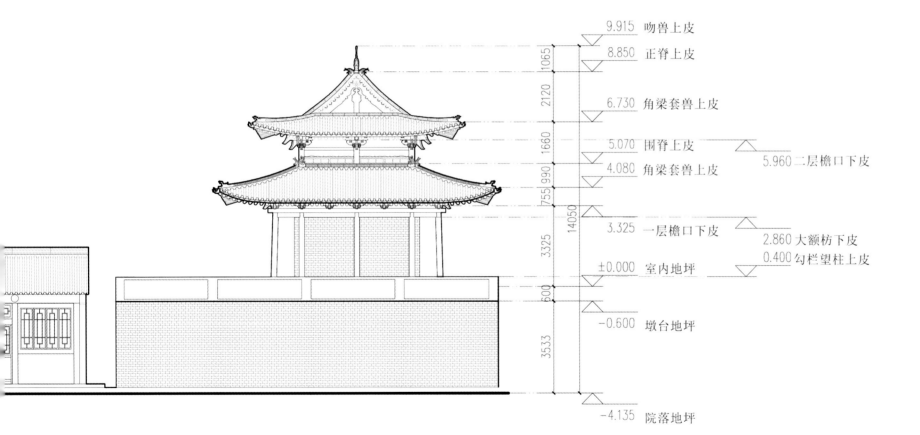

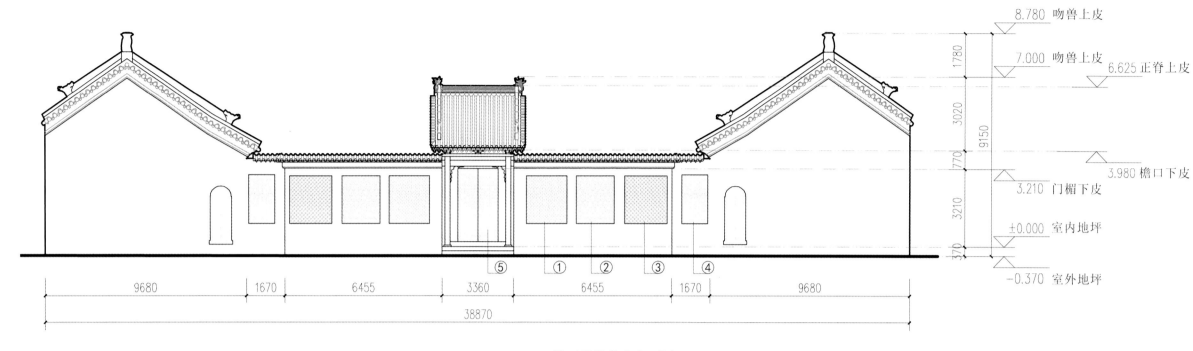

第三进院落北立面图
North elevation of third courtyard

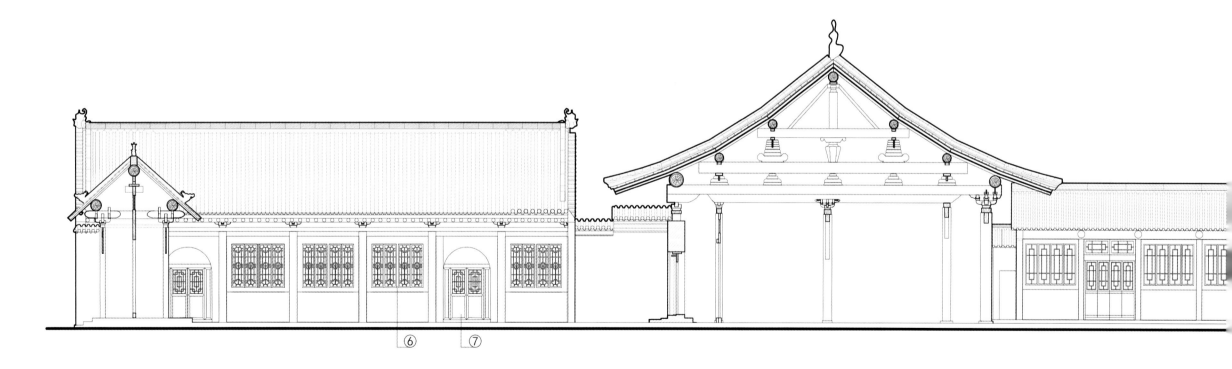

第三、第四进院落纵剖面图
Longitudinal section of the third and fourth courtyards

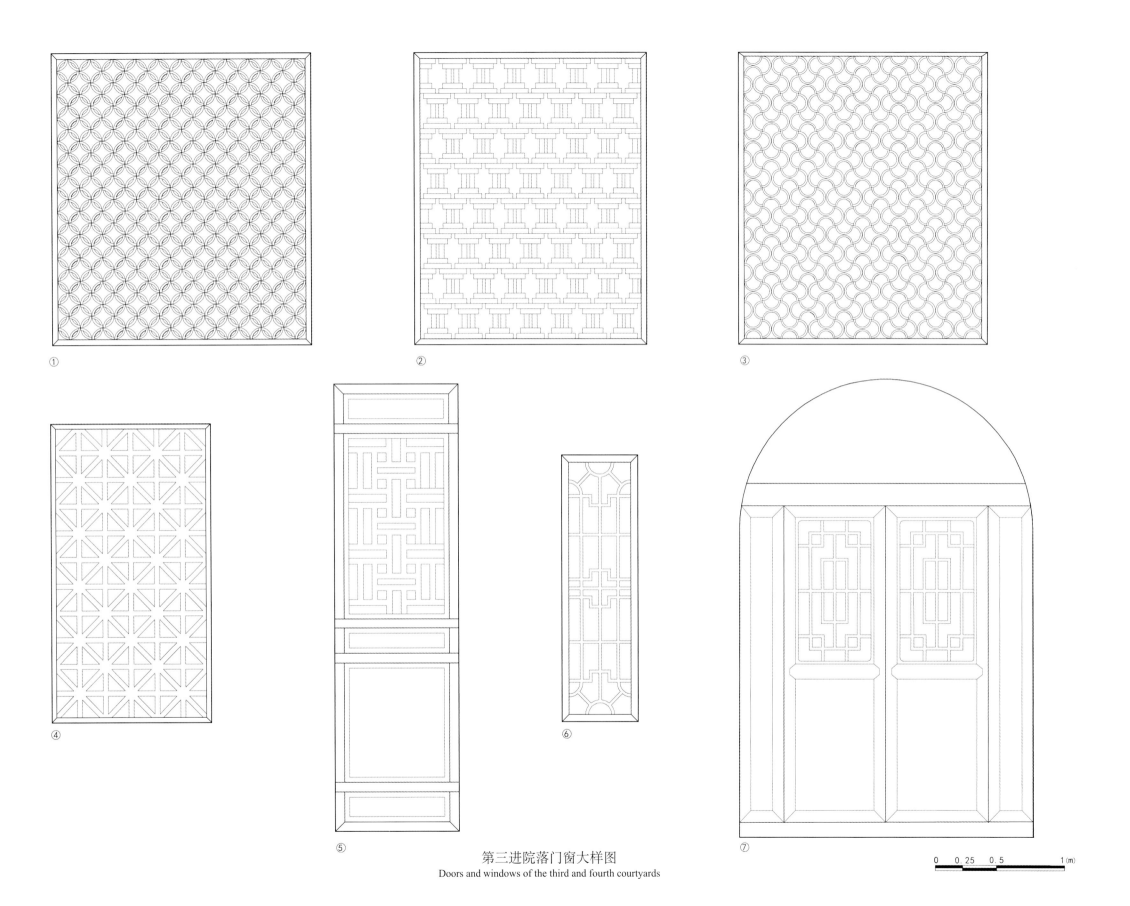

第三进院落门窗大样图
Doors and windows of the third and fourth courtyards

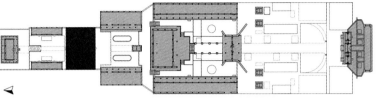

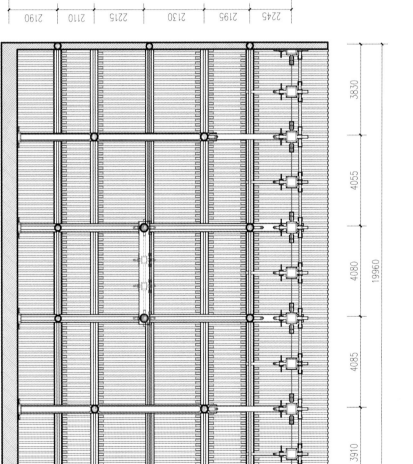

明伦堂梁架仰视图
Framework of Minglun Hall as seen from below

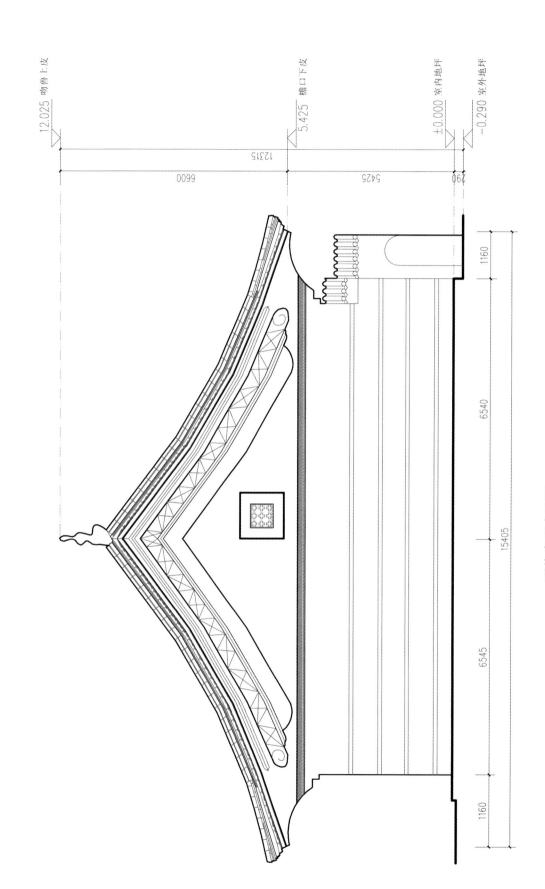

明伦堂西立面图
West elevation of Minglun Hall

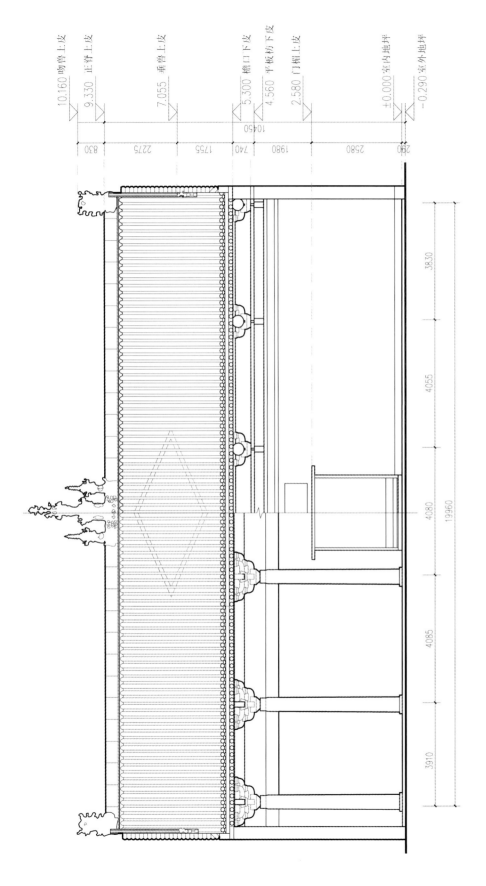

明伦堂南-北立面图
South elevation of Minglun Hall

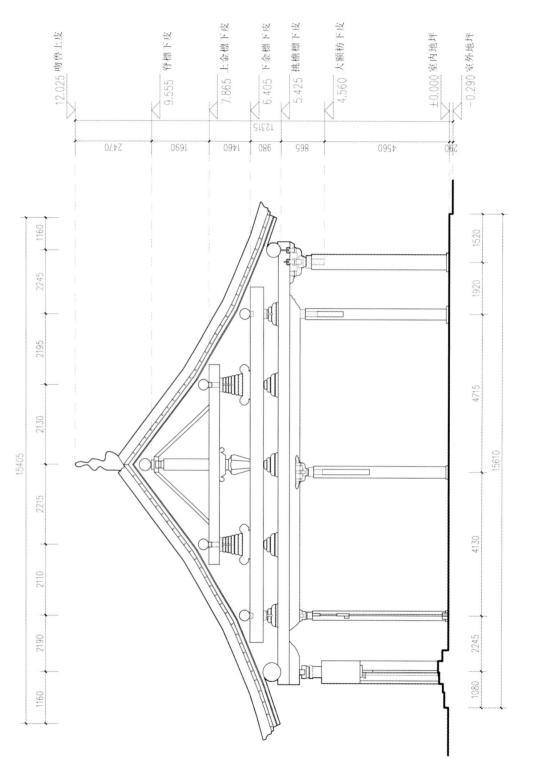

明伦堂当心间横剖面图
Cross-section of central bay of Minglun Hall

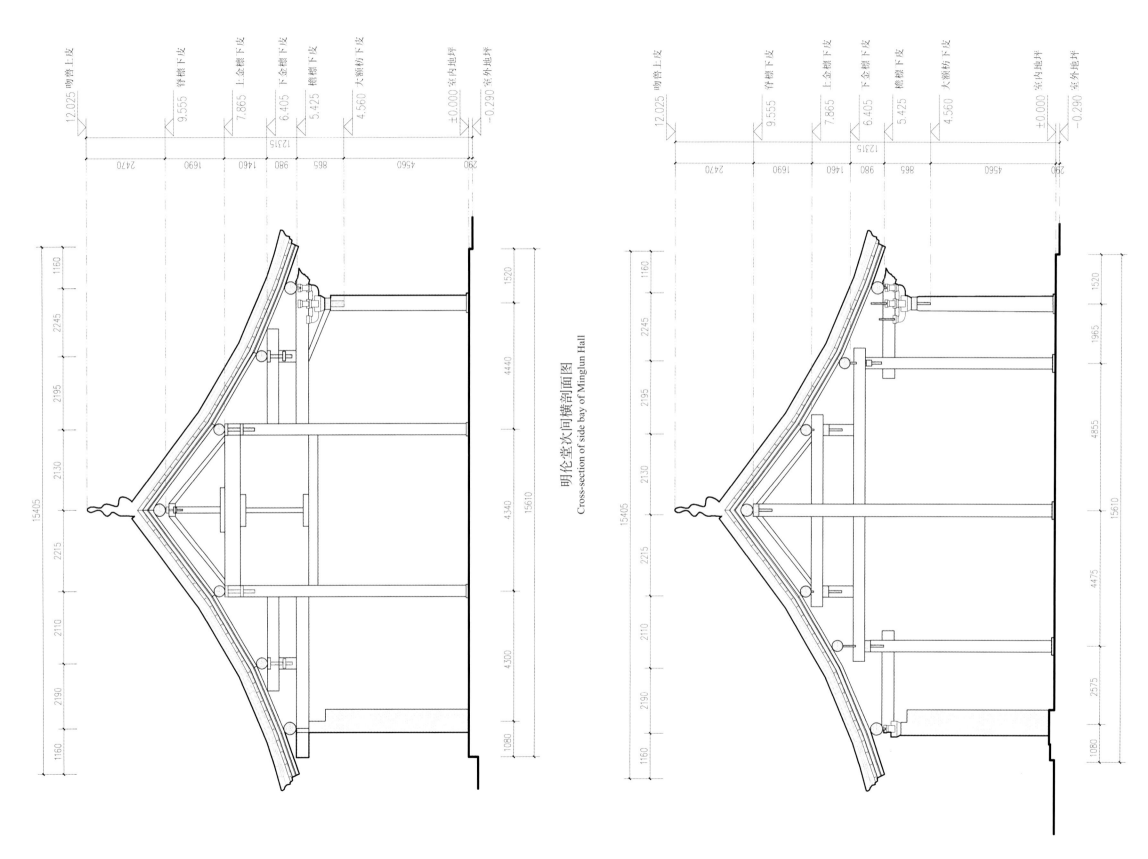

明伦堂次间横剖面图
Cross-section of side bay of Minglun Hall

明伦堂梢间横剖面图
Cross-section of second-to-last bay of Minglun Hall

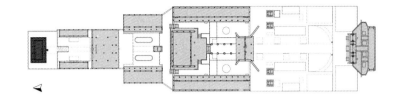

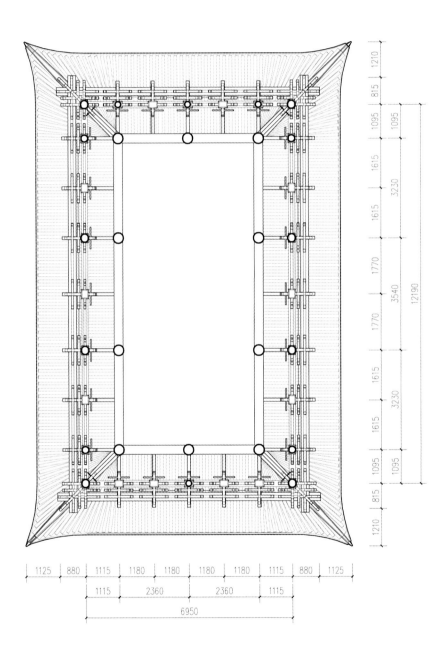

尊经阁一层梁架仰视图
Plan of first-floor framework of Zunjing Pavilion as seen from below

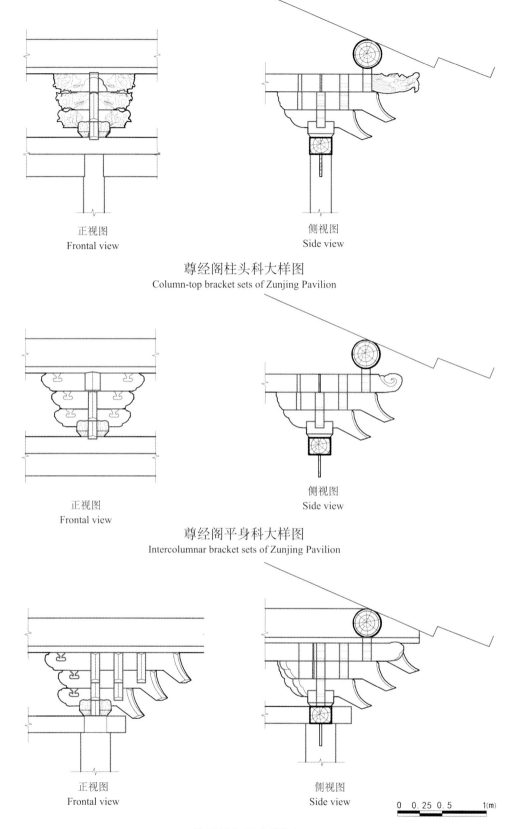

尊经阁柱头科大样图
Column-top bracket sets of Zunjing Pavilion

尊经阁平身科大样图
Intercolumnar bracket sets of Zunjing Pavilion

尊经阁角科大样图
Corner bracket sets of Zunjing Pavilion

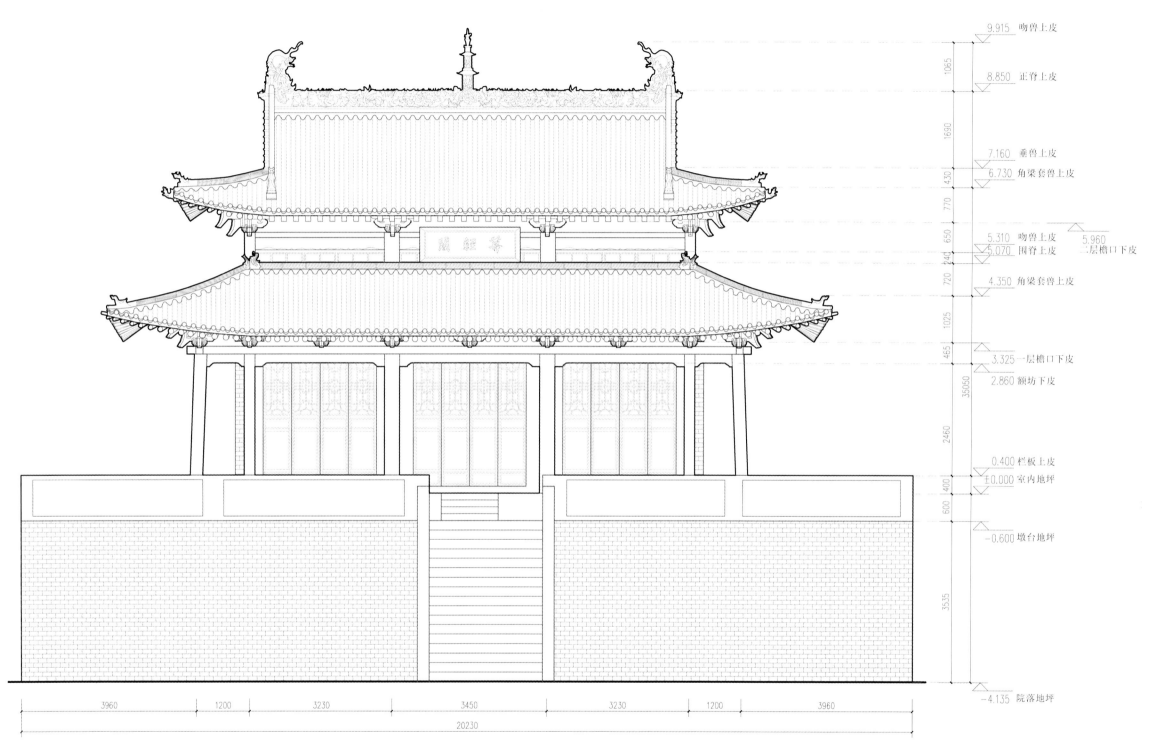

尊经阁南立面图
South elevation of Zunjing Pavilion

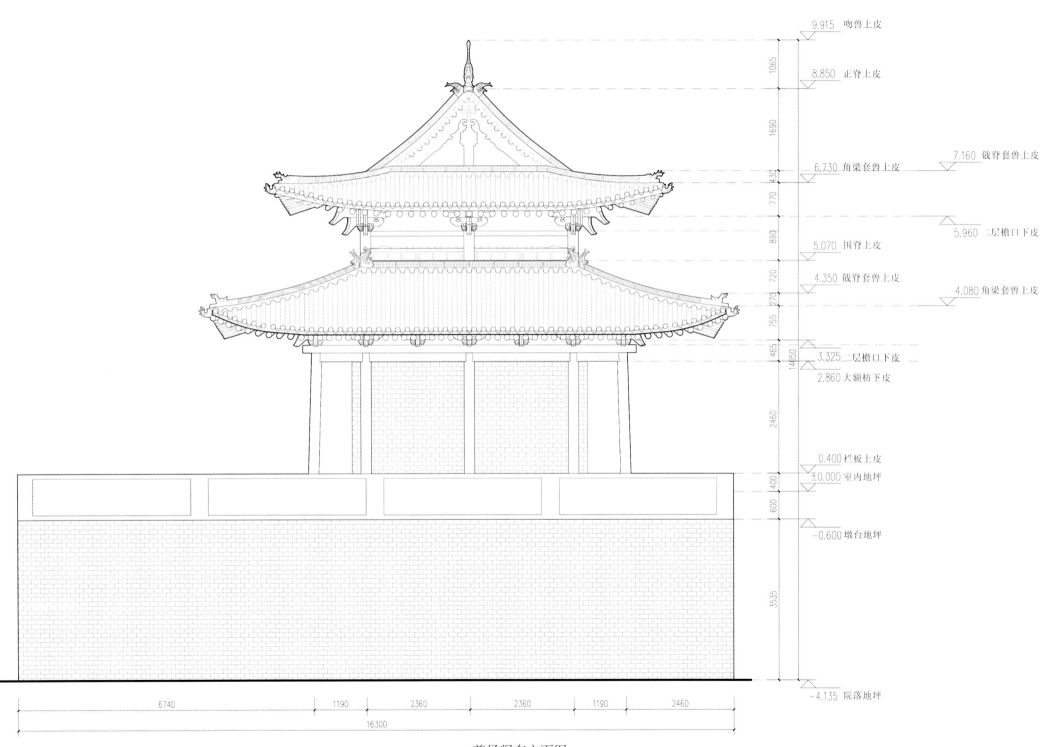

尊经阁东立面图
East elevation of Zunjing Pavilion

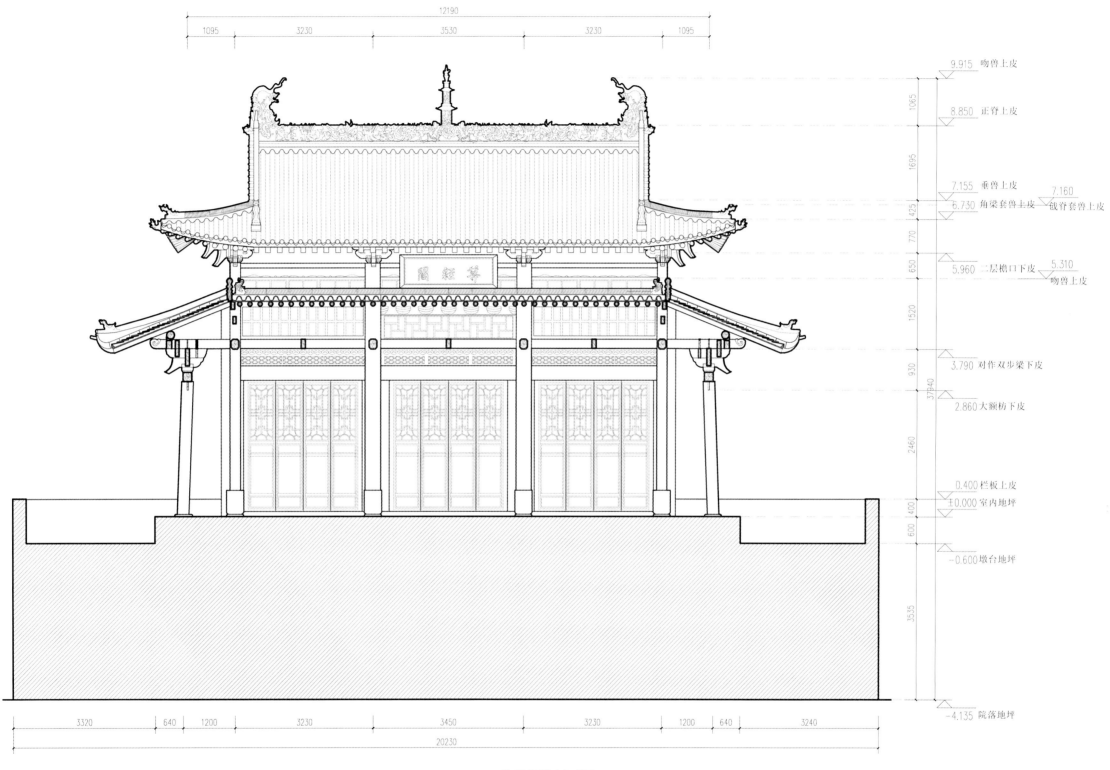

尊经阁纵剖面图
Longitudinal section of Zunjing Pavilion

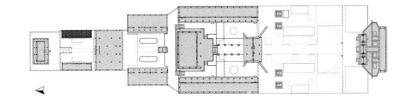

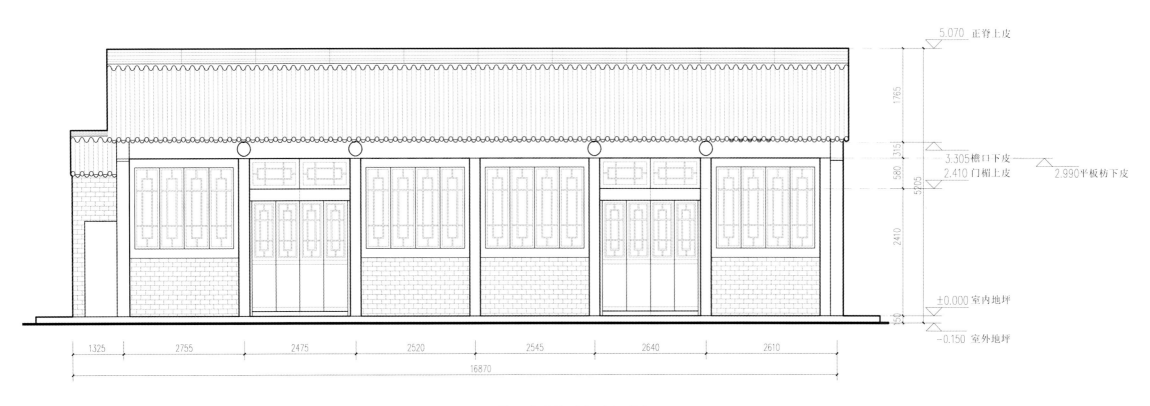

第四进院落厢房西立面图
West elevation of wing-room in the fourth courtyard

华阴西岳庙
Xiyue Temple of Huayin

Location: Yuezhen Street in Huayin, Shaanxi province

Construction Date: Ming and Qing dynasties

Protection Level: National Priority Protected Site

地　　址：陕西省华阴市岳镇街

年　　代：明—清

保护级别：全国重点文物保护单位（第三批）

Introduction

Located on Yuezhen Street in Huayin, the Xiyuemiao or Temple to the West Peak (referring to Mount Hua or Huashan, the West Mountain of the Five Great Mountains) faces Mount Hua ("Flower Mountain") to its due south. Measuring 525m (north-south) by 225m (east-west), the temple is a rectangular walled enclosure with the main structures laid out along a longitudinal axis. This includes, from south to north, a glazed-tile seven-dragon screen wall, Haoling (Grand Spirit) Gate, Wufeng (Five-phoenix) Building, Lingxing Gate, a stone *pailou*, Jincheng (Golden City) Gate, Jinshui (Golden Water) Bridge, Haoling (Grand Spirit) Hall, a resting hall, an imperial library known as Yushulou, and Wanshou (Longevity) Pavilion. A bell tower, a drum tower, auxiliary buildings, and steles (and stele pavilions) are positioned on the sides of the axis. What is noteworthy is that the magnificent temple architecture still stands tall and erect today. From the platform atop Wufeng Building one still has an excellent view of the five peaks of Mount Hua. The front platform (*yuetai*) of Haoling Hall is surrounded by a winding corridor. Inside are hung plaques handwritten by Qing emperors, for example "*jintian zhaoduan*" (bright and just Gold Heaven [here referring to the West]) and "*xianyun*" (celestial clouds). The complex is also full of lush trees and historical steles dating to the Eastern Han dynasty (25-220 BCE; *Xiyue Huashanmiao bei*), the Northern Zhou dynasty (557-581; *Xiyue Huashan shenmiao bei*), the reign of Tang emperor Xuanzong (r. 685-762; *Huashanming*), and the reign of Qing emperor Qianlong (*Yuelian lingshu*). In 1988, the site was declared a National Priority Protected Site.

Mount Hua looks back on a very long history of worship, but the establishment of the first temple—Jilinggong, or Palace of Gathering Spirits—dates back to emperor Wu (156-87 BCE) of Western Han (206 BCE-24 CE). However, due to the close proximity to Mount Hua, it was difficult to perform the *wang* ritual (watching a sacred mountain from a distance while conducting rituals). Thus the temple was moved to its present-day site on the route connecting the two traditional capitals of the Chinese empire—Chang'an and Luoyang. The relocation is confirmed by various sources including a Qing copy of the originally Eastern Han stele inscription from 165 (*Xiyue Huashanmiao bei*) and other Han stone figures and inscribed bricks. A chapter in *Huashan Gazatteer* (*Huashanzhi*, section Jinshi) records the erection of temple steles in 165, 179, and between 196 and 220, and this information is consistent with the material evidence.

概述

西岳庙位于陕西省华阴市岳镇街上，庙坐北朝南，正对华山，外侧建有城墙一周，南北长525米、东西宽225米。中轴线上依次排有琉璃七龙壁、灏灵门、五凤楼、棂星门、石牌楼、金城门、金水桥、灏灵殿、寝宫、御书楼、万寿阁等系列建筑，两侧辅以钟鼓楼、配殿、碑亭等。庙宇气势恢宏，于五凤楼城台之上远眺华山，五峰历历在目；灏灵殿前设凸字形月台，周围回廊围绕，殿内悬有康熙、道光、慈禧所题『金天昭瑞』、『仙云』等匾额。院内林木繁茂，殿宇辉煌，历代碑刻极多，现存东汉《西岳华山庙碑》、北周《西岳华山神庙碑》、唐玄宗御制《华山铭》残碑、乾隆御书『岳莲灵澍』石额等。1988年公布为全国重点文物保护单位。

祭祀华岳的历史非常悠久，但庙祭始自汉武帝创集灵宫。东汉时因其距离华山较近，难以实现望祭，加之山路崎岖，故整体迁移到靠近两京间官道的今址。根据在庙内发现的汉桓帝延熹八年（165年）立、清代重刻的《西岳华山庙碑》残石和汉代石人、文字砖等文物资料，可知其确切创建时间。

图3 西岳庙"天威咫尺"石牌坊

图2 西岳庙棂星门

图4 西岳庙"天威咫尺"石牌坊细部

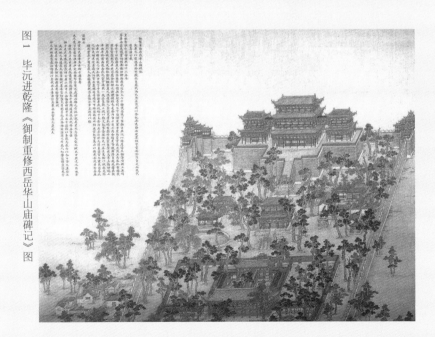

图1 毕沅进乾隆《御制重修西岳华山庙碑记》图

Fig.1 Map from Qianlong-period stele entitled *Yuzhi chongxiu Xiyuemiao beiji* by (governor) Bi Yuan
Fig.2 Lingxing Gate of Xiyue Temple
Fig.3 "*Tianwei zhichi*" stone archway, Xiyue Temple
Fig.4 Detail of "*Tianwei zhichi*" stone archway, Xiyue Temple

Worshipping rituals came to a halt during the decline of the Han dynasty, but were restored by emperor Wu (236-290) of Jin (266-420) in the last decade of the third century. Emperor Wu also ordered to plant thousands of cypress trees that should provide shade on the road leading from the temple to Mount Hua and enhance the sense of solemnity. The situation during the chaotic period of the Sixteen Kingdoms (304-439) remains unknown, but we know that, after order was restored in northern China, emperor Wencheng (r. 452-465) of Northern Wei (386-557) sent an envoy to Mount Hua in 454 to repair the temple. Rituals were performed again in 532 under emperor Xiaowu (r. 532-534) of Northern Wei. During his westward (military) expansion, emperor Jing (r. 585-587) of Western Liang (585-587) sent his minister Xiao Du to offer sacrifices at Mount Hua. Worshipping rituals reached a peak under the Northern Zhou. In 563, emperor Wu (r. 560-578) ordered Da Xi, the magistrate of Tongzhou (present-day Dali), to hold a ceremony and pray to the gods and spirits of Mount Hua for help in the struggle against the drought that had happened in that year. The emperor ordered further repair of the temple in 567. An imperially commissioned stone inscription by the high-ranking official Wanniuyu Jin commemorates this event.

Later in 614, emperor Yang (r. 604-617) of Sui (581-618) offered not only sacrifices to the mountain god but also built another site (a square) near the temple. In 724, emperor Xuanzong of Tang conferred the title of "Jintianwang" (King of Gold [Metal] Heaven) on the mountain god and changed the temple name accordingly, as recorded on a stone stele by the local magistrate Xu Zhiren. This huge stele—five *zhang* tall, one *zhang* wide and three quarters of a *zhang* thick—was erected on the street outside Yingtian (Complying with Heaven) Gate, today known as Lingxing Gate. A line of the inscription reads "*gaobiao heri, banbi feiyu*" (its top reaches the sun and its cliff overlooks rainclouds). Emperor Xuanzong commissioned further repair in 750, but at the end of his reign, in 880, the temple was razed to the ground by Chao Huang's rebel army.

Emperor Taizu (r.960-976) of Song ordered rebuilding in 962, as recorded in the stele inscription by Yang Zhaojian:

"...the temple was repaired and its appearance was enhanced. Old principles were interpreted into new form, transferring the coarse into the refined and the narrow into the wide. The new buildings were magnificent."

Thereafter, imperial worship at Mount Hua became annual routine. In the fifth lunar

《华山志·金石篇》中也有延熹八年（179年）、建安年间（196—220年）曾在此立碑的记载，两者可互为佐证。

汉末战乱，庙祀中绝，晋武帝太康年间（280—289年）予以恢复，并在西岳庙至华山的路旁植下数千株柏树，更增庄重森严。十六国时期西岳庙兴废情况不详，直到北魏孝武帝太昌元年（532年）才恢复遣使祭祀，文成帝三年（454年）正月又遣使诣华岳修庙。南朝梁敬帝太平二年（557年）车驾西征时，也曾派大臣杜晓祭华岳。北周时祭祀华岳最为频繁，武帝保定三年（563年）大旱，命同州刺史达溪武祭西岳；武帝天和二年（567年）又修庙，令万纽于瑾撰文勒石纪念。

隋唐时期，炀帝曾于大业十年（614年）祭祀华岳并在岳庙旁筑场。玄宗开元十二年（724年）封华山神为『金天王』，改西岳庙为金天王神祠，并令华州刺史徐知仁勒石纪功，碑刻成后立在应天门（今棂星门）外通街上，碑身通高五丈，阔一丈，厚四尺五，碑铭『高标赫日，半壁飞雨』，体量极为巨大；天宝九年（750年）又对庙宇重加修缮。唐僖宗广明元年（880年），黄巢军烧毁了金天王庙。

宋太祖建隆三年（962年）对西岳庙进行了大规模整修，据杨昭俭碑记载：『……庙貌时加修建，

图5 西岳庙东南角楼

图6 西岳庙八角亭

图7 西岳庙御碑亭

图8 西岳庙金城门

Fig.5 Southeast corner building of Xiyue Temple
Fig.6 Octagonal pavilion of Xiyue Temple
Fig.7 Imperial stele pavilion of Xiyue Temple
Fig.8 Jincheng Gate of Xiyue Temple

month of 1009, emperor Zhenzong (997-1022) of Song performed sacrifices to dispel ill fortune and pray for rain. Two years later, the emperor bestowed a honorific title upon the mountain god while performing the *tailao* (large beast) sacrifice i.e. sacrificing an ox, goat, and pig and the *sanxian* (three offerings) ritual i.e. inviting the spirit to take part in the feast. Historical records about the event note:

> "The emperor visited the temple to pay respect together with his ministers. His imperial guards of honor lined up in rank and file both inside and outside the temple. The officials were given the task of offering sacrifices to various deities. And the mountain god was named Shunsheng jintianwang (Obliging and Sagely King of Gold [Metal] Heaven)."

A month later, the title was changed to "Jintian shunshengdi" (Obliging and Sagely Ruler of Gold [Metal] Heaven). In 1265, during the Yuan period, Kublai Khan (r. 1260-1294) regulated and standardized the worshipping rituals and in the first lunar month of 1291, awarded another honorific title upon the deity—"Xiyue jintian dali shunshengdi" (Xiyue, Most Beneficial, Obliging, and Sagely Ruler of Gold [Metal] Heaven). These secular titles were not used for long. Shortly after the founding of the Ming dynasty, however, emperor Taizong (1368-1398) ordered the title of the deity to be restored to "Xiyue Huashan zhishen" (Xiyue, God of Mount Hua), which possessed only a religious meaning. The Ming emperors came to record every major event that happened, ranging from war to the accession to the throne, natural disasters or epidemics. Starting in 1497, the temple underwent renovation on a large scale, and during the next three years, the complex was greatly expanded. Li Rong's nineteenth-century gazetteer *Huayuezhi* records a stele inscription (*Zhongxiu Xiyuemiao*) composed by the Minister of Rites, Zhong Hongmo, and erected to commemorate the repair:

> "Since the buildings were deteriorating daily, the highest ranking eunuch Tan Ping and the censor-in-chief Cheng Zong were granted permission by the emperor to conduct rebuilding as requested by them…Construction began in autumn 1479 and ended in summer 1482. The new architecture has a public hall in the front and private rooms in the back, and in-between are five longitudinally positioned buildings that are connected with each other. A holy kitchen (*shenchu*) is to the left and a holy storage (*shenku*) to the right. Galleries are attached to the hall on the front and the sides, so that the total hall length measures 84 *chi* (0.32 m). The main entrance to the temple is located in front of the hall. Inside the walled temple enclosure stands Yuxiang (Imperial Incense) Pavilion, and ancient and modern stone steles are lined up right and left. Taoist priests reside in a building in the western part of the temple. Outside the main temple gate is a

阐旧规而从新制，起卑陋而为显敞。土木之制，尽其壮丽。"从此朝廷每年遣使致祭成为定制。真宗大中祥符二年（1009年）五月祭西岳庙禳灾祈雨，大中祥符四年（1011年）五月为西岳神上尊号，用太牢三献之礼，真宗"亲谒岳庙，群臣陪位。庙垣内外列黄麾杖，遣官分祭庙内诸神，加号岳神为『顺圣金天王』"，一个月后又改为『金天顺圣帝』。

元世祖至元二年（1265年）规范祭祀华山制度，并于至元二十八年（1291年）春正月加封西岳神为『西岳金天大利顺圣帝』等。

明太祖建国后取消了西岳神的帝号，恢复其本名『西岳华山之神』。有明一代凡国家大事均要遣使祭告岳神，如用兵、即位、遭遇自然灾害与疫情等。明宪宗成化十五年（1479年）对西岳庙进行了大规模修复，前后历时三年告成。修缮后规模大为增扩，据礼部尚书周洪谟《重修西岳庙》碑记（载于清道光间李榕《华岳志》）称："栋宇瓦墁日浸腐败，镇守太监覃平公、都御史程公宗辈奏允重修……经始于成化己亥秋，落成于壬寅夏。前为堂，后为室，其间贯以纵屋，连栋者五。其前为重门，重门之内有御香亭，古今碑石罗列于左右。西有屋一区，以栖道流；重门之外，又为台门，建重屋其上，巽、坤维皆有角楼，大凡八十四尺。其左为神厨，右为神库，堂之前左右为廊，

图9 西岳庙灏灵殿

图10 西岳庙灏灵殿前檐当心间平身科斗栱

图11 西岳庙灏灵殿（左）与寝殿（右）院落

图12 西岳庙寝殿

Fig.9 Haoling Gate of Xiyue Temple
Fig.10 Bracketing between central-bay front eaves columns of Xiyue Temple
Fig.11 Courtyard with Haoling Gate (left) and resting hall (right), Xiyue Temple
Fig.12 Resting hall of Xiyue Temple

platform (gate), a multi-story building with watchtowers installed on its southeast and southwest corners. The architecture totals 187 bays."

The second imperially commissioned repair during the Ming dynasty took place in 1541, and was described in *Fuxiu Yuemiao beiji* (by Xia Yan) as follows:

"What used to be shabby is renewed, and what had collapsed has been erected. The craftsmen managed to finish in time. Hence, the buildings are magnificent, the layout is spacious, the walls and foundations are firm…the decorations are brilliant. The architecture is as high as the sun and the moon…but also provides vantage points for watching the three peaks (West Peak North Peak, South Peak of Mount Hua) and (the scenic spot of) Xuanzhang (located on East Peak)…All kinds of rooms are present here, ranging from exquisitely decorated formal chambers to kitchens and slaughter-houses. Such a splendid temple must appear inviting for the gods and spirits of Mount Hua, and during the annual worship, they will all gather here…"

Historical texts also describe the architecture of the temple after repair:

"The main hall has five (literally columns, but here more broadly) bays. The resting hall behind has two columns on each side (in other words, if including the central bay then a three-bay hall). In front of the main hall stand the seven-door Lingxing Gate, the five-door Tou (Head) Gate and a Ming-period stele pavilion dating. Tou Gate was restored because it had deteriorated. Newly reconstructed were nine wing buildings (*sifang*) on the left and right sides, two halls dedicated to (the door god) Yulei, historical stele buildings, and two "land" or model boats. The structures outside were linked to the corner towers. The architecture adds up to more than two-hundred bays."

From the above description we can know that, in comparison to the 1497 repair, the temple has considerably grown. But only fourteen years later, in 1555, a catastrophic earthquake took place in present-day Shaanxi, and Xiyue Temple suffered severely from it. Repair work was not finished before 1562, because the power of the empire was not great enough to carry out construction properly. And yet, the temple was not restored to its original splendor, as described in *Chongxiu miaoji*, a stele inscription composed by Qu Jingchun:

"Walls that collapsed, members that broke, and bricks that crumbled were all removed and reconstructed to restore the temple's pre-earthquake appearance. With a total of two-hundred and twelve bays of architecture restored, the whole project took two years and cost 12,000 taels of silver to complete."

图 13　西岳庙御碑楼

Fig.13 Imperial stele building of Xiyue Temple

Even so, the great earthquake of 1556 was not the only disaster for the temple during this period, although later damage was much less severe. *Xuke Huashan zhi* (1606; by Wang Minshun) and *Huayinxian zhi* (1614; by Wang Jiuchou) provide illustrations of the temple. The accompanying text gives the following account:

"Newly were built the six-column (i.e. five-bay) Haoling Hall, the four-column (i.e. three-bay) resting hall and two wings (*sifang*) of eighty bays. A bell tower and a drum tower are at the bottom of the (hall) podium, as well as two ponds enclosed by bamboo fences in the middle of the complex. In front of the ponds stand Jincheng (Golden City) Gate, outside which are a hall dedicated to (the door god) Shentu and a storehouse for sacrificial utensils both facing west, as well Yulei Hall and Yifu Pavilion both facing east. Lingxing Gate is located further down south flanked by a stele pavilion (in the east) and Yuxiang Pavilion (in the west). Continuing in this direction, one reaches seven stele buildings and Tai (Platform) Gate with five doorways and a multi-story building atop…The north end of the complex features a big fish pond, and to its near north stands the Buddhist library…Outside of the temple stand two wooden memorial pillars (*chuoxie*) with a music (concert) pavilion to its south."

Similar to the Ming, the Qing also treated the mountain god as a divine ruler and authority to which every major event had to be reported including disasters, rebellions, bestowing titles and birthday ceremonies of emperors and empresses. Throughout the Qing dynasty, large-scale repair was carried out on three occasions. First in 1703, during a visit of emperor Kangxi (r. 1661-1722) who "granted several thousand taels of silver" for repair of the temple and mountain road, with the goal to "enhance the brilliance of the mountain god's earthly abode," as recorded by a stele inscription entitled *Yuzhi chongxiu Yuemiao*. Lan Shen, a famous painter of the time, who created an album with thirty-four paintings of Mount Hua (*Xiyuetu*) depicts the temple on his twenty-sixth leaf. Although the painting itself is lost today, the accompanying text as quoted in *Guangyang zaji*, a Qing anthology of essays composed by Liu Xianting, says:

"Enclosing walls, although slightly shorter than their Tang counterparts, were constructed for defense. Stele pavilions and flanking archways and gates stand in the courtyard in front of Wufeng Building. Platforms and towers sit on the four corners. From here, entering through Lingxing Gate, one will pass a second gate, main hall, third gate, resting hall, and fourth gate, before one arrives at a pond with channeled-in water. In the pond are a bridge and a platform. Atop the platform stands Wanshou Pavilion."

年）才陆续补修完成，据瞿景淳《重修庙记》碑称：「垣墉有倾颓者，栋宇有折挠者，瓦石有毁败者，悉撤而新之，务完其初。全部工程阅二年始成，自寝殿以及门亭凡二百一十二，费金凡一万二千有奇」，此次重修无异新建。隆庆二年（1568年）六月又遭地震，万历三十年（1602年）因水灾、火灾又有毁损，因是重整，「先是，灏灵、角楼遭回禄，比岁庙宇为霖潦所噬，丹雘剥落，咸次第修举，由殿寝、御香亭、神厨、斋所渐于金城诸门，灏灵诸楼，周围环除约二百余楹」。明代庙貌，有万历三十四年（1606年）王民顺《续刻华山志》图和四十二年（1614年）王九畴撰《华阴县志》庙图，志曰：「今制灏灵正殿六楹，寝殿四楹，两翼司房八十间。阶下钟鼓楼各一，中竹栏池二，泓外金城门，门外神荼殿、祭器所西向列，郁垒殿、易服亭东向列。再前为棂星门，其外左碑亭，右香亭。碑楼七，又前台门五，台上有楼……最后鱼池一，大泓近北修藏经阁……庙外树两绰楔，南对又有亭，用以备乐」。

清朝对待西岳神，同样是逢事必告，水旱之灾、荡平叛乱、帝后生日或加封号等均要祭告。清代对西岳庙进行过三次较大规模的修建：其一是在康熙四十二年（1703年），西巡谒华岳神祠，「特发帑金数千两」修复宫观及登山道路，以「增辉少昊之下都」，事载《御制重修岳庙》碑，

The second repair was carried out in 1777. Bi Yuan, the governor of Shaanxi, reported to the imperial court the desperate condition of the temple and was granted 120,000 taels of silver for its restoration. The result was a renewed magnificent temple. *Huayin xianzhi* describes the new temple in detail:

"…A monumental archway known as Taihuashan (Great Mount Hua [Flower Mountain]) Gate stands at a distance of half a li (250 m) away from the temple. Outside the temple entrance are also erected a glazed-tile screen wall and, on Qipan Street, two iron flagpoles, and two steles that encourage visitors to dismount their horses. After entering through the main temple gate, one passes a bell tower and a drum tower and then Haoling Gate crowned by Haoling Building also known as Wufeng Building. West of Lingxing Gate stands the stele pavilion of the Tang emperor Xuanzong. The stele must have been extraordinary beautiful, but it is broken, and only four characters have survived.

Additionally, more than two hundred stele fragments have survived here, dating to as early as the Tang. Governor Bi Yuan ordered pavilions and stone railings built in 1778 to give them shelter and protection. Most stele pavilions are named after the dynasty or patron that had commissioned them, for example, the Song dynasty and the Ming emperors Hongwu and Shenzhong.

There are corner entrances on the east and west sides of Haoling Gate, and an old tree named Qingniu Tree is standing nearby. According to legend, Laozi tied the string of his oxen to Qingniu in 978 BCE. In the same courtyard also stand two other legendary trees not far from each other—a Chinese scholar tree and a cypress tree. Their branches are interwoven so that it looks as if they are hugging each other. The three trees (each of them more than two thousand years old) are protected by stone railings. North of Haoling Gate stands Lingxing Gate and further north stands Jincheng Gate, which is flanked by a storage building for sacrificial utensils, Gengfu Pavilion, four corner towers, and other religious and secular buildings. Statues are lined up left and right of Jincheng Gate including the door gods (Shentu, Yulei) and the Yama of the Ten Courts (Shidian lingguan). Passing through the east- and west-side halls that connect two courtyards (*chuantang*), one reaches a pond filled with water channeled in from outside. Three longitudinally positioned bridges span over the pond; the largest one in the center is named Wangxian (Watching Immortals) Bridge.

The main hall is known as Haoling Hall and has nine (literally columns, but here more broadly) bays, and a stone archway stands in front of it. This *pailou* has three plaques, with the middle one saying '*zunyan jun*' (the most venerable and solemn), the left one saying Shaohao *zhidu* (abode of Shaohao), and the right one saying

当时的画家蓝深创作《西岳图》三十四帧，第二十六幅即为华岳庙图，图已逸失，文字见载于《广阳杂记》，称：「今筑城为卫，较唐稍隘。五凤楼前为壁亭，左右为门，四角为台，为根星门，为宫门，为大殿。次入内宫门，引水为池，为桥，为台，台上为万寿阁」。第二次是乾隆四十二年（1777年），因陕西巡抚毕沅奏称西岳庙岁久倾颓，急需葺治，朝廷拨银十二万两重修，修成后规模宏壮，据乾隆五十三年（1788年）《华阴县志》记载：「距庙半里许有坊曰太华山门。庙门外有琉璃影壁，棋盘街铁旗杆二、下马碑二。甬道、岳庙门、钟楼、鼓楼、灏灵门，门上为灏灵楼，即五凤楼。根星门西为古碑亭，唐明皇碑史称其伟绝特嘱，经兵燹断坏已尽，今尚存四字，又唐宋以来残碣计二百余枚，乾隆四十三年巡抚毕公建亭覆之，护以石栏。又有宋碑亭、明太祖碑亭、神宗碑亭、提点碑。灏灵门两翼有东西角门，门内有青牛树，相传周昭王二十三年老子系青牛于此。又有槐抱柏，柏抱槐，虬枝胶葛，偃盖扶疏，皆数千年物，置石栏围之。灏灵楼后为根星门，再后为金城门。旁有祭器所，更服亭，角楼四翼，道流宫观参处其间。东西穿堂两座，正中望仙桥，左右石桥城门外东西翼为神荼、郁垒、十殿灵官、门神、厩马诸像。

'Rushou zhifu' (the Autumn God's mansion). The hall has a front platform (yuetai) extending from its interior, and bamboo railings are installed to its east and west. Behind the hall are Libu (Courteous Steps) Gate, a resting hall, a hall connecting two courtyards (chuandian), and auxiliary buildings placed on the east and west sides (peidian and sifang). Behind the resting hall are the imperial library and Wanshou Pavilion (built by the Taoist monk Tan Kui in the Ming period). Even further behind are Youyue (Visiting the [West] Mountain) Archway and a platform. In front of the Buddhist library stand Lyvzu Hall dedicated to the famous Taoist immortal Lyv Dongbin and Fangsheng Pond. These buildings create the fine scenery of Xiyue Temple."

The second imperially commissioned repair was also captured in a painting (Chixiu Xiyuemiao tu), which provides the most detailed historical account of the temple. Additionally, the 1831 edition of Huayuezhi describes the temple architecture at that time:

"The architecture in the temple has changed over the course of history, but today it includes the nine-bay Haoling Hall which is the principal building of the complex and behind it, Libu Gate, a resting hall (qingong), a connecting hall (chuandian), and side halls; in front of the main hall are Wangxian Bridge and to the left and right, the eighty-bay wing buildings (sifang). South of the bridge stands Jincheng Gate, flanked by Gengfu Pavilion (east) and a storage for sacrificial utensils (west), and west and east stand statues of the door gods (Shentu, Yulei), the Yamas of the Ten Courts (Shidian lingguan), as well as other religious and secular buildings.

There are seven stele pavilions, five of them inside Jincheng Gate and the remaining two outside the gate. Further south is Lingxing Gate along with Qingniu Tree. South of the tree, and north of Wufeng Building, stands an old stele erected by Tang emperor Xuanzong and destroyed in the Huang Chao Rebellion at the end of the dynasty. Further south of Wufeng Building stands Haoling Gate which is surrounded by walls and crowned with four corner towers. Wanshou Pavilion is located at the northern end of the temple. The imperial library lies to its south, Youyue Archway to its north, and two rotating sutra cabinets to its sides. Qipan Street lies outside the main temple complex, leading to Huashan Gate, the starting point of the route ascending the mountain. This is a general description of Xiyue Temple."

During the Dungan Revolt in 1862, Haoling Hall, Wufeng Building, and Wanshou Pavilion were burnt down by rebels. Five years later, general Zuo Zongtang and governor Liu Dian initiated the third round of repair in the Qing dynasty, which lasted for four years and cost 29,000 taels of silver and 100,000 labor units to complete. An inscription on one

为池，引水注之。正殿曰灏灵殿，殿九楹，前有石坊，中曰"尊严峻极"，左曰"少昊之都"，右曰"蓐收之府"。并有月台，东西竹槛，殿后为礼步门、寝宫、穿殿、两翼司房，寝殿后有御书楼、万寿阁，明神宗时道士席演魁建阁。后有游岳坊、平台。藏经楼前为吕祖堂、放生池。此则岳庙之胜概也。"此次重修，留下了《敕修西岳庙图》一幅，记录最为详细。到道光辛卯年编《华岳志》时，其规制为"按庙制代有增损，今制：灏灵正殿九楹，殿后礼步门、寝宫、穿殿、配殿；正殿前望仙桥、东西翼司房八十间。桥前金城门，门旁更服所、祭器所，东西翼神荼、郁垒十殿；灵官、门神，厩马诸神，道流宫观错处其间。碑亭七，门内五、门外二。前为棂星门，青牛树在焉，树之南为古碑石，明皇御制碑，黄巢之所燔者也，石在五凤楼北。楼南为灏灵门，绕以周垣，角楼四翼。最后万寿阁，阁前御书楼。阁后游岳坊，左右转藏楼各一座。庙门外棋盘街不数武即华山门，上山路自此始，此西岳庙之大概也"。同治元年（1862年）关中地区回民暴乱，同年九月十六日乱民烧毁了西岳庙灏灵殿和五凤楼、万寿阁。同治六年（1867年）左宗棠与巡抚刘典商议重修，历经四年，用银两万九千两，用工十万人次修成，这是第三次重修（灏灵殿内上梁文记："同治八年岁维大荒落仲冬月二十五日日辰时，钦差大臣太子太保一等恪靖伯陕甘总督左宗棠，钦命帮办陕

of the beams of Haoling Hall records the date and the officials in charge of the work. In 1878 Wanshou Pavilion was rebuilt, and the imperial library, Wanghe (Watching the [Yellow] River) Building, Wusheng (Five Saints) Shrine, two corner towers, and Fangsheng Pond were restored, breathing new life into the place.

In 1911, after the Xinhai Revolution, the temple fell into oblivion and became desolated. In 1932, General Feng Yuxiang stationed his troops here, turning the complex into an arsenal, but an accidental fire in the armory caused an explosion that destroyed Wanshou Pavilion. In 1979, the Xiyue Cultural Heritage Administration Bureau was established and gradually restored the architecture along the temple axis, repairing the stone carvings and inscriptions and the historical buildings including the Jincheng, and Lingxing gates and the west perimeter wall that had collapsed, as well as demolishing illegally built houses on Qipan Street. In 1988, the temple was nominated as a National Priority Protected Site.

Six years later, the temple was handed over from the Commission for Science, Technology and Industry for National Defense (COSTIND) to the Shaanxi Provincial Government. Afterwards, remains of the steles that encouraged visitors to dismount their horses, iron flagpoles, and pailou foundations were unearthed in archeological excavations. During this period seven hundred cypress trees were planted to enhance the environment. In 1996, the temple was opened to the public and has remained so ever since.

甘军务署理陕西巡抚刘典率同陕西按察使布政使潼商道华阴知县等』）。在此基础上，光绪四年（1878年）又修复了万寿阁，并补修了御书房、望河楼、五圣祠、两角楼、放生池等，使之重焕生机。

辛亥革命之后，西岳庙迅速遭到废弃。1932年，冯玉祥部进驻，将其改造成为兵工厂，并因弹药库失火炸毁了万寿阁。1979年，西岳庙文物管理所正式成立，逐步回收中轴线上各建筑的管护权，对石雕、石刻、古建筑采取了保护措施，并先后重修了金城门、棂星门及西城墙的部分塌陷段，拆除了庙门前棋盘街违建房屋。1988年，西岳庙被公布为全国重点文物保护单位。1994年将西岳庙正式由国防科工委移交陕西省人民政府。此后陆续发掘出下马石、铁旗杆、牌楼基座等遗址，新植柏树近七百棵，庙宇环境大为改观。1996年起，西岳庙正式对外开放。

Survey and Mapping Information

Responsible Department: Department of Architecture (Class of 2011), School of Architecture, Xi'an University of Architecture and Technology

Team Members: SHEN Yijun, LIU Yueyi, LI Pengfei, YANG Xi, LUO Yichen, WANG Changshuo, WU Fan, LI Tong, HU Yihong, WANG Ruinan, FU Qiuyuan, HE Jiaxuan, SU Ye, WANG Yizhi, SUN Weiyi, CHEN Qian, DING Yike, YU Dongxing, FAN Yuting, GAO Xin, HE Mengyun, LIU Yutong, WEI Boyang, WU Mufei, LIU Jiayuan, QIN Yang, HAN Yuqing, YIN Shiwen, LI Yining, ZHANG Ning, LIANG Kangqi, WANG Yirui, WANG Ye, YOU Yixing, ZHANG Chuang, ZHANG Boya, WANG Yuyang, QIN Qi, GAO Jie, QIAO Zhen, ZHANG Yige, YANG Yijie, HE Yifeng, SHANG Dan, YIN Mengyun

Supervisors: LIN Yuan, YU Mengzhe, YUE Yanmin
Editor of Drawings: LEI Honglu
Survey Time: May 2014

华阴西岳庙测绘的人员名单

测　绘：西安建筑科技大学建筑学院建筑学2011级

沈逸君　刘悦怡　李鹏飞　杨茜　罗怡晨　王昌硕　吴凡　李通
胡已宏　王瑞楠　付秋源　何嘉轩　苏晔　王怡智　孙唯一　陈茜
丁一珂　于东兴　范宇廷　高欣　贺梦云　刘宇彤　魏伯阳　吴慕飞
刘家源　秦阳　韩宇清　尹诗雯　李怡凝　张宁　梁康琦　王一睿
王晔　由懿行　张闯　张博雅　汪钰洋　秦祺　高杰樵
张弋戈　杨祎洁　贺一丰　尚丹　殷梦芸
指导教师：林源　喻梦哲　岳岩敏
图纸整理：雷鸿鹭
测绘时间：2014年5月

References 参考文献

[一] 华阴县志编纂委员会编.陕西地方志丛书·华阴县志[M].西安：陕西人民出版社.2000.
[二] 赵立瀛主编.陕西古建筑[M].西安：陕西人民出版社.1992.
[三] 国家文物局主编.中国文物地图集·陕西分册[M].西安：西安地图出版社.1998.
[四] 刘宇生.救修西岳庙记碑与陕甘回民起义[J].文博.2013（11）.55-59.
[五] 何修龄.华阴西岳庙的古代建筑[J].文物.1958（4）.54-58.
[六] 刘宇生.明清西岳庙修缮纪略[J].文博.1992（3）.18-23.

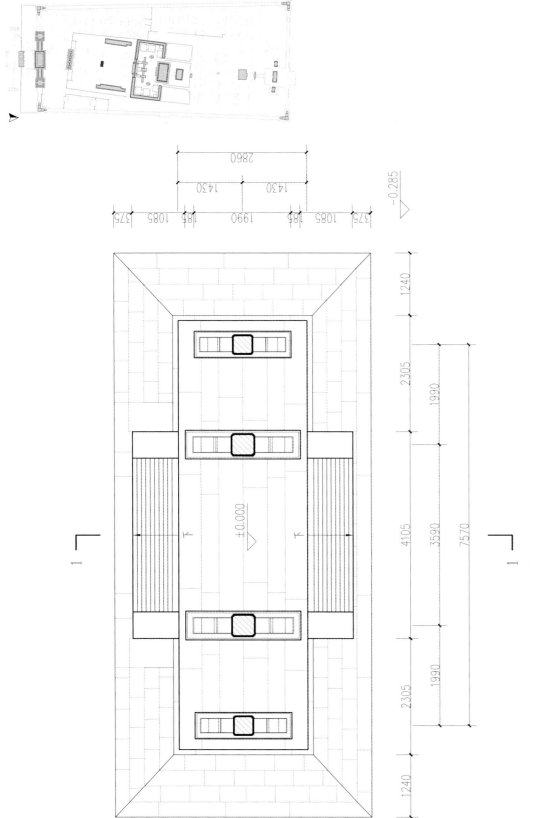

"天威咫尺"石牌坊平面图
Plan of "tianwei zhichi" stone archway

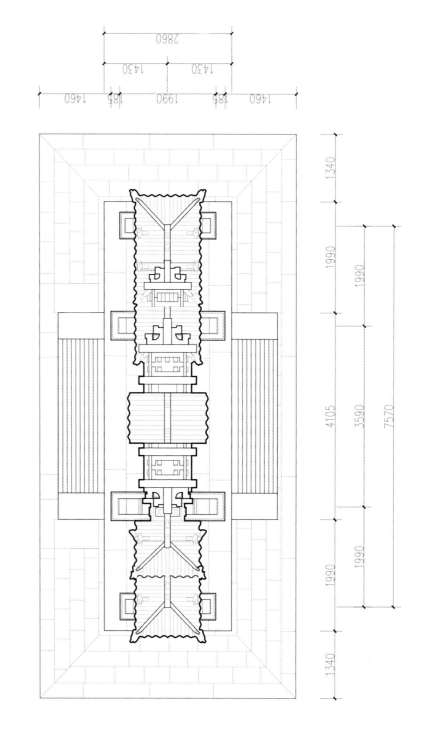

"天威咫尺"石牌坊屋顶平面图
Plan of roof of "tianwei zhichi" stone archway

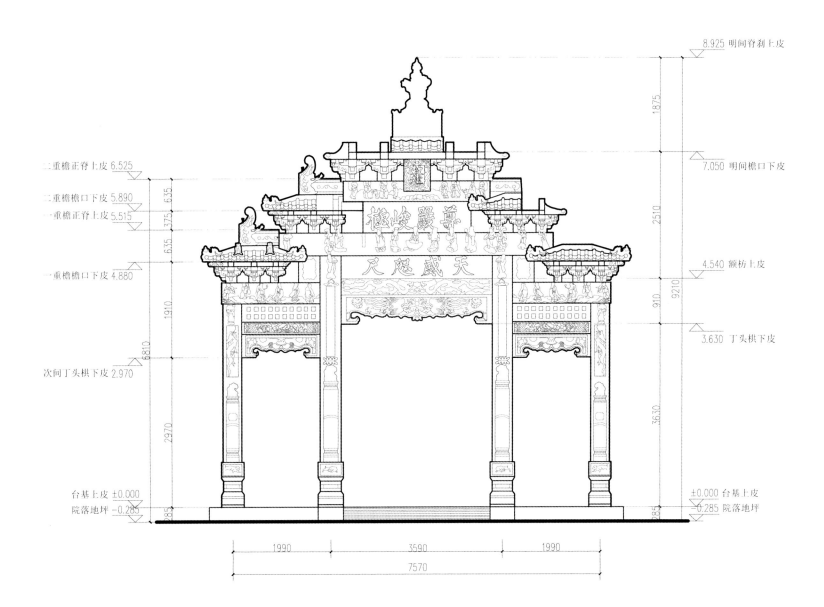

"天威咫尺"石牌坊南立面图
South elevation of *"tianwei zhichi"* stone archway

"天威咫尺"石牌坊 1-1 剖面图
Section 1-1 of *"tianwei zhichi"* stone archway

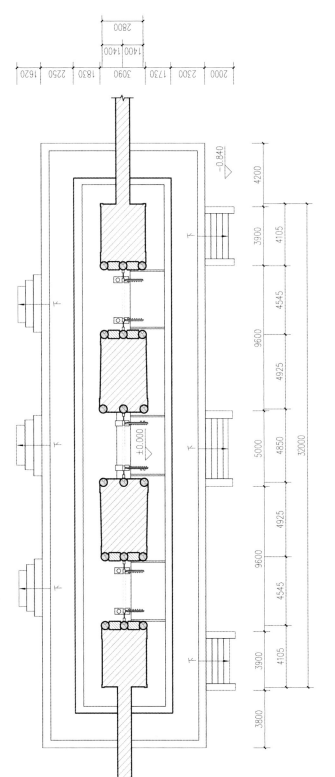

棂星门平面图
Plan of Lingxing Gate

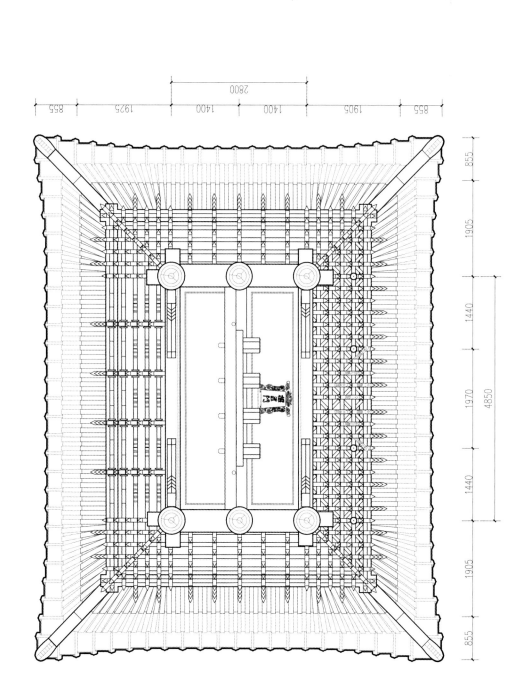

棂星门次间梁架仰视图
Plan of framework of Lingxing Gate as seen from below

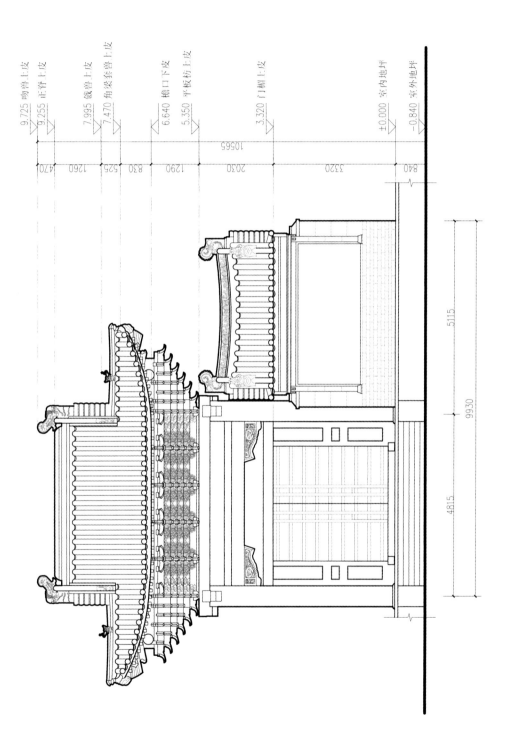

棂星门梢间北立面图
North elevation of second-to-last bay of Lingxing Gate

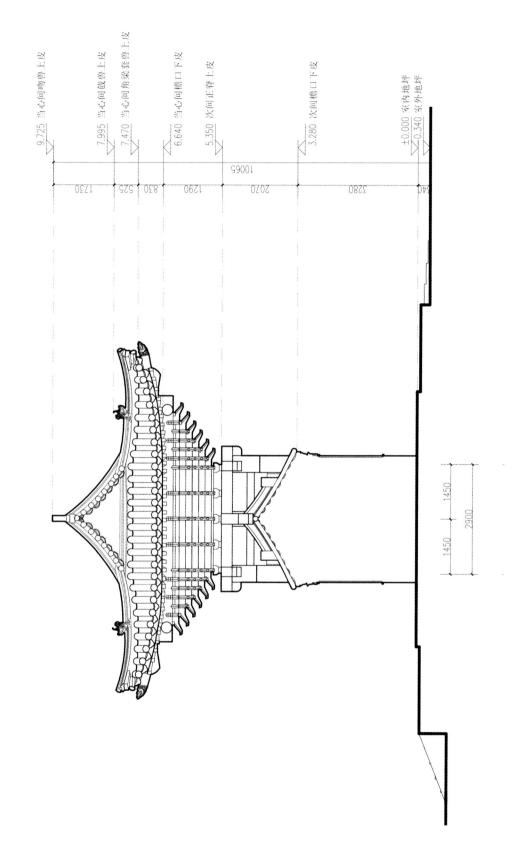

棂星门东立面图
East elevation of Lingxing Gate

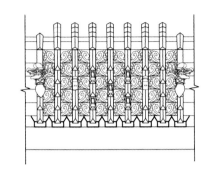
正视图
Frontal view

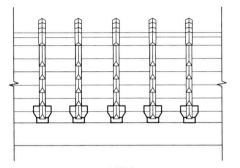
正视图
Frontal view

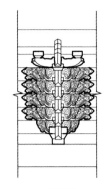
正视图
Frontal view

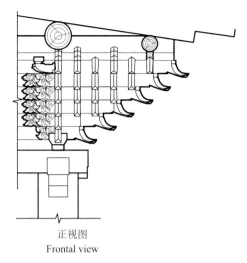
正视图
Frontal view

仰视图
View from below

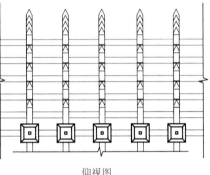
仰视图
View from below

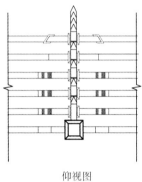
仰视图
View from below

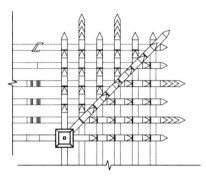
仰视图
View from below

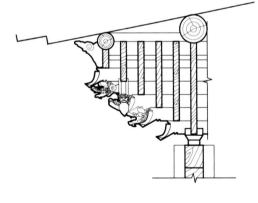
侧视图
Side view

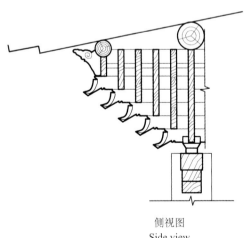
侧视图
Side view

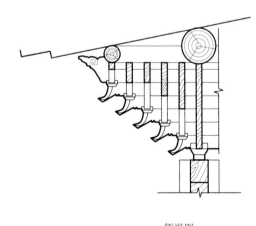
侧视图
Side view

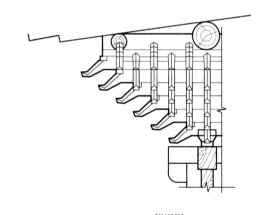
侧视图
Side view

棂星门正面平身科大样图
Bracketing between front columns of Lingxing Gate

棂星门侧面平身科大样图
Bracketing between side columns of Lingxing Gate

棂星门背面平身科大样图
Bracketing between rear columns of Lingxing Gate

棂星门角科大样图
Corner bracketing of Lingxing Gate

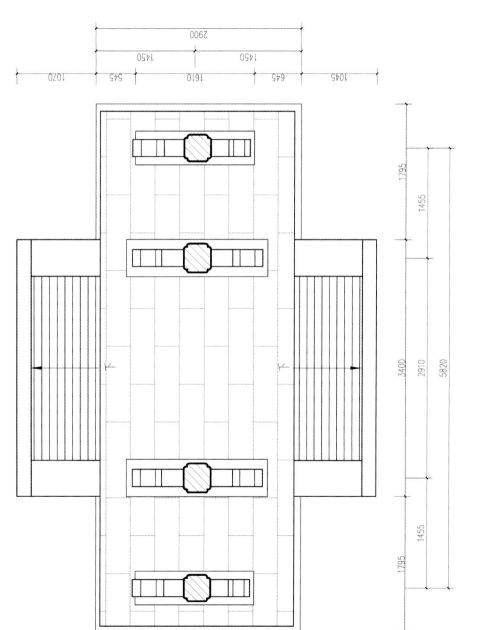

"少昊之都"石牌坊平面图
Plan of "Shaohao zhidu" stone archway

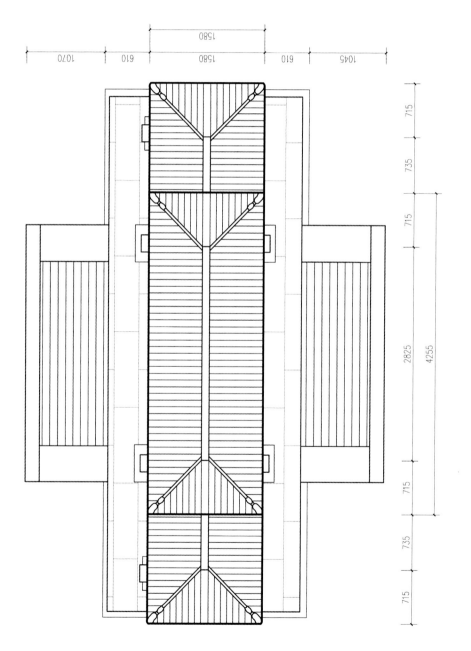

"少昊之都"石牌坊屋顶平面图
Plan of roof of "Shaohao zhidu" stone archway

"少昊之都"石牌坊南立面图

South facade of "Shaohao *zhidu*" stone archway

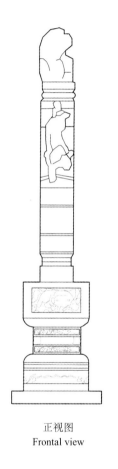

侧视图
Side view

正视图
Frontal view

"少昊之都"石牌坊抱鼓石大样图
Drum stone of "Shaohao *zhidu*" stone archway

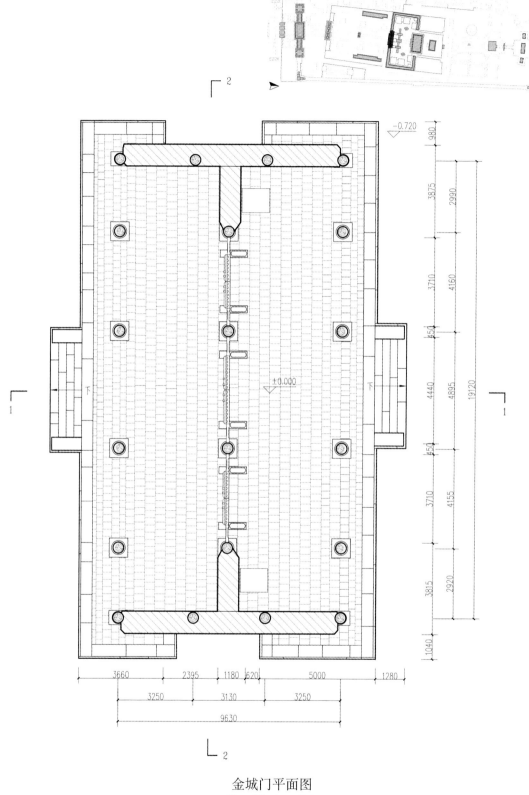

金城门平面图
Plan of Jincheng Gate

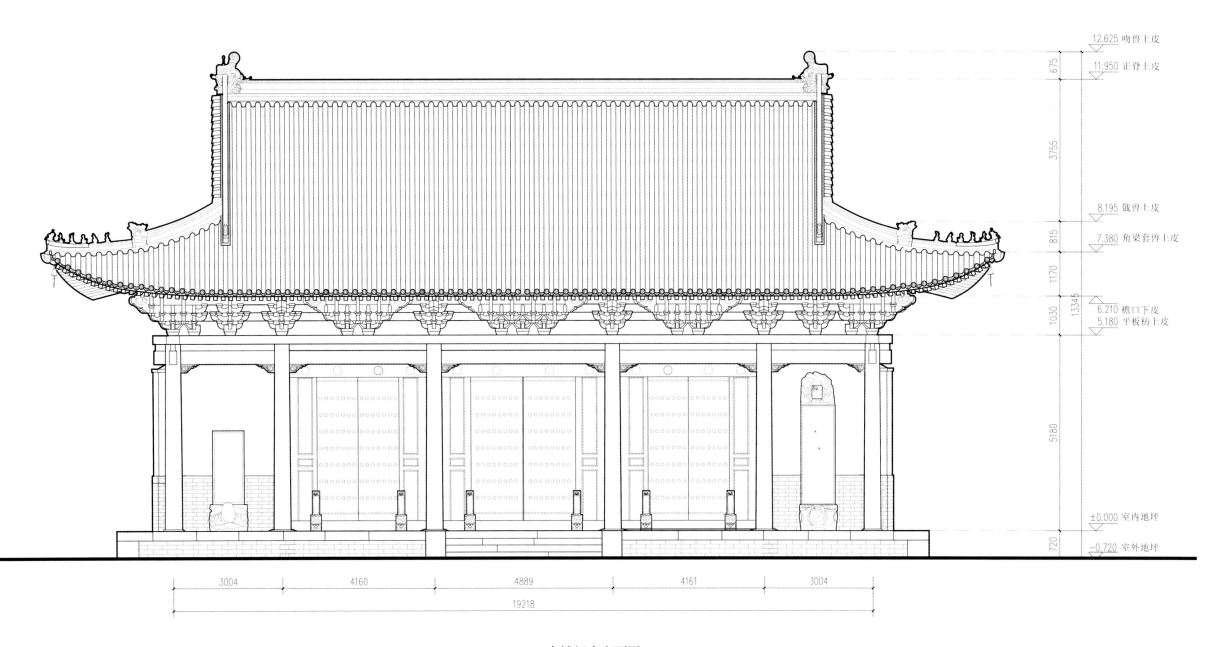

金城门南立面图
South elevation of Jincheng Gate

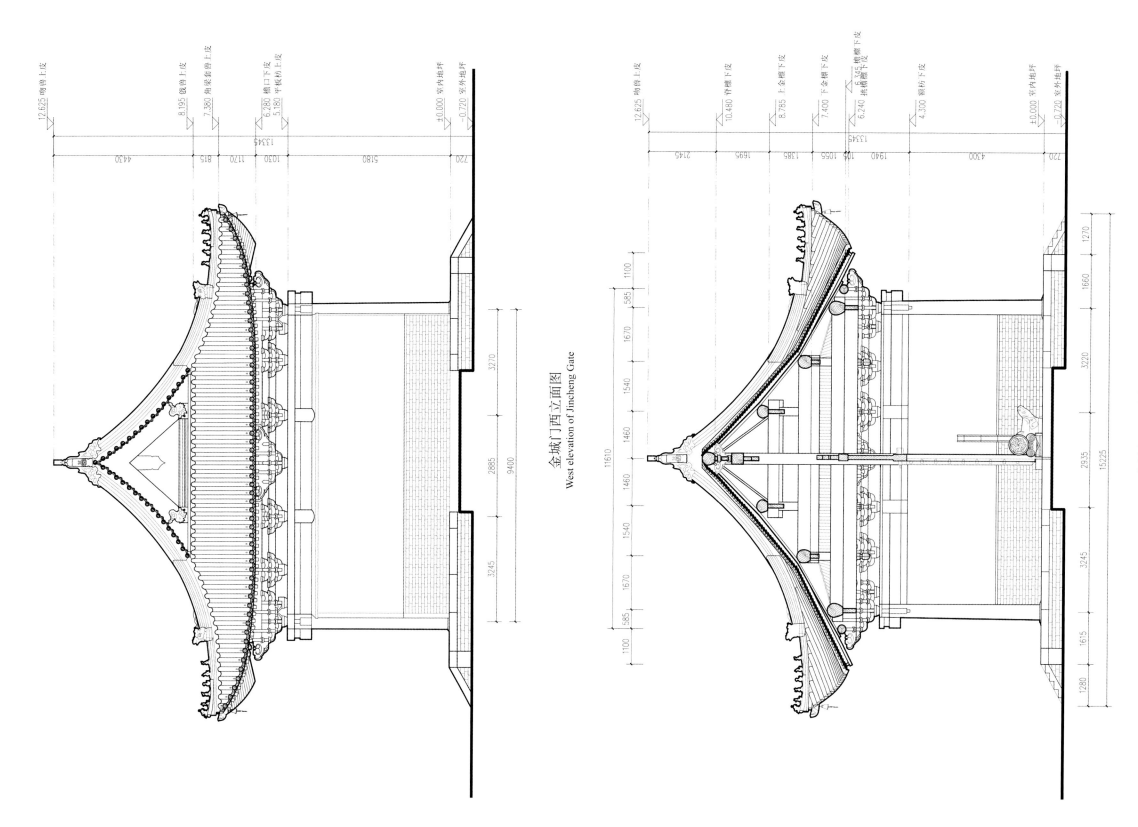

金城门西立面图
West elevation of Jincheng Gate

金城门 1-1 剖面图
Section 1-1 of Jincheng Gate

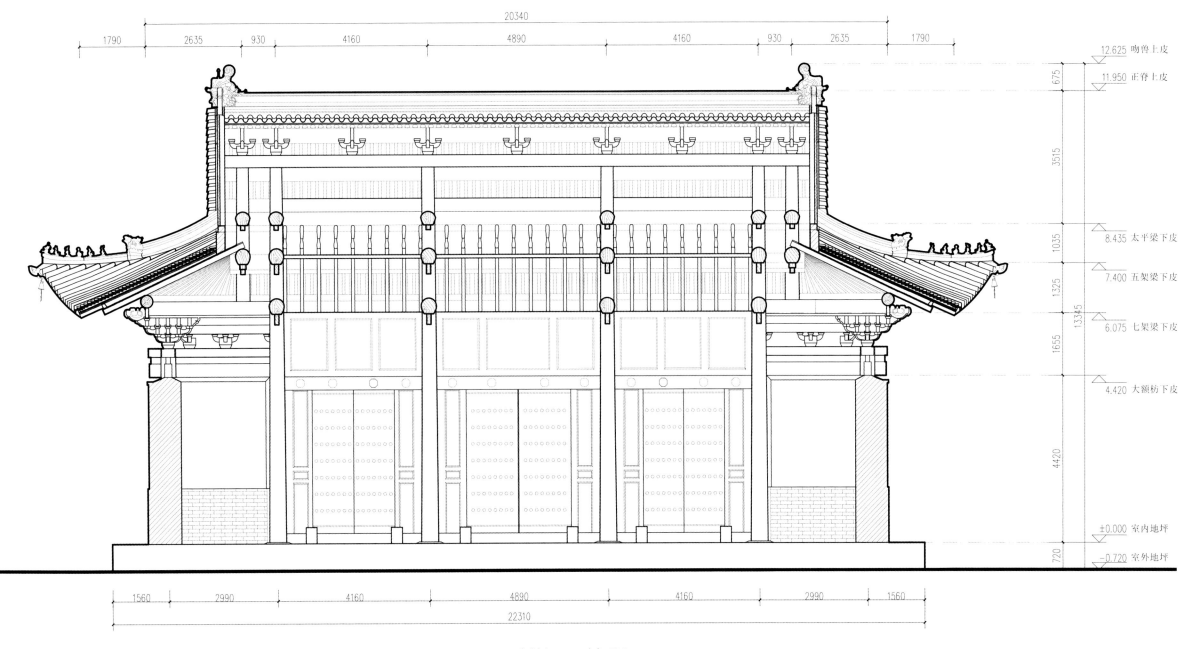

金城门 2-2 剖面图
Section 2-2 of Jincheng Gate

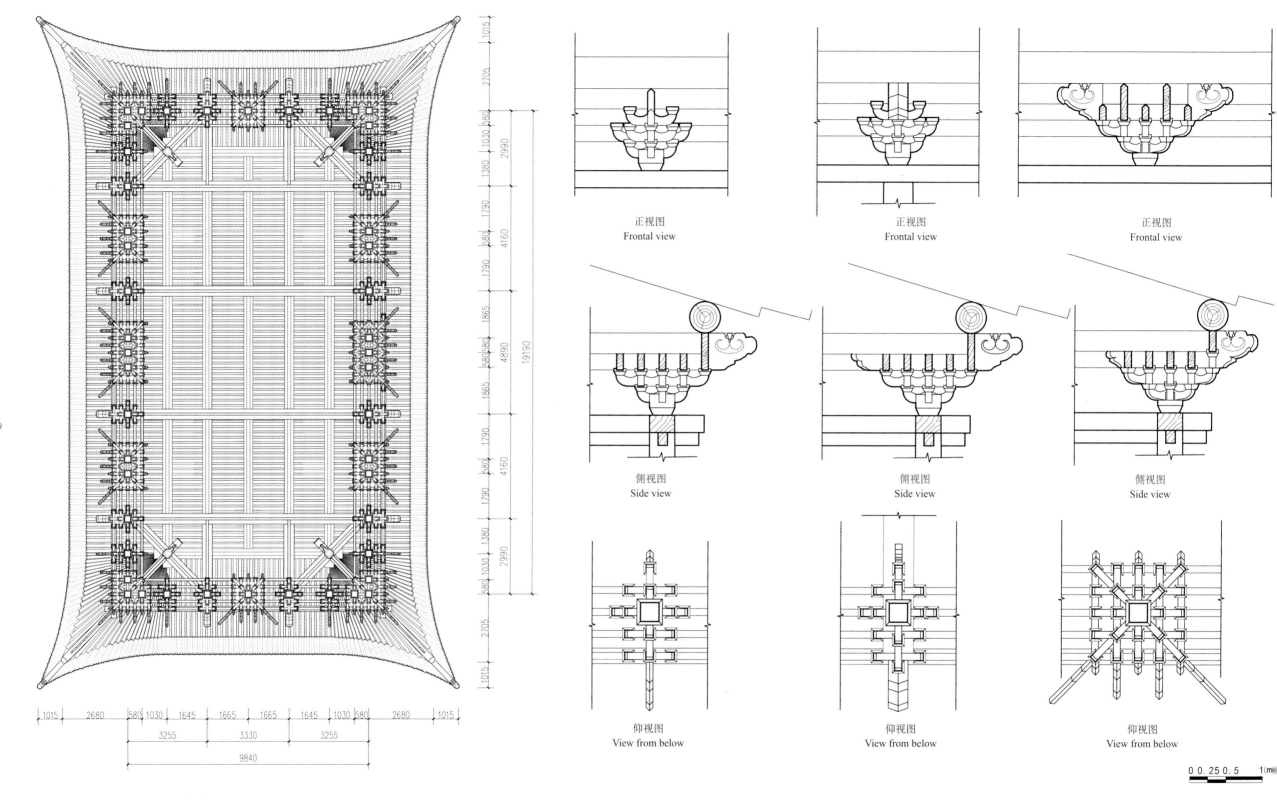

金城门梁架仰视图
Plan of framework of Jincheng Gate as seen from below

金城门尽间平身科大样图
Bracketing between end-bay columns of Jincheng Gate

金城门柱头科大样图
Bracketing atop columns of Jincheng Gate

金城门山面明间平身科大样图
Bracketing between gable-side central-bay columns of Jincheng

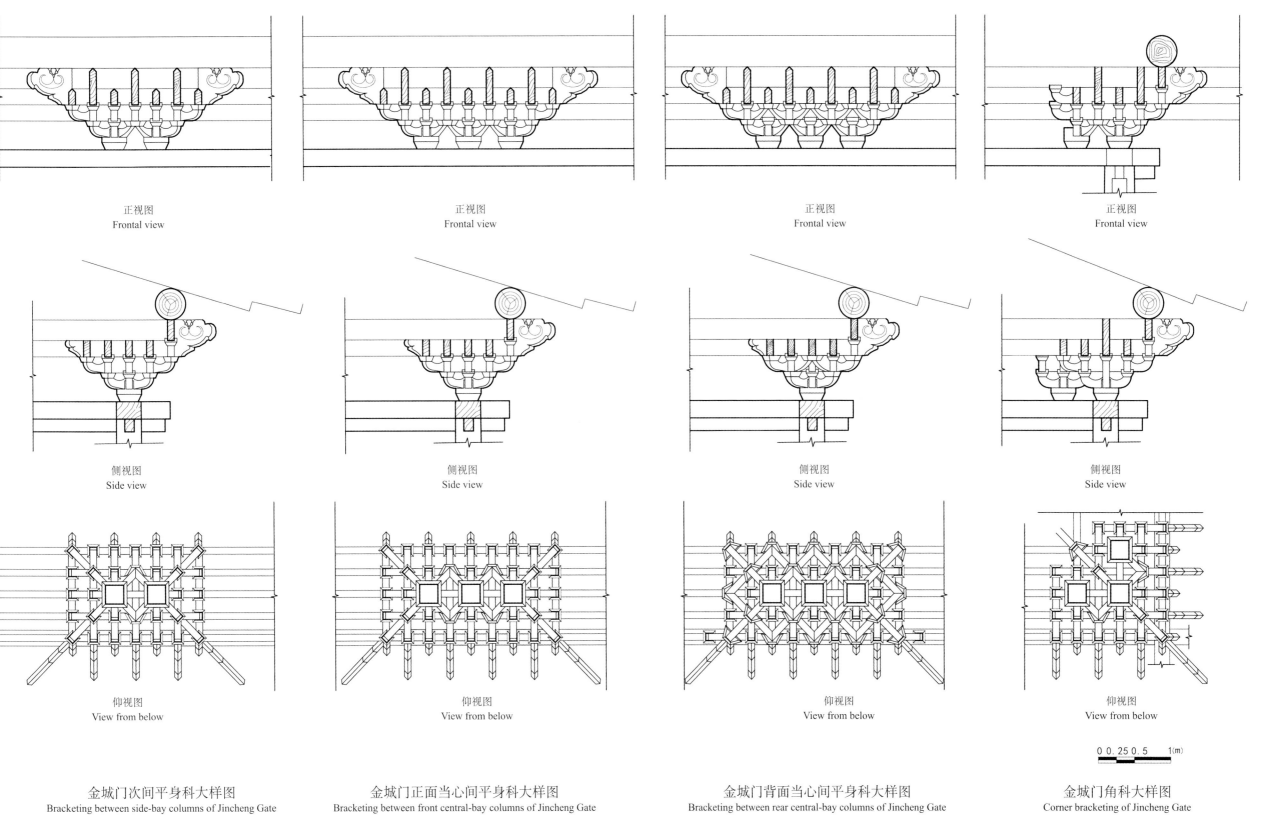

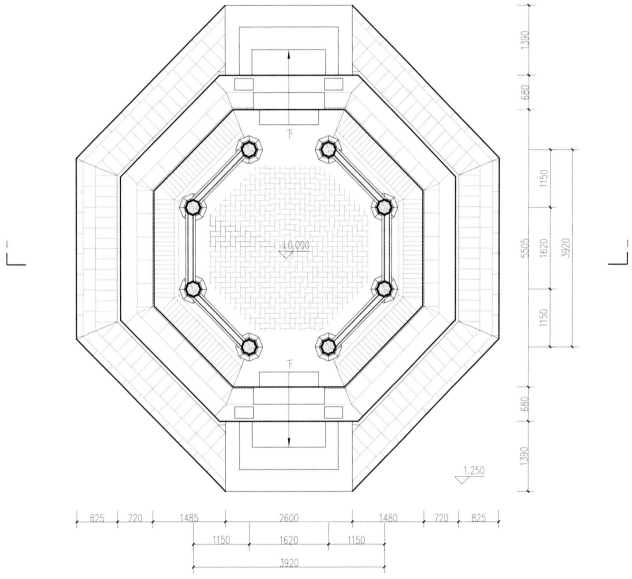

东八角亭平面图
Plan of eastern octagonal pavilion

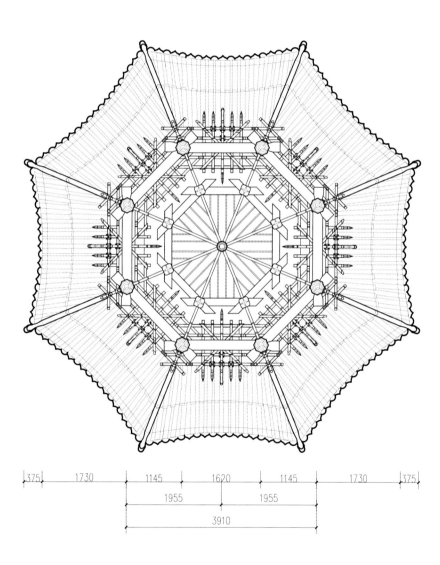

东八角亭梁架仰视图
Plan of framework of eastern octagonal pavilion as seen from below

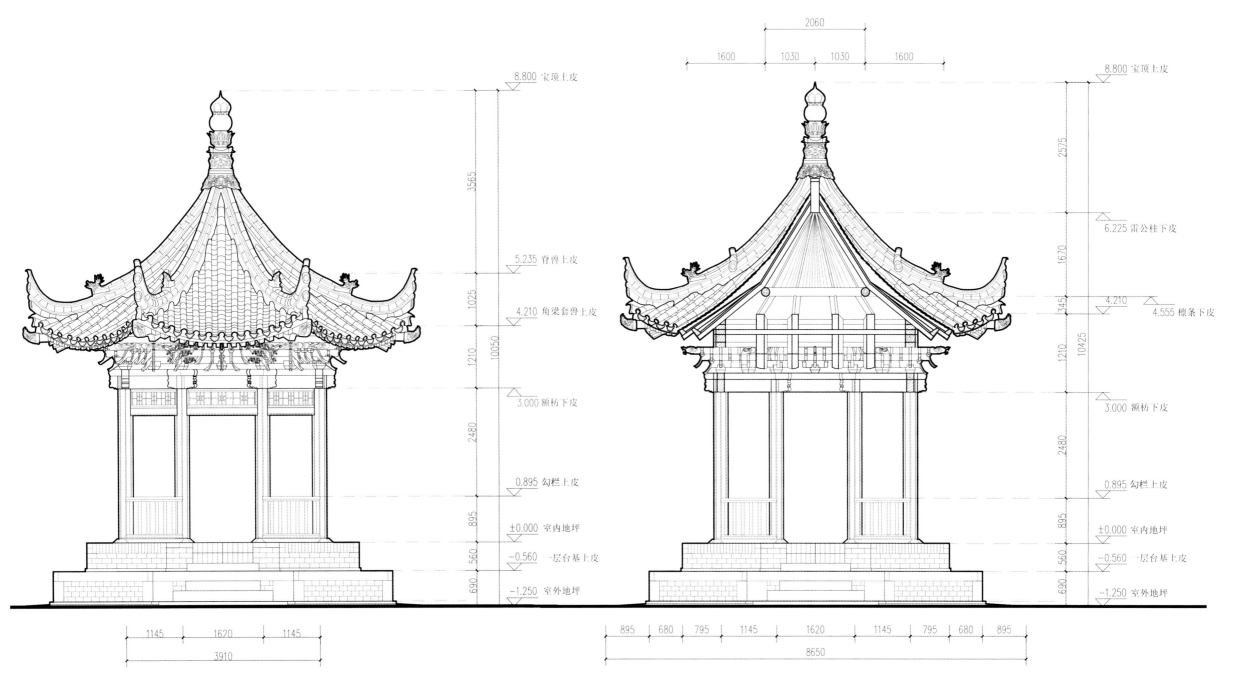

东八角亭西立面图
West elevation of eastern octagonal pavilion

东八角亭 1-1 剖面图
Section 1-1 of eastern octagonal pavilion

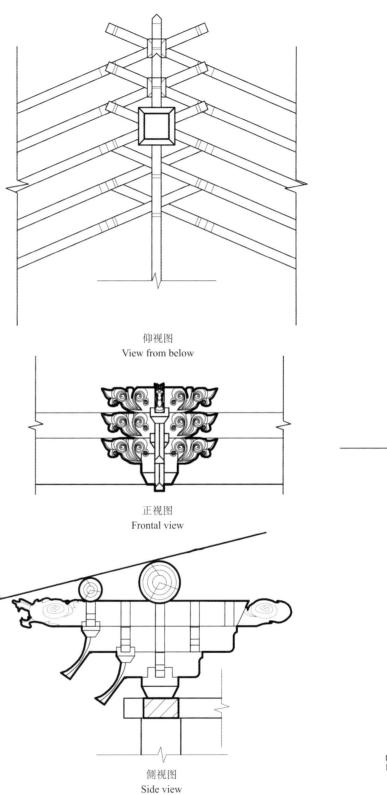

仰视图
View from below

正视图
Frontal view

正视图
Frontal view

仰视图
View from below

东八角亭柱头科大样图
Column-top bracketing of eastern octagonal pavilion

东八角亭宝顶大样图
Baoding of eastern octagonal pavilion

灏灵殿平面图
Plan of Haoling Gate

灏灵殿西立面图
West elevation of Haoling Gate

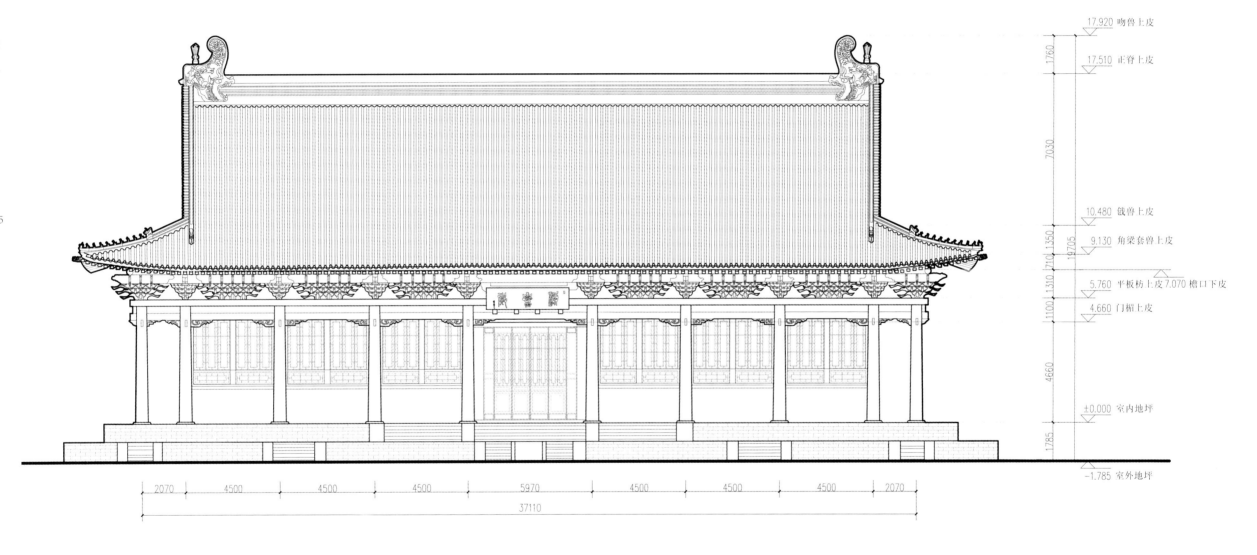

灏灵殿南立面图
South elevation of Haoling Gate

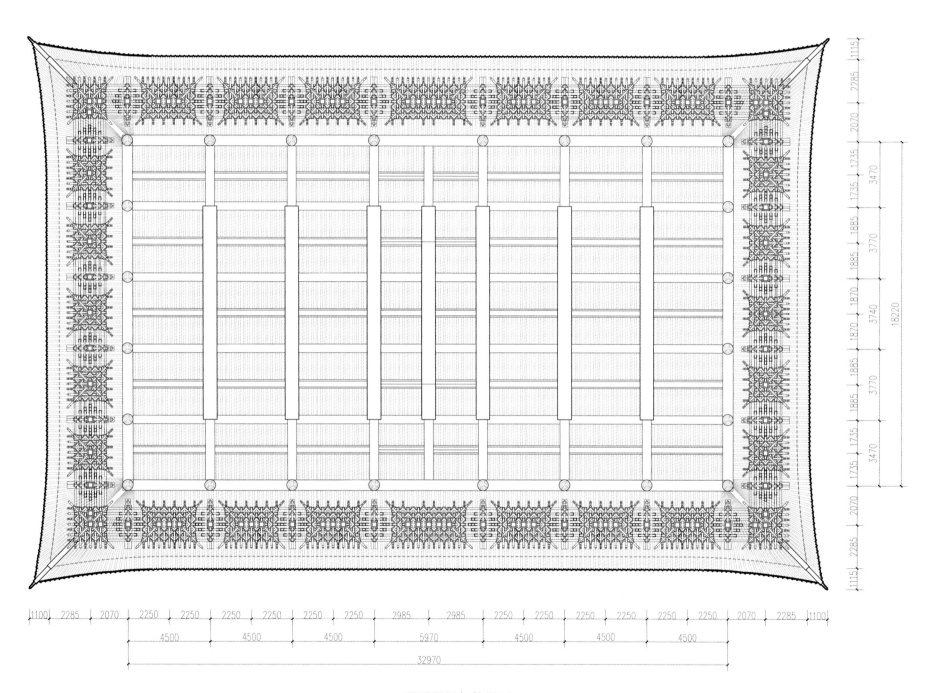

灏灵殿梁架仰视图
Plan of framework of Haoling Gate as seen from below

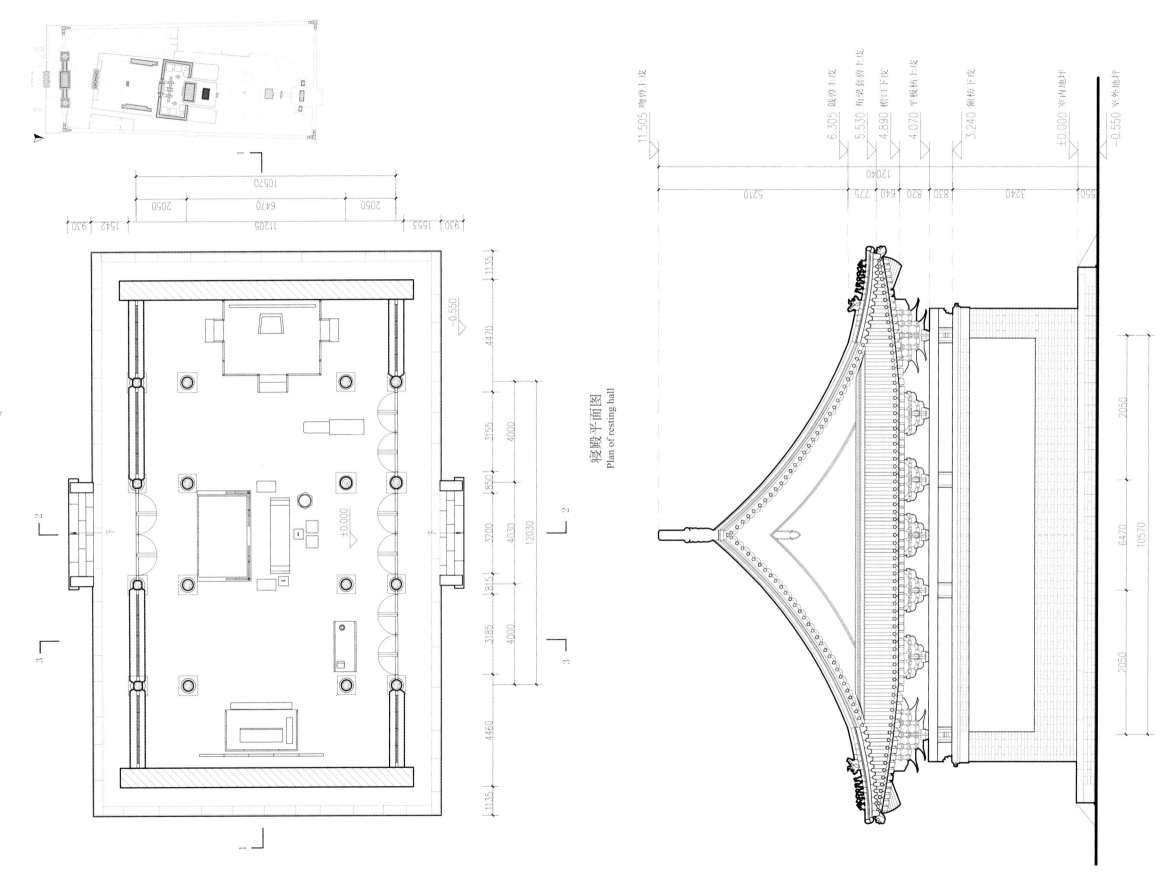

寝殿平面图
Plan of resting hall

寝殿西立面图
West elevation of resting hall

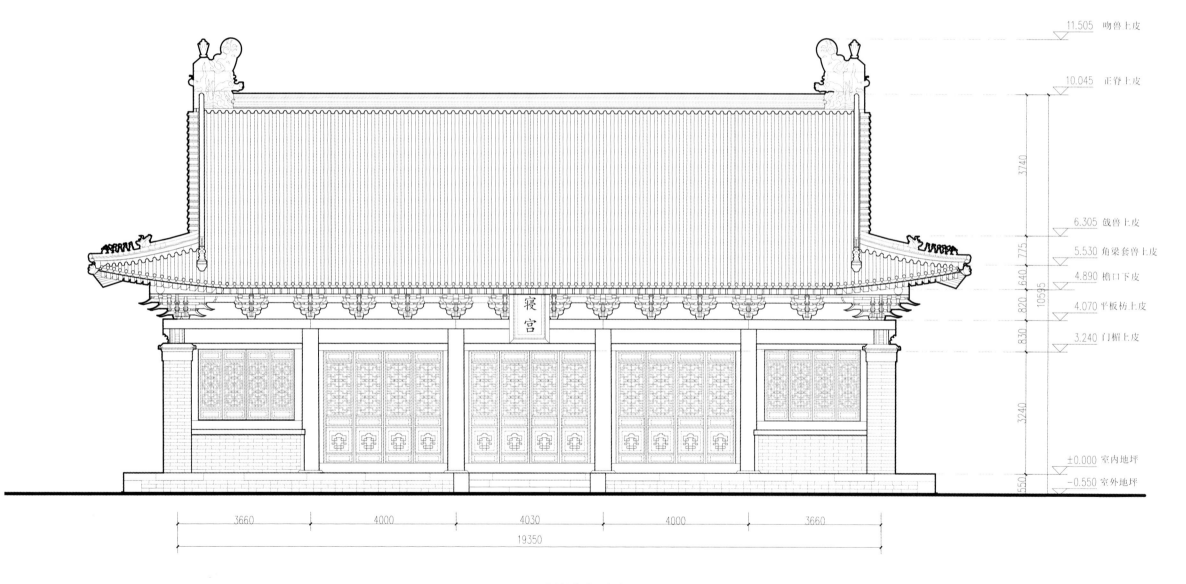

寝殿南立面图
South elevation of resting hall

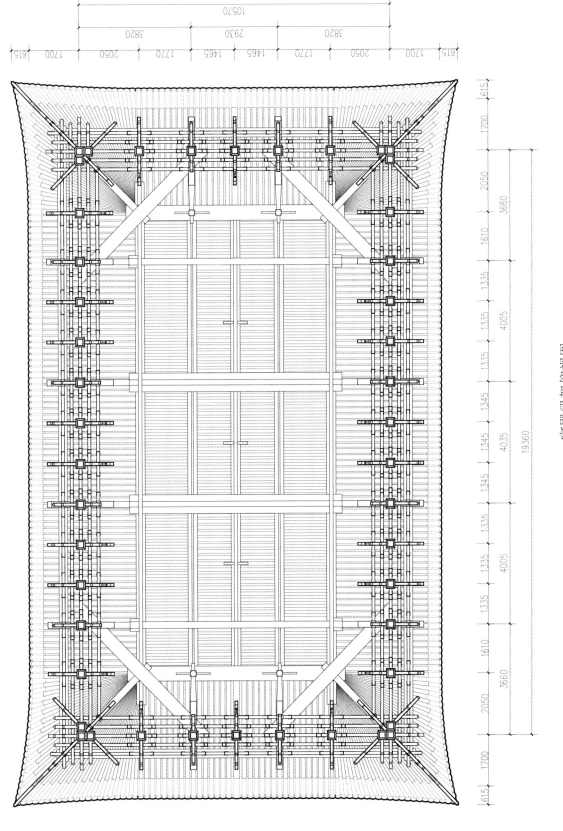

寝殿梁架仰视图
Plan of framework of resting hall as seen from below

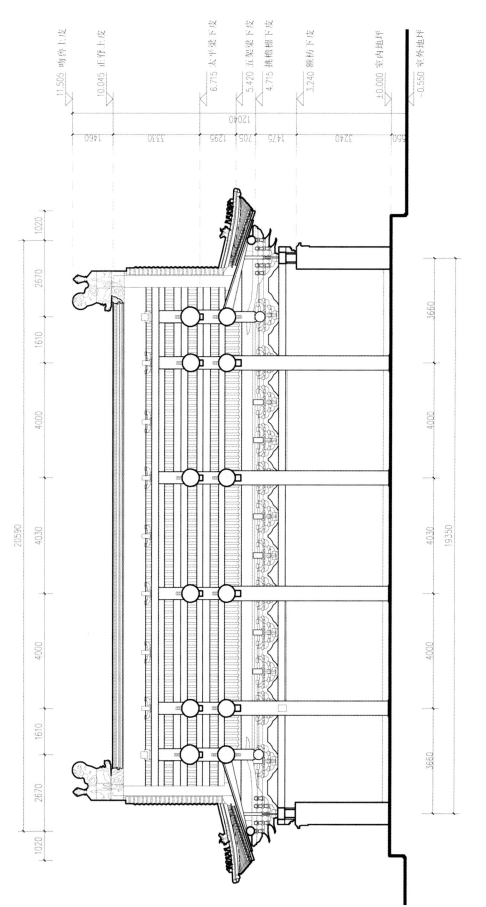

寝殿 1-1 剖面图
Section 1-1 of resting hall

寝殿 2-2 剖面图
Section 2-2 of resting hall

寝殿 3-3 剖面图
Section 3-3 of resting hall

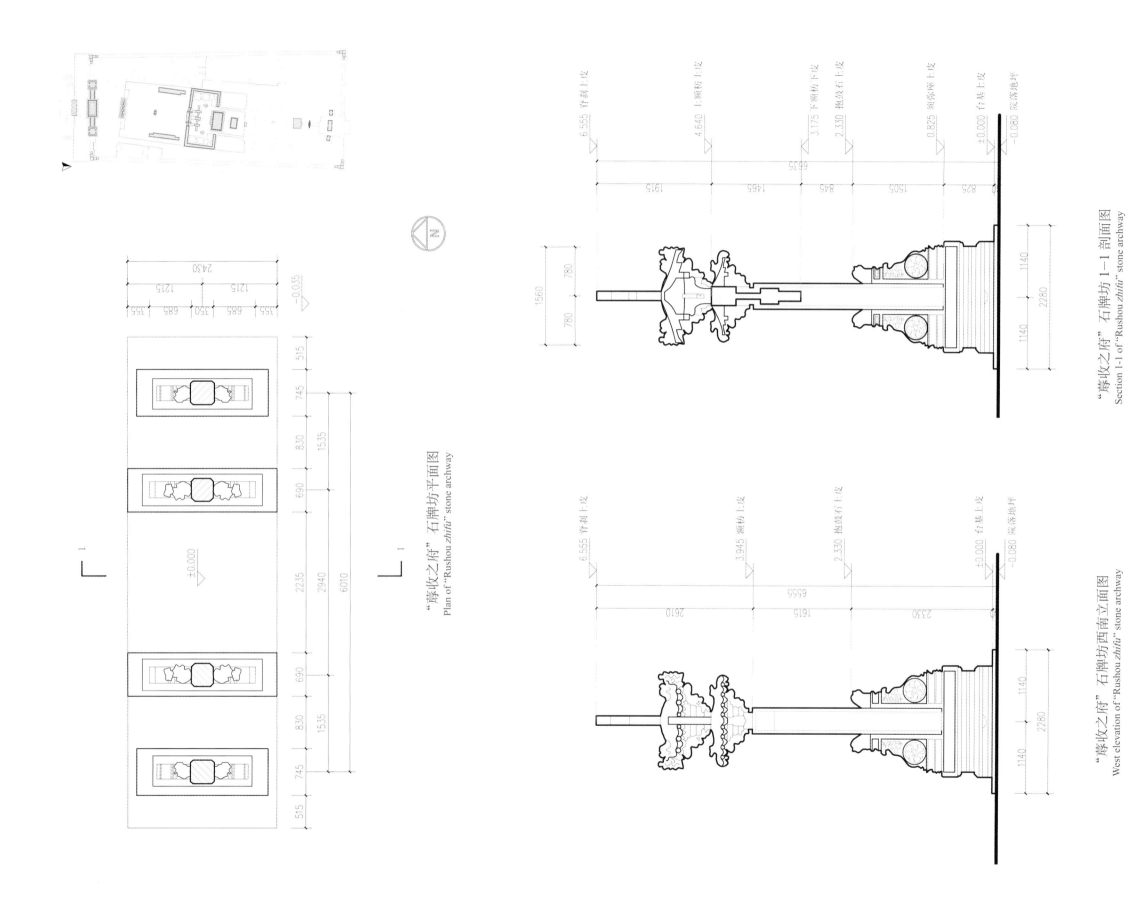

"蓐收之府" 石牌坊平面图
Plan of "Rushou zhifu" stone archway

"蓐收之府" 石牌坊1—1剖面图
Section 1-1 of "Rushou zhifu" stone archway

"蓐收之府" 石牌坊西南立面图
West elevation of "Rushou zhifu" stone archway

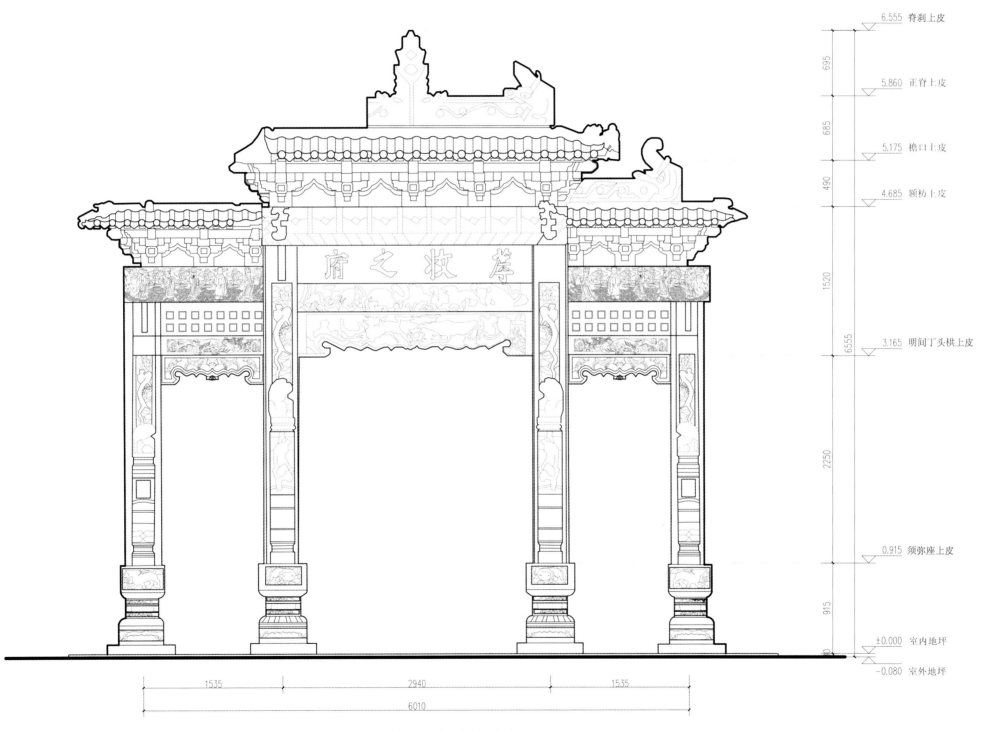

"蓐收之府"石牌坊南立面图
South elevation of "Rushou zhifu" stone archway

本卷编写人员名单

文字撰写：林 源　喻梦哲

英文翻译：林 溪

图版编排：汶武娟

图纸整理：仝梦菲　雷鸿鹭　王茹悦　汶武娟　文 娟
李双双　夏 楠　申佩玉　黄思达　陈斯亮
孟 玉　李宛儒　李 祯

Credits

Text: LIN Yuan, YU Mengzhe

English Translation: LIN Xi

Layout Editor: WEN Wujuan

Drawings Compilation: TONG Mengfei, LEI Honglu, WANG Ruyue, WEN Wujuan,, WEN Juan, LI Shuangshuang, XIA Nan, SHEN Peiyu, HUANG Sida, CHEN Siliang, MENG Yu, LI Wanru, LI Zhen

测绘工作记录 Survey Record

附表 陕西地区现存祠庙建筑一览表
Attachment: Existing Temple in Shaanxi region

序号	建筑名称	年代	保护级别	地区
01	西安文庙（碑林博物院）	明—清	国保（第一批）	西安市
02	户县文庙	清	省保	西安户县
03	咸阳文庙	明	国保（第六批）	咸阳市
04	泾阳文庙	明—清	省保	咸阳泾阳县
05	兴平文庙大成殿	明	省保	咸阳兴平市
06	旬邑文庙	明	省保	咸阳旬邑县
07	礼泉文庙	清	省保	咸阳礼泉县
08	合阳文庙	明	国保（第七批）	渭南合阳县
09	韩城文庙	明	国保（第五批）	渭南韩城市
10	渭南文庙大成殿	明—清	省保	渭南市
11	华县文庙大成殿	明	省保	渭南华县
12	蒲城文庙	明	省保	渭南蒲城县
13	富平文庙大成殿	明	省保	渭南富平县
14	耀县文庙	明	国保（第五批）	铜川耀县
15	铜川文庙大成殿	清	省保	铜川市
16	汉中文庙	明	省保	汉中市
17	洋县文庙大成殿	清	省保	汉中洋县
18	城固文庙大成殿	清	省保	汉中城固县
19	安康文庙大成殿	元—清	省保	安康市
20	汉阴文庙大成殿	清	省保	安康汉阴县
21	旬阳文庙	明—清	省保	安康旬阳县
22	洛南文庙	明	省保	商洛洛南县
23	西安都城隍庙	明—清	国保（第五批）	西安市

一 此表仅统计陕西地区现存的列入全国重点文物保护单位（表中简称为『国保』）和陕西省文物保护单位（表中简称为『省保』）的祠庙建筑。国保单位在括号中注明公布批次。各建筑的年代以保护单位公布名单为准。灰色部分是本卷收录的建筑。

续表

序号	建筑名称	年代	保护级别	地区
24	三原城隍庙	明	国保（第五批）	咸阳三原县
25	武功城隍庙	明	国保（第七批）	咸阳武功县
26	澄城城隍庙神楼	明	国保（第七批）	渭南澄城县
27	扶风城隍庙	明	国保（第六批）	宝鸡扶风县
28	韩城城隍庙	明	国保（第五批）	渭南韩城市
29	白水城隍庙	明—清	省保	渭南白水县
30	洋县城隍庙戏楼	明—清	省保	汉中洋县
31	城固城隍庙	明—清	省保	汉中城固县
32	宁陕城隍庙	清	省保	安康宁陕县
33	商州城隍庙	明—清	省保	商洛市
34	西岳庙	明—清	国保（第三批）	渭南华阴县
35	西安东岳庙	明—清	省保	西安市
36	户县东岳庙（化羊庙）	明	省保	西安户县
37	岐山周公庙	明—清	国保（第六批）	宝鸡岐山县
38	仓颉庙	明—清	国保（第五批）	渭南白水县
39	司马迁墓和祠	西汉—宋	国保（第二批）	渭南韩城市
40	勉县武侯祠	明—民国	国保（第六批）	汉中勉县
41	留坝张良庙	明—清	国保（第六批）	汉中留坝县
42	韩城法王庙	宋—清	国保（第六批）	渭南韩城市
43	韩城北营庙	元	国保（第六批）	渭南韩城市
44	韩城东营庙	明	省保	渭南韩城市
45	韩城玉皇后土庙	元	国保（第六批）	渭南韩城市
46	韩城大禹庙	元	国保（第六批）	渭南韩城市
47	韩城九郎庙	元	国保（第七批）	渭南韩城市
48	韩城关帝庙正殿	元	省保	渭南韩城市
49	柳枝关帝庙	明	省保	渭南华县
50	武功关帝庙	明	省保	咸阳武功县

图书在版编目(CIP)数据

陕西祠庙/林源，喻梦哲，岳岩敏主编. —北京：中国建筑工业出版社，2016.1
 (中国古建筑测绘大系·祠庙建筑)
 ISBN 978-7-112-19901-3

Ⅰ.①陕… Ⅱ.①林… ②喻… ③岳… Ⅲ.①祠堂-介绍-陕西 Ⅳ.①K928.75

中国版本图书馆CIP数据核字（2016）第228378号

丛书策划：王莉慧
责任编辑：李　鸽
书籍设计：付金红
英文审稿：[奥] 荷雅丽（Alexandra Harrer）
责任校对：王　烨

中国古建筑测绘大系·祠庙建筑

陕西祠庙

西安建筑科技大学建筑学院　编写
林　源　喻梦哲　岳岩敏　主编

*

中国建筑工业出版社出版、发行（北京海淀三里河路9号）
各地新华书店、建筑书店经销
北京方舟正佳图文设计有限公司制版
北京雅昌艺术印刷有限公司印刷

*

开本：787×1092毫米　横1/8　印张：32½　字数：861千字
2019年12月第一版　2019年12月第一次印刷
定价：258.00元
ISBN 978-7-112-19901-3
　　　（29162）

版权所有　翻印必究
如有印装质量问题，可寄本社退换
(邮政编码 100037)